RECOVERY

OF A LIFETIME

THE INSPIRATIONAL JOURNEY OF A SUPER BOWL HERO SON
AND HIS FATHER'S BATTLE AGAINST MULTIPLE ADDICTIONS

MIKE AND CHRIS REIS

WITH MIKE YORKEY

F·S PUBLISHING

Photography and cover design by Leigh Germy
www.LeighGermy.com

Interior design by Catherine Thompson
phatphamly@yahoo.com

Mike and Chris Reis are represented by The Keynote Group, Yolanda Harris, President and Speaker Agent, P.O. Box 2444, Mt. Pleasant, SC 29465.

Mike Yorkey is represented by WordServe Literary Group, Ltd., Greg Johnson, Literary Agent, 10152 S. Knoll Circle, Highlands Ranch, CO 80130.

Published by FS Publishing, a division of RBG LLC, 2450 Atlanta Highway, Suite 604b, Cumming, GA 30040.

Our mission is to inspire, encourage, and empower others to live intentionally through God's truth and love.

For the lost and broken, may you realize
that it's never too late to live for more.

CONTENTS

FOREWORD BY JEFF FOXWORTHY xi

A NOTE TO THE READER xiii

1. AMBUSH 1

2. A BRUSH WITH HISTORY 25

3. COMING OF AGE 41

4. JUST A FORMALITY 61

5. SEEDS OF DESTRUCTION 75

6. THE RAZOR'S EDGE 93

7. LONG-DISTANCE DAD 109

8. THE SLIPPERY SLOPE 125

9. PRESSURE TO PERFORM 145

10. THE PERFECT SON 165

11. ARRIVING AT A CROSSROADS 175

12. COLLEGE GAMEDAY 195

13. SECOND-CLASS FAMILY 223

14. A TIME OF TRANSITION 241

15. BEATING THE ODDS 263

16. AMAZING GRACE 281

17. SWEET SURRENDER 301

18. LIVING FOR MORE 317

ACKNOWLEDGEMENTS 331

INVITE MIKE AND CHRIS TO SPEAK AT YOUR EVENT 335

ABOUT THE AUTHORS 337

FOREWORD
BY JEFF FOXWORTHY

COMEDIAN AND CREATOR OF
YOU MIGHT BE A REDNECK IF . . .

Years ago, my grandfather walked out to get a pack of cigarettes and never came back—and that's no redneck joke. My mother found him twenty years later living in another city with another family.

His sin was passed on to the next generation. When I was nine years old, my father walked out on his marriage and left Mom to raise me and my younger brother and sister. I watched my mother struggle to keep a roof over our heads and food on the table from the money she made as a keypunch operator.

Dad ended up marrying six times with a thousand affairs in between. I grew up in the carnage of his cavalier decisions. I witnessed the collateral damage he left behind.

That's why I identify so much with Mike and Chris Reis' book, *Recovery of a Lifetime*. As you'll learn in the following pages, Chris was only two years old when his father, Mike, left him and his family to live with a woman he had met in a bar.

As a little kid, when your dad chooses to leave, you always think: *I wasn't worth staying for. Someone else was more important than me.* Yet everybody on the planet wants to be worth something. Everybody wants to be significant.

Recovery of a Lifetime explores this search for significance in a compelling narrative that will keep you turning pages. I first met Chris a couple of years ago when he joined our Bible study group that meets every Thursday morning in the back of a barbecue restaurant in downtown Atlanta. Chris immediately fit in with guys like former Braves players John Smoltz and Terry Pendleton and TBS announcer Ernie Johnson.

As a Falcons fan, I had to sneer at Chris a bit since he played for the New Orleans Saints, but I found out quickly that he was a great guy. He was so humble and vulnerable, which is what we wanted in our small group—someone who didn't succumb to the applause of the world.

When Chris told me that he was working with his father on a book about their lives, I immediately identified with their mission. I loved the title *Recovery of a Lifetime* because I read somewhere that God is the God of "re-" as in *re*demption, *re*surrection, and *re*covery. One of the biggest delights of God's heart is *re*storing things. He understands our fallibilities.

Think about it: we know that God said David was a guy after His own heart, but when you study his life, there were more than a few moments that he wasn't proud of—like when he watched a woman take a bath and decided he wanted to have her, which led to her getting pregnant, which led to David having her husband killed on the field of battle.

Why God would still say that David was after His own heart? Answer: because David recognized his sins and walked toward God with a contrite heart. David sought restoration.

That's why I believe you will be uplifted by this amazing account of restoration and recovery. Chris and his father, Mike, tell their story with humility and honesty that I've rarely seen in a book.

And we are the beneficiaries.

A NOTE FROM MIKE AND CHRIS REIS

What you are about to read is not a sports book or a self-help book. *Recovery of a Lifetime* is a father-and-son story of inspiration, faith, hope, and recovery.

Some of the stories we share may make you uncomfortable and could be difficult to read. By sharing intimate details of our lives, we are not glorifying or excusing bad behavior or poor choices. Our intent is to shine a light on these circumstances as an example of God's redeeming love.

This is a true story; we have rendered the events from our recollection as faithfully as we remember them. Some names and descriptions of individuals have been changed to respect their privacy. The conversations depicted in our story are based on our best effort to recollect and reenact them as accurately as possible. These are meant to capture what happened to us and communicate the spirit of the moments that shaped our lives.

We hope you can see a part of your life in our story and feel inspired to let God make a recovery of a lifetime in you.

AMBUSH

Chris Reis

How does one express the amazing thrill of jogging onto the field for the opening kickoff of a Super Bowl?

It would be insane to try, but there I was, loosening up near the red-white-and-blue NFL logo at midfield, flexing my legs and making sure my chin strap was buckled up. My senses were on overload as I attempted to soak in the biggest game of my football career.

As my Nike cleats punctured the natural grass of Sun Life Stadium in Miami Gardens, Florida, the time was 6:32 p.m. on Sunday, February 7, 2010. Two weeks of highly pitched anticipation would soon give way to the kickoff of Super Bowl XLIV—a marquee match-up pitting my team—the New Orleans Saints—against the Indianapolis Colts, led by All-World quarterback Peyton Manning.

There were several storylines going into the game, but the biggest one was this: four-and-a-half years after Hurricane Katrina destroyed 70,000 homes and flooded 85 percent of the Crescent City, resulting in human misery on a massive scale, a Saints victory would go a long way toward restoring the city's fragile psyche. The talking heads on ESPN said that bringing home the Lombardi Trophy would raise the spirits of downtrodden Big Easy residents and bring the city back from oblivion.

No pressure or anything.

But it did feel like we had the weight of New Orleans' future on our padded shoulders. The Saints had never been to a Super Bowl before during the team's up-and-down forty-three-year history, and it wasn't that long ago that New Orleans fans were wearing brown paper bags over their heads and calling their home team "the Aints." Now we had a chance to rewrite history and give our hungry fans something to *really* cheer about.

Our team, led by quarterback Drew Brees—who had resurrected his career after being blown out of San Diego by Katrina-like headwinds—was something special. Throughout the 2009 NFL season and into the playoffs, we stepped up when it counted the most. Our great fans filling the Superdome hoisted home-made signs that read, "Who dat?"—shorthand for "Who dat say dey gonna beat dem Saints?"

And now we were about to take on the Indianapolis Colts in the NFL title game. There were only 111,300,000 persons watching the game on TV, which would make the forty-fourth Super Bowl the most-watched television show in U.S. history. But I wasn't nervous to be playing in front of so many people. Let's just say that I was really excited to be a part of this big game.

We had won the pregame coin toss when our team captain Drew Brees correctly yelled heads. "We want the ball!" our leader said. But there was another reason we elected to receive, and it was because our head coach, Sean Payton, had something special up his sleeve for the second-half kickoff.

All that was yet to come.

The voluminous noise filling Sun Life Stadium crescendoed as referee Scott Green blew his whistle and circled his right arm to start the game. When kicker Pat McAfee of the Colts lifted the ball into the air, I turned and sprinted back toward our return man, Courtney Roby. We had a "return left" play set up, so my job was to block or throw my body at the nearest blue-shirted Colt in my vicinity. Perhaps my block would blow a hole in Indianapolis' coverage and spring Courtney free for a long runback, which would jumpstart our team.

I couldn't believe the thousands and thousands of flash bulbs popping off at the moment McAfee put his foot on the ball. It was like *tch-tch-tch-tch*—ten thousand flashes from handheld cameras and smartphones sparkling everywhere. The strobe effect was the coolest thing, but that impression quickly left me because I had an important job to do—create a running lane for Courtney. On this kickoff return, though, the Colts bottled us up and tackled our runback guy at the 23-yard line.

Mike Reis

My heart was beating rapidly as I watched Chris turn and get into position for the runback. I was seated at the 25-yard line—about twenty-five rows behind the left side of the Saints' bench. Seated next to me were an assortment of family and ex-family members. To my left was my third wife, Celia. On my right sat my oldest son, Mike Jr.; his then girlfriend Sandra; my first wife, Stephanie; Chris' wife of two years, Michelle; and Stephanie's mother, Kathy.

Five members of Michelle's family were perched several rows below us: Bob and Melissa Tyree; her brother, Michael; sister Kelly; and her brother-in-law Jesse Dalton. Michelle would have sat with her parents and siblings, but that's how the tickets broke down.

All told, there were twelve in our group. It wasn't hard to tell that we were cheering on Chris because everyone wore a gray long-sleeved T-shirt with a Super Bowl XLIV logo on the breast pocket and a big black number 39 and REIS silkscreened on the back. Michelle had the custom T-shirts made for everybody.

Many football fans don't realize that players from both teams in the Super Bowl do not receive *any* comp tickets. Instead, the NFL league office gives them the "opportunity" to purchase a limited number of tickets for family and friends at face value—$800 per seat.

After New Orleans went into overtime to beat the Minnesota Vikings, 31-28, in the NFC Conference Championship game and reach the Super Bowl, Chris generously offered to write a $9,600 check to pay for all of our tickets. All we had to do was cover our transportation costs from our home in Atlanta as well as our hotel and meal expenses in South Florida.

As far as I was concerned, that was a done deal because I wouldn't have missed Super Bowl XLIV no matter how much Super Sunday cost. To think that my son—my flesh and blood—was playing football in the biggest game of the year made me immensely proud.

That pride turned to concern, though, as the Saints were held to a three-and-out on their first series and the Colts easily moved the ball down the field. Their quarterback, Peyton Manning, seemingly passed at will. A false start stalled their drive at the New Orleans 20-yard line, which led to a Colts field goal. Indianapolis had grabbed a quick 3-0 lead.

Chris

I was the backup strong safety behind starter Roman Harper, so I didn't figure to see any action in the defensive backfield. I was a role player on the Saints—a special teams guy playing the "core four": kickoff, kickoff return, punt, and punt return.

Everybody builds up the Super Bowl in his or her minds, and there's no doubt that the National Football League's annual championship game is the biggest sporting event of the year in the United States. After the opening kickoff jitters, though, it felt like any other football game. The white-striped grass field was still 100 yards long, the sidelines were still 53$^{1/3}$ yards apart, and yellow goalposts were planted in the center of each end zone.

At least, that's how I tried to view the Super Bowl—by making it into just another game. But Peyton Manning didn't give us any time to get settled. He had our defense retreating throughout the first quarter, forging a 10-0 lead. Fortunately, we got a field goal to narrow the gap. We were driving late in the first half to tie the game when we had a fourth-and-goal on the Colts' 1-yard line. Coach Payton didn't hesitate to keep our offense on the field. He said we're going for it, but the Colts' stout defense stuffed running back Pierre Thomas at the goal line.

That huge stop took a considerable amount of wind out of our sails, but the good news was that we could play field position with the Colts' backed up near the end zone. We held on three downs and got the ball back at our 48-yard line, but there were only 35 seconds left in the half.

With Drew Brees at the helm, though, there was plenty of time: few NFL quarterbacks were better at working the two-minute offense and managing the game clock. None of us were surprised when Drew got us close enough for a 44-yard field goal as time expired in the first half, and Saints fans cheered us on as we jogged into the locker room underneath the stands.

Down 10-6, we were still in the game. But our defense was ranked 25th out of thirty-two NFL teams, and everyone had the feeling that defending against Peyton Manning was like sticking a finger in a leaking dam. Eventually, the breach would give way.

Mike

I was surprised that the capacity crowd was not that loud. I knew the Super Bowl was contested on a neutral field, but this game had a different sound and feel. I think it's because there weren't that many fans from New Orleans or Indianapolis. Corporate people and diehard NFL fans filled the seats.

Normally, I would leave my seat at halftime to hit the restroom and maybe have an adult beverage or two, but I wasn't going anywhere this time—not when the Super Bowl halftime show was coming on. The British rock band from the Sixties, The Who, was playing, and while I wasn't the biggest Who fan growing up, they were legends. Super Bowl halftime shows were always over-the-top spectacles, and this time The Who didn't disappoint, opening their mini-set with "Pinball Wizard" and "Baba O'Riley."

Chris

I couldn't have cared less *who* was playing on a darkened stage in the middle of Sun Life Stadium. All I knew was that in order to put on a big halftime show that would keep 100 million sets of eyes glued to their flat screens, the NFL extended the halftime intermission from 12 minutes to 30 minutes—which had the potential to throw the players off our rhythm. It sure felt different having a lot of time to kill during the halftime break.

We filed into our locker room, where my teammates took off their helmets and removed their jerseys, shoulder pads, and gloves. Those who needed to go to the bathroom did so.

I drifted over to a nearby table and grabbed a cold bottle of Gatorade—choosing fruit punch, my favorite flavor—and a banana. That's what I've always consumed during halftime. Then we broke up into offensive and defensive team meetings to go over what had happened during the first half and hear from the coaches about what adjustments we needed to make.

I was part of the defensive team meeting in one corner of the locker room. Dennis Allen, our defensive backs coach, was using a white dry erase board to diagram how Peyton Manning was finding seams and open spots in the coverage when I looked up and noticed that Coach Payton had stuck his head inside our meeting. Something had to be up because he usually spent half-time with the offense.

I remember Coach looking at me and then at Roman Harper, who also played special teams. "We're doing Ambush to start the half, so get ready."

Ambush.

My heart skipped a beat. That was an onside kick play that we had put into the playbook before the NFC Conference Championship game against the Minnesota Vikings. Coach told us to be ready to run Ambush against the Vikings, but the opportunity had never presented itself. I didn't think he'd be crazy enough to try an onside kick in the middle of a Super Bowl game.

But Coach Peyton wanted to roll the dice. The decision to *start* the second half with an onside kick was either a stroke of genius or would go down as one of the dumbest coaching decisions ever in a Super Bowl.

Normally, onside kicks come at the end of the game when your team is down by a touchdown or less and can't stop the clock. In other words, desperate times call for desperate measures. Our situation was totally different: at that moment, we were only behind 10-6 with a whole half left to play.

But Coach wanted to do something dramatic to change the tenor of the game. I think he and the coaching staff felt that Peyton Manning would be pretty much unstoppable in the second half, so we needed the ball one more time than they did if we were going to win.

A successful Ambush would give us that extra possession. I loved that Coach was willing to take such a huge risk.

"Man, this is good," I whispered to Roman.

A grim-faced Roman didn't say a word. I knew what he was thinking: *The ball is coming my way. I better not blow it.*

The way Ambush was designed, our kicker Thomas Morestead would make it look like he was making a regular kickoff, but at the last second, he would stop in his tracks and squib the football to his left.

The bouncing football would stay low to the ground for ten yards and roll into a part of the field that had been vacated by the Colts players, who would presumably turn and run back to block for their return man. Ambush was designed for Roman to either pick up or fall on the ball; my job was to back him up in case the slippery football popped out.

We ran Ambush eight or nine times in practice leading up to the Super Bowl—but never when the media was watching. The onside kick worked every time during rehearsal, but I attributed that to the work ethic of Thomas Morestead, who was also our punter. He was extremely detail-oriented and always precise on his kicks, and I figured he had practiced making that squib kick a hundred times off in some far-flung corner of our practice field.

Thomas, however, had *never* attempted an onside kick in an NFL game—and now Coach Payton was asking him to come through in one of the riskiest gambles in Super Bowl history.

Mike

Celia left and joined the long line for the restroom, but I stayed in my seat because I wanted to see The Who and not miss anything when the second half started. I knew the Saints were kicking off and that Chris would be on the field.

During the first half, my eyes were glued to his movements every time he was in the game. He had performed admirably, and nothing bad had happened on special teams.

At the same time, though, I was a bit depressed. I didn't see how we could stop Peyton Manning. The guy was too good at picking off receivers. We could have been down 24-6 quite easily at the half, a blow-out in the making. I knew I'd feel better about our chances if I had a drink.

Normally when I went to Saints games in New Orleans, I'd tell Celia that I was going to the restroom during intermission. I'd never make it to the urinal, however. Instead, I'd draw a beeline for one of the eight bars in our club section, where I'd order two vodkas on the rocks. I'd drink one after the other and then make my way back to my seat. Celia would be none the wiser.

Not tonight. This was the freaking Super Bowl, and I wanted to be in touch with all my faculties. The other thing to consider was that I never knew when a lens would be pointed at me. TV cameras and newspaper photographers often scanned the "family section" trolling for reaction shots. Not that Chris was in the same stratosphere as Drew Brees, but you never knew who was watching.

When The Who finished their twelve-minute set with "Won't Get Fooled Again," the lights went up, and a massive crew went to work disassembling the stage. Meanwhile, players from both teams came onto the field to warm up for the second half.

The Saints would be kicking off since we had received to start the game. I noticed Celia slip into her seat as Chris jogged onto the field. There was a lot of commotion, though, because the aisle was clogged with fans trying to get to their seats before the start of the second half.

Down in front!

I kept trying to find Chris, but my view was blocked.

Chris

I was nervous about what was going to happen. The last instructions from Coach Payton in the locker room were this: "Hey, pay attention. One quick thing. We're gonna start the half kicking off—Ambush. Roman Harper, you recover it. I don't want this thing going out of bounds. Now listen, men. Let's go get this @#$%-ing game!"

You should have heard the hoops and hollers filling the locker room. All our heart rates shot up because we knew Ambush could change the arc of this contest.

The Saints players had to act like nothing unusual was about to happen while we loosened up for the second half. We went through our usual routine—jogging up and down the sideline, tightening gloves, and putting on helmets. All our stomachs were churning—and I know mine was. Several fleeting doubts crowded my subconscious thinking, but I reminded myself that I had a job to do and the abilities to perform the task at hand.

The only thing out of the ordinary was when Coach Peyton told the refs that we wanted to kick the ball from the right side of the field. We were supposed to kick the ball from the left side toward the right, but the kickoff team has the option to choose which direction to go.

The reason why Coach Payton wanted to kick off from the right side was because Thomas Morestead was going to dribble the ball to his left. We wanted his onside kick coming toward the Saints bench, not the Colts sideline. There were stories around the league about weird things happening whenever you made an onside kick toward your opponents' bench. Sometimes people ended up in the pile who weren't on the field to begin with.

No one on the Colts' bench showed any signs of reacting to our plans. Ambush was working.

Time to roll. Our kicking team jogged out onto the field to start the second half. Business as usual. Nothing in our demeanor—an extra-long glance between the players, different positioning on the field, or even the way Thomas Morestead placed the ball on the kicking tee—could be different. We had to sell this moment.

At the same time, I harbored some doubts that this was going to work. Onside kicks are generally successful 25 percent of the time, but those who study these stats say that a surprise onside kick has a much greater chance for success—60 percent. Either way, it was a jump ball on whether we'd come up with the recovery, but we had to give the appearance that we were super confident in what Coach Payton was doing and trust that his decision was the best call.

Five Saints players lined up to the right of Thomas and five players lined up to the left. Roman Harper was furthest left and closest to the Saints sideline. I was No. 4 man—fourth in from the left. My role was to circle behind our No. 2 and No. 3 guys, who were supposed to blast any blockers out of the way. Thomas would dribble the ball toward our sideline, and I would loop in behind Roman so that I would be available in case something unexpected happened. When an egg-shaped ball with pointed ends hits the ground, you can get some crazy bounces.

Mike
The aisle was still jammed, and I strained to see what was happening on the field. On kickoffs, I rarely watched the flight of the ball. I always kept my eyes on Chris, but my view was partially blocked.

Chris

Ambush was kind of like the D-Day landing: things don't always go like you planned. Thomas approached the ball like he was going to side-wind it into the end zone, but instead of swinging his leg, he tapped the ball with the instep of his right foot.

The bouncing ball skittered in Roman's direction, but one of our guys whiffed on blocking the Colts' Hank Baskett. Instead of cleanly scooping up the ball near an empty sideline, Roman was fighting Baskett to reach the bouncing ball first. The Colts defender lunged, but the leather spheroid caromed off his chest. The ball then squirted out right in front of me, and I didn't hesitate. I threw my hands and body at the ball instantly, but what happened over the next sixty-three seconds will forever be etched in my memory.

I knew exactly what to do—cradle the ball in my arms and get covered up as quickly as I could to prevent other players from ripping the pigskin out of my arms. But I couldn't get a quick handle on the shiny and smooth ball, which slipped out of my grasp and lodged between my legs.

No way I could maintain possession with the ball there. I was on my side, reaching down for the ball, but I was being pummeled by players from both teams diving headfirst into the pile. Hank Baskett plunged under me and was getting his hands on the ball when teammate Jonathan Casillas saved the day by spearing Baskett and driving him away. That gave me a split second to secure the ball with one arm even though it felt like there were a hundred other arms grabbing at my treasure, yanking on my arms, and ripping at my fingers.

Suddenly everything went black as even *more* players launched themselves into the pile. I felt like I'd just been run over by a Mack truck, but I was still fighting for the ball. I was hearing grunting noises, and the skirmish for the ball had escalated. Nobody's weak in the NFL; everyone is strong as an ox. I had one arm locked on the ball and was straining to bring it to my chest, but I still didn't have absolute control.

The laws of the jungle apply in a dog pile like this. I've always likened NFL fumbles to having a street fight lying down. People were trying to pull my arms out of my sockets and break my fingers. Fortunately, nobody was grabbing at my nuts. This was like gang warfare. I had to tuck that ball close to my chest. I had to win.

Then, in a split-instant, with all the strength I could summon, I secured my second arm around the ball—and hung on for dear life. As the seconds ticked by, keeping the ball was all passion and will—who wanted it more.

I desired that ball in the worst way because I knew the outcome would probably determine the winner of the Super Bowl. My hands hurt from holding on to the ball so tightly, and my forearms burned. The scrum seemed to last *forever.*

And then I saw some light. The refs were pulling off bodies one by one, yelling, "You get out of here!" It was taking a long, long time to pull everyone off, but that's probably because eighteen players had dove into the pile of bodies.

I remember one of the refs was kneeing me. Then he stood up and cried out, "Blue ball!" But he wasn't signaling with his arm.

What was he talking about? I had the ball in my arms, but I couldn't show him that I had possession lest a Colt player rip it out of my hands. My attitude was that I wasn't leaving that pile until I came out with the football.

And then I heard the words I was waiting for: "White ball!"

I pulled myself to my feet and jogged off the field with the football lifted high. I didn't hear the crowd's reaction, but my elated teammates were slapping me and yelling, "Good job!" and "Way to fight!"

Greg Williams, our defensive coordinator, was the first coach to greet me. He stopped me in my tracks and looked me in the eyes. "That had nothing to do with Xs and Os," he said. What he meant was that no matter how well Coach Payton drew up Ambush and put everyone in the right place, hanging on to that football had everything to do with passion and heart.

Coach Mac—Greg McMahon—was our special teams coach. He found me with the widest grin splashed across his gray-goateed face. "I don't know if anybody else could have come up with the ball except for you. We had the right guy in the right place for Ambush."

Before I sat down to rest my burning arms, I looked for one of our equipment managers. "Here, hold onto this ball," I directed. Equipment managers are used to stowing away game balls that were part of big plays—a touchdown catch, an interception, or a fumble recovery. I had a feeling that this would be the most important football I'd ever hold.

Man, it felt good to come up with that recovery. I was super glad that it was me and not them.

Mike

I couldn't tell what the heck was happening down there. As bodies flew and the refs struggled to figure out what had transpired, there was mass confusion.

I had never seen it take the refs so long to determine who had the ball. Players from both teams wouldn't give up. I think they sensed that this onside kick was bigger than a battle for the ball. This was a battle for the Super Bowl.

I heard somebody yell, "Chris has got the ball! He's got the

(AP Photo/ J. Pat Carter)

ball!" That was good news because if he didn't recover the onside kick, we were in big trouble.

People were going crazy with excitement, and then I heard the public address announcer say, "Onside kick recovery by Jonathan Casillas!"

What a minute! That was my son running off the field, carrying the ball high. Chris had the ball in his hand. I jumped to my feet and gave Celia and Mike a high-five—plus a few Saints fans in the row in front of us.

Minutes earlier, The Who had just finished singing "We won't get fooled again." This time the Colts had been fooled by some outside-the-box thinking from Coach Payton. His gamble paid off big time. The Saints took over, marching 58 yards in just six plays to score the go-ahead touchdown in just over three minutes of play. Instead of Peyton Manning coming onto the field with a 10-6 lead, he and his Colts teammates were behind 13-10. Big psychological difference.

I have to hand it to Manning, however. He quickly moved the Colts down the field to score a touchdown and retake the lead, but I felt that Chris' recovery had inspired the Saints to take this game.

Chris

The entire second half was *We score, they score.* We forged a 24-17 lead with less than six minutes to go, but that was more than enough time for Peyton Manning to take the game into overtime. The Colts were driving late in the game when our defensive back Tracy Porter jumped a route on Peyton Manning for a pick-six. Tracy raced 74 yards to the house, and just like that, we had broken this game wide open, 31-17.

We were within three minutes of setting off New Orleans's

biggest celebration in its 300-year history. When the final gun went off and giant fans swirled the air with multi-colored confetti, I was super excited. It was surreal. I had always dreamed of playing in the NFL and winning a Super Bowl, but to have played in such a big game—and literally have my hands on the outcome—was the pinnacle of my football career.

I suddenly found news cameras and reporters thrusting microphones at me. Before the Super Bowl, I think I could count on one hand the number of times I'd been interviewed by someone other than a reporter from the *New Orleans Times-Picayune*. After this game, though, I must have done a dozen stand-up interviews. The reporters all wanted to know how I managed to come out of that pile with the ball.

Mike

Of course, there were hugs all around and great joy among the twelve members of Team Reis.

Time to party!

The Saints were hosting a post-Super Bowl bash at the team hotel after the game, which ended around 10:30 p.m. As far as I was concerned, I had some catching up to do. My alcohol consumption up to that point had amounted to a couple of beers at the NFL Experience before we entered the stadium.

We reached the InterContinental Miami hotel just after midnight to the invitation-only event for Saints players, their families and significant others, Saints management, and tons of celebrities, including Kim Kardashian and James Carville, the national political figure with New Orleans ties. Dennis Haysbert, the African-American actor with the deep baritone voice who does those Allstate commercials, appeared to be enjoying himself.

An alternative rock band based in New Orleans, Better Than

Ezra, opened up the musical entertainment portion of the evening, and they were followed by country singer Kenny Chesney. Since the Saints had just registered a monumental upset of the Colts, everyone was in a great mood. The ballroom was packed.

I loved that there were open bars everywhere you looked, and the liquor was flowing. Celia really didn't approve of me drinking very much, so I'd excuse myself and make my way to one of the open bars, where I'd order my favorite libation—vodka on the rocks. I would get two or three drinks and stand there and knock them down.

And then I'd go back to the table and check on Celia and everyone else to make sure they were having a good time.

Chris

Michelle and I had a great time celebrating with family and team-mates. The party started breaking up around three o'clock in the morning. What a day! But I was ready for bed, so Michelle and I walked toward the lobby to take an elevator to my room. We ran into the equipment manager to whom I had given the ball—the onside kick recovery that changed everything about Super Bowl XLIV.

"Do you still have that ball I gave you?" I knew that the equipment managers marked them and put these footballs in gunny sacks for safekeeping.

"Nope," he said.

I couldn't believe what I was hearing. "How come? I gave it to you."

"After the game, an official with the NFL came up and took it. He said that this was the first recovered onside kick in Super Bowl history before the fourth quarter, and they wanted to put the ball into the Hall of Fame." I knew the NFL Hall of Fame was in Canton,

Ohio, the birthplace of pro football—and where I was born.

I smiled. I wasn't a big sentimental guy when it came to sports memorabilia. Actually, I thought it was pretty cool that future generations could see that Super Bowl XLIV football that I recovered. Little did I know that my onside kick recovery would become the defining moment of the big game. NFL Films would later make an eight-minute film about Ambush, calling it "the greatest heist in Super Bowl history."

Mike

I was on the top of the world. In fact, I was just getting warmed up at three o'clock in the morning. So was a lot of the crowd. I kept putting away vodkas on the rocks, and I'd say I probably had twelve or fourteen drinks by the time 5 a.m. rolled around. Celia was making noises about leaving, and so was my son, Mike, and his girlfriend. Okay, time to go.

I had rented a nice luxury car for the Super Bowl weekend. While we waited for the valet to fetch the vehicle, Celia sidled closer to me. "Don't you think you should . . . you know . . . let me drive?"

The question ticked me off. Actually, I was pissed because I wasn't drunk. Feeling good, yes, but I was far from smashed.

"I'm perfectly fine," I replied. "There's nothing wrong with me."

Inwardly I seethed, however. I didn't like being told that I may have had too much to drink. I tried to hide my outrage. I didn't have a problem with drinking. I reminded myself to give Celia some grace, though. She and I had been married almost two years, so she wasn't really aware of how much I could drink when I set my mind to it.

Besides, couldn't she cut me a little slack? I was feeling on top of the world. My son was the hero of Super Bowl XLIV, so I *deserved* a few drinks.

When our car rolled up to the hotel entrance, I moved quickly to the driver's side and handed the valet a generous tip.

Mike, however, refused to get in the car. "Dad, don't you think you should let Celia drive?"

I glared at my son. "No, there's no way I'm letting her drive. I'm fine."

Mike took a step closer. "Dad, there's no way in hell I'm getting in the car with you behind the wheel."

I was getting angrier by the minute, but something in my mind told me that it wasn't worth arguing with my son. After all, we just won the Super Bowl, and I didn't want to ruin the night. I looked toward my wife, who was sitting in the shotgun seat. "Celia, can you drive?"

There wasn't much conversation on the drive back to the hotel, which was a good thing because that gave me time to calm down. I shrugged my shoulders. Even though I felt some shame in not driving, I had to admit that it had been an awesome day.

Two weeks later, back home in Atlanta, I drove to a thirtieth birthday party for Mike's then girlfriend, Sandra, given by some friends in Roswell. I decided I wasn't going to drink that night even though Celia was out of town attending a real estate convention hosted by her company, Keller Williams. For some reason that escapes me, I thought I needed to lay low that weekend.

We were having a good time hanging out when Mike approached me. "Dad, how come you're not drinking?" He knew how unusual it was for me *not* to have a vodka on the rocks in my hands in social settings like this.

I didn't have a good answer, except that maybe I was playing the martyr. "Okay, you changed my mind. I'll just have one."

I had more than one. I had one vodka on the rocks and then

another. And I had another, plus two more. The party broke up early, around 10:30, but I was just getting started. I drove to Wild Wings in Alpharetta, where I had two vodkas straight on the rocks. I got bored and wanted to find another place, so I drove over to the Lone Star Bar & Grill, also in Alpharetta, where I had two more. I downed them pretty quick.

It was around 11:30 when I got into my car and proceeded north on Georgia State Route 400, a four-lane highway that led to my hometown of Cumming. Then I decided to do something dumb—text a message on my BlackBerry. While keeping half an eye on the highway, I tapped out a text message to Celia saying that I was going home and would call her after I arrived.

That's when I saw the bright blue lights of a Forsyth County Sheriff's Department cruiser on my tail. I muttered a four-letter word. I had probably swerved a bit since I was texting and driving. Not a good thing to do on a Saturday night.

I pulled over to the shoulder and waited for the sheriff's deputy to approach. I rolled down my window and adopted a winning smile. The deputy shined a flashlight in my face. "Have you been drinking?" he asked.

"Two," I replied. "I had two."

"Sir, if you could step outside the car."

I did as I was told, and then the sheriff's deputy said he was going to conduct a field sobriety test. It's just like you see in the movies: first, he asked me to look into his flashlight, no doubt to check how much my eyes were dilated. Then he asked me to stand with my arms outstretched and try to touch my nose.

I did as ordered, touching my nose with the tip of my forefingers. I thought I had aced the test.

"Now I'd like you to walk in a straight line, toe to toe," the deputy said.

"Well, I can't do *that* sober," I joked. My attempt at making light of the situation failed, however.

I tried walking in a straight line, but this time around, I don't think I did so hot. I also teetered a bit when he told me to stand on one leg. This wasn't going well, so it was time to play my hole card.

"Don't you know who I am?"

The policeman looked at me with a blank face. "Should I know who you are?"

"Two weeks ago, my son recovered the football during the onside kick at the Super Bowl."

"Well, isn't that great? You have the right to remain silent. Anything you say can and will be used against you in a court of law. You have the right to an attorney. If you cannot afford an attorney, one will be provided to you. Do you understand the rights I have just read to you? With these rights in mind, do you wish to speak to me?"

"What's going on?"

"You're being arrested. Turn around so I can put the handcuffs on."

I was 'cuffed and then stuffed into the rear bench of the police cruiser. You know those police reality shows like *Cops* where they show the officer putting his hand on the perp's head and shoving him into the back of patrol car? I was living that reality. The thoughts racing through my mind were:

- *This is going to be expensive.*
- *I could lose my job.*
- *I'll be humiliated.*
- *I could lose my driver's license.*
- *I could get divorced . . . again.*

Then a deep sense of shame overcame me as I thought, *I'm the father of a Super Bowl champion, and this is the way I behave.*

I felt so humiliated being booked for a DUI at the Forsyth County Sheriff's Department. This wasn't my first rodeo, so I knew what to expect. I bailed myself out and took a taxi home at 4 a.m.

I did a lot of thinking that weekend. I thought about my son Chris, who—through nothing I did—became not only a great guy but a great man of God. When he was growing up, people told him over and over that he couldn't do certain things or achieve certain goals, but he showed them anyway.

Something else gnawed at my conscience. Four-and-a-half years earlier, at a Fellowship of Christian Athletes event hosted by Chris, I had heard and responded to the gospel message that Jesus welcomed sinners like me. All I had to do was believe in Him and place my trust in Him.

I asked Jesus to come into my life that day, which I'll describe in greater detail later in this book. Yet here I was, attending church and professing to be a man of God, but I was still behaving like one who didn't believe in God at all. That's why I felt incredible shame and low self-respect. Once again, I had blown it.

My son had just made the most famous recovery in Super Bowl history. Now I needed my own recovery—a recovery from my addiction to alcohol, sex, and a life filled with bad choices and poor decisions.

Little did I know how that play would change both our lives as father and son forever. Chris would be there again when I needed him most, and together we would make a recovery of a lifetime.

2

A Brush with History

Mike

I'm here because my mother and her best friend Rosie were sitting on the front steps outside their rundown apartment building in a poor neighborhood on the northwest side of Chicago.

Lois Marie Slaughter was thirteen years old when a Fuller Brush salesman stumbled upon the two girls one afternoon. Standing before Lois was a handsome eighteen-year-old named James Reis. The smooth-talking door-to-door peddler with movie star good looks didn't miss a beat.

"Hi, there," Jim said, sizing up the opportunity to make a different kind of sale. "I'm a Fuller Brush salesman, and your street just happens to be in my territory. Mind if I sit down and rest for a while? You're really cute, young lady. Let's say you and I go out Friday night."

Lois blushed at his forwardness, but at age of thirteen, she had never gone out on a date. When Jim saw that he wasn't getting anywhere, he left his phone number on the back of his business card.

The year was 1953, and there was an influx of rural white families and various racial and ethnic groups that made Chicago the fifth largest city in the world halfway through the 20th century.

Born in Virginia, Lois was literally a coal miner's daughter. When work in the coal mines dried up during the Depression, many fled the grinding poverty of the Appalachian mountains and struck out for Chicago in search of manufacturing jobs and a better future.

I wish that was the case with my mom's family. Her father, Reedy Slaughter, journeyed to Chicago in search of Lois' mother, who had run off to stay with friends after receiving a drunken beating from the hands of her husband. Instead of traveling to Chicago in search of a better life, an episode of domestic violence brought the Slaughter family to the Windy City.

When James Reis and his box of Fuller brushes came walking up that day, a spark was lit but nothing happened until Rosie dared Lois to call Jim a few weeks later. It wasn't long before the young salesman was calling on Lois after hours. Her father, a player himself and wise to the world, wouldn't allow the young suitor anywhere near his blonde-haired, freckled-faced daughter. The reason was obvious: he was eighteen and she was thirteen, so there was quite an age and maturity gap between the pair.

Jim, however, would not be deterred, and Lois was naturally flattered by the attention. She started sneaking out to see her new beau whenever she heard his secret whistle from several houses away. That was her signal to tell her parents she was going across the street to visit Rosie. Lois would jump into Jim's car and drive downtown to do what teenagers do at that age.

These clandestine dates occurred over the next two years. They began talking marriage, even though she was just a sophomore at Wells High School. There was a formidable obstacle, however—her age. She was fifteen years old, and it was illegal to marry in Illinois at that young age. But they couldn't wait.

So the young couple hatched a plan: they would get married

in Clinton, Iowa, where age restrictions were more lenient, but Lois still needed parental consent. Even though Jim was twenty years old, he needed at least one parent to give consent to marry a fifteen-year-old. Jim's mother objected and pleaded with him not to marry the "little hillbilly." She even tried to bribe him by offering him money *not* to make such a big mistake. Jim wouldn't think of it, however, and his mother eventually gave her blessing.

As for Lois, her mother reconciled herself to the fact that the young couple was dead set on marrying, but her father would have none of it. She agreed to sign the consent form.

On the day of their wedding, Jim had to take Lois out of school for the trip to Clinton. She remembers someone in the principal's office telling her that "your dad is here to check you out of school for the day." As the young couple and their respective mothers were pulling out of the neighborhood, they saw Reedy stumble out of a bar. He was "three sheets to the wind" as they asked him to come to Clinton. Reedy started crying and pleading with his daughter not to marry Jim, telling her she was making the biggest mistake of her life. Eventually, though, he agreed to get in the car.

After tying the knot at a small church just down the street from the county courthouse in the Iowa border town, the young couple honeymooned in Hot Springs, Arkansas. When they returned to Chicago, they settled into a small $40-a-month apartment closer to the north side of the city.

A short time later, Dad joined the Navy as a seaman and was stationed in Norfolk, Virginia. Mom lived in naval housing on the base until they purchased a small white trailer for $1,200 with money Dad borrowed from his mother. I came along three years into their marriage and was born August 30, 1958. Mom was still a teenager and a kid herself when I arrived, just eighteen years old.

Dad was twenty-three. Three days after I was born, Dad left for sea.

We eventually returned to Chicago after Dad was discharged from the Navy. Three sisters were born after me: Debbie, Ellen, and Patty.

My father was good with his hands, the type of guy who could fix anything, given the right tools. During the 1960s, everyone wanted residential air conditioning, which was coming down drastically in price. Today, we leave our air-conditioned homes, jump into our air-conditioned cars, and drive to our air-conditioned workplaces or shopping malls and think nothing of it, but fifty years ago air conditioning was limited to movie theaters and a few restaurants.

My father was in the right place at the right time. Since everyone was talking about this new thing called "central air," he decided to start a one-man business of installing and repairing central air conditioning units in the summer as well as heating systems for the winter.

My father was a blue-collar guy, which fit his aptitude. He was far different in temperament and drive than his younger brother, Fred, who was his only sibling. Where Jim Reis was always a grease-under-the-fingernails type of guy who graduated from Lane Technical High School on the north side of Chicago, Fred was the blond-haired, blue-eyed All-American type. A fantastic basketball player, skilled tennis player, and scratch golfer. Great grades in the classroom, too.

Guess who got all the praise growing up? And guess who got all the beatings?

One time, when my father was a young boy, his father, Ben Reis, caught him fooling around with the gas burners on the kitchen stove.

"Stop monkeying around, you stupid son of a bitch!" Ben

roared. "I'm going to teach you a lesson you'll never forget!"

Ben Reis turned on a burner, grabbed his son by the scruff of the neck, and held his hand over the blue fire. A scream stopped the punishment, but my father's hand had been burned and a lesson learned.

How did such a cruel event happen? My grandfather was a huge alcoholic who drank nearly every day and every night. That was his way of coping with his miserable life and my grandmother. He was the son of Polish immigrants who died when Ben was young. He grew up a foster child with a hardscrabble existence in some of Chicago's toughest neighborhoods. But if you're thinking that Reis is *not* a Polish name, you'd be correct. Reis wasn't my grandfather's last name growing up.

Confused? Me, too! Here's what happened. My paternal grandfather was born Bernard Boldiga, as befitting his Polish background. After he married Clara Ellen Reis (Clare) in 1934, she unilaterally decided that her husband and family would never get anywhere in Chicago with a Polish surname since there was a certain prejudice against "Polacks," as they were called back in the day. She announced that they were going to change their last name . . . to her last name!

Henceforth, my grandfather would become known as Ben Reis—pronounced *Reece*. It's a Swedish name, a given since Clare Reis was the daughter of Swedish immigrants.

Clare Reis wore the pants in the family, and she's an important part of my story as you'll soon discover. My parents would often leave my sisters and me in her care whenever they could, no doubt to get a break from child-rearing duties. During the summer months when Ben and Clare Reis would look after us, my grandfather would trudge out to the screened-in back porch where he'd watch a TV with rabbit ears broadcasting a Cubs game. He'd pop the tabs on beer after beer until he was so obliterated that he'd pass out. His snoring was loud enough to make the neighborhood dogs howl.

With her husband sawing logs, Grandma Clare was free to . . . really mess me up. I was probably five years old when I first remember Grandma walking around the house without a bra under a loose-fitting revealing top—or sometimes nothing at all. I can remember her approaching me, topless and wearing no bra, and asking, "Don't you want to touch my puppies?"

I'd look up and stare. I'd never seen anything like those before. Things got more bizarre when it was time for bed. With Grandpa passed out on the back porch, I would often sleep in her bed. Grandma would change into a thin nightshirt while I put on my pajamas. When she finished getting ready for bed, she'd order me to lie down on the floor. Then she would stand over me, and I'd look up and see that she wasn't wearing any underwear. She'd force me to look for a long time, and I was confused. I was too young to be aroused, but I was definitely curious about what I saw.

Her abusive behavior didn't end there. There were occasions over the years when Grandma would climb in bed and get real close to me—real, real close. I may have been eight years old by then, but I didn't know what fondling was or what to do about it. All I knew was that it was futile to resist or say anything against her.

I had learned early on not to cross Grandma Clare because she had a volcanic temper and a dominating personality. I never questioned her because I never wanted to experience her verbal wrath. She was an evil woman who loved to humiliate me every chance she got and liked to argue with everyone in the family. She was one of those persons always telling others what to do and how to live.

The only time I saw Grandma Clare smile was when she took

my cousin Whitney and me on Saturday afternoon outings to State Street, Chicago's main shopping district. Her favorite stop was the Marshall Field's department store. I thought shopping was boring and could never understand why Grandma liked to look at racks of clothes for hours and never purchase anything.

One time, we were in the women's department when Grandma Clare called Whitney and me together.

"Listen, you two. I need you to do me a favor. I'd like you to go over there"—she pointed to a corner of the store—"and pick a fight with each other. Yell, scream, and call each other every name in the book. Make sure that people around can hear you."

"But why, Grandma—" I didn't see the point.

"Shut up! Do as you're told. *Now.*"

So that's what Whitney and I did. We walked to where Grandma pointed and then I pulled on my cousin's hair. She screamed, and then we started fighting and calling each other names. Sure enough, it wasn't long before we created a big scene. Several sales clerks rushed over and separated us.

Years later, I would learn why Grandma wanted us to act out in a big downtown department store. While we were screaming, "Don't hit me!" and shoving each other, sales clerks would leave their stations to find what the commotion was all about. That gave Grandma an opportunity to slip scarves, jars of make-up, and cheap costume jewelry pieces into her oversized purse. In other words, Grandma used our diversion to shoplift.

There was an even darker side to Grandma, and that was her behavior with Whitney. I later learned that when my cousin was five or six years old, Grandma would stick objects in her and perform unspeakable sexual acts. The woman was sick!

I never knew any of this happened to Whitney growing up, but I always wondered why she was so frustrated and angry as a child.

She says that my grandmother would babysit her at her house and then go off on a tirade, grabbing books off the shelves and throwing them to the floor. Then she'd turn furniture over and empty dresser drawers on the carpet. Whitney was dumbfounded why her grandmother would halfway destroy her bedroom.

When her parents returned, they would see her bedroom in shambles and demand to know what happened.

"Whitney didn't want to go to bed, so she threw another one of her temper tantrums," Grandma would say, waving at the destruction.

How was Whitney going to win that one? Of course her parents believed Grandma Clare. And then Whitney would get spanked and severely punished for a crime she did not commit.

Whitney has spent most of her life in therapy and struggled with alcohol until she quit drinking three years ago. Neither of us can understand why our parents would leave us so much in Grandma Clare's care, but they never suspected she was severely abusing their children.

We later learned why Grandma was such a sick individual. Born October 14, 1913, she was the youngest of five children. She was only four years old when her mother died unexpectedly of pneumonia in 1917. Her father, William, rounded up all five kids and dropped them off at Angel Guardian Orphanage, founded in 1865 by five German Catholic parishes to help preserve the German cultural heritage.

"Here, they're yours," the father said. "I can't take care of them."

Clare never saw her father again. She was separated from her siblings and lived with other orphaned children her age.

Clare was at the mercy of the nuns. I can only imagine the living hell that she endured. It is believed today that hundreds of children were sexually abused behind the walls of Angel Guardian. I suspect my grandmother was doing things to me and my cousin that had been done to her.

Whatever happened, she was screwed up by her upbringing. In modern-day language, we would classify her as bipolar, but people didn't know much about mental illness in the 1960s or how to explain Grandma's massive mood changes and bizarre behavior—from mania to depression. Nor were they aware that vulnerable young children like me and my sisters, along with my cousins, were the victims of her abuse.

It would be years before I found out how much and in what ways Grandma's sexual abuse messed me up.

∽∾

While I was wary of Grandma Clare, I thought Grandpa Ben was a really cool guy. He was always good to me, but what I liked most about him was that he stood up for me against my grandmother. That may have made his life sheer torture when he and Grandma Clare got home, but that's who he was. I just wish he had stood up more for himself against my grandmother.

While Grandma liked to take me shopping so that she could pilfer a few things, Grandpa liked to escort me to the local bars. Saloons, taverns, pubs, and brewery-sponsored Tied Houses—they seemed to be at every intersection in Chicago.

When I was seven or eight, I loved tagging along with Grandpa whenever he went to the corner tavern. First of all, everyone was friendly. Grandpa's friends always seemed to be in a good mood, laughing and swapping stories. I could tell they were having a good time when they had a drink in one hand, and that made a big impression on me—more than I knew at the time.

When Grandpa would sit me down on a tall stool at the bar, I'd feel very grown-up sipping a Coke from a glass-molded tumbler. Every so often, he would let me take a sip of his beer and whiskey. I loved the dark, cool surroundings of the tavern illuminated by the light of neon beer signs coupled with the grainy smell of alcohol in the air.

Occasionally, he'd let me get off the barstool to play shuffleboard bowling with those silver pucks sliding down the lane on sawdust. Other times, Grandpa would play cards or pitch pennies with me, watching and giving me a share of the winnings to avoid the wrath of Grandma if she ever found out.

Grandpa Ben was mainly an auto mechanic and ran through a number of odd jobs back then. He'd tell me stories about how he drove for the gangster Al Capone at times in the 1930s. He also chauffeured Babe Ruth, the New York Yankee home-run hitter who was the most famous person alive, to Comiskey Park when the Babe was making his farewell tour following his retirement.

My grandfather wasn't a gangster, but he looked like he could have been cast in a movie like *The Untouchables*. He was five feet, eight inches tall with an olive complexion and pencil-thin moustache. He liked to dress nattily in double-breasted suits with two-tone shoes, but he usually wore brown slacks and a white button-down short-sleeve shirt when he took me to his favorite watering holes. I felt special being the oldest grandchild and being escorted into his favorite bars.

I was a normal-sized kid growing up, but the chicken pox did me in. Somehow, lesions of the virus got into my nose, setting off a nasty rash inside my nasal passages. Next thing I knew, I couldn't stop bleeding. My parents' attempts to stem the flow were unsuccessful, so they rushed me to the emergency room. I ended up staying at the hospital for thirty days, bedridden the entire time.

A combination of prescription medicine, lack of exercise, and a growing appetite caused me to add weight. Seemingly overnight, I became a chubby kid. I had apple red chipmunk cheeks, too.

Grandma Clare was embarrassed by me and hated to see her oldest grandchild with a Michelin tire around his waist. She decided she was going to do something about that—by offering a running commentary about how fat I was and taking any chance she could to publicly embarrass and humiliate me.

Here's an example. I was fairly young, still under ten years of age, when we celebrated my Uncle Fred's accomplishment of obtaining another advanced degree. The setting was a dinner party in the banquet room of an upscale steak house with family and friends. I didn't like the grisly fat that ringed my steak, so I sliced off that part and didn't eat it.

A friend of the family said, "Hey, you need to eat that fat. That gives the steak all the flavor!"

Grandma Clare saw her opening. "As fat as he is, he doesn't need to be eating any more fat. Just look at him. He's disgusting!" She spoke loudly enough for everyone to hear. No one came rushing to my defense.

Then again, my grandmother was always muttering things like, "You'll never amount to anything in this world," or how disappointed my dad was to have me as a son.

That was a common theme with her. When I was twelve years old, I was home sick from school when Mom was about to give birth to Patty. When the labor pangs grew too frequent, she and Dad rushed to the hospital while Grandma came over to watch me.

Several hours later, the phone rang.

She listened to my father telling her that after a son and two daughters, one more daughter had joined the world.

"Congratulations," she said as she hung up the phone with my father. "I'll be sure to tell Mike."

Hearing whether I had a new baby brother or sister was a big deal for me. I heard footsteps and then saw Grandma come into my bedroom.

"Well, do I have a brother or a sister?" I'm sure the anticipation was written all over my face.

"It's a girl," Grandma said with no emotion or hint of happiness. "We were hoping for a boy because you've been such a massive disappointment."

Hot tears formed in my eyes from the humiliation, but Grandma wasn't finished turning the knife.

"Your dad is really upset that he didn't have a boy. We don't think you'll amount to anything. You'll be lucky to become a trash collector."

Grandma wasn't just sadistic on me. She also got after my mom and said things that were entirely inappropriate for any mother-in-law, mouthing off opinions like:

- "You're a terrible wife and mother. I told Jimmy he could have done better than you. He should have married Susan, that cute girl down the street from us. She came from a good family."
- "All your kids are worthless and will never amount to anything. Jimmy should just leave you all."

When my grandfather would take the side of those who'd been on the receiving end of Grandma's mean-spirited barbs, the two would really get after it. He would kick her in the rear end, calling her a "dumb Swede," and she'd retaliate by grabbing an ashtray and flinging it at him. I witnessed constant knock-down fights with the two of them throwing things at each other and furniture getting turned over. Holes punched in the walls, slammed doors—it was always violent.

I never met my maternal grandfather because he died a year before I was born while driving home after spending some cuddle time with his mistress. Mom's dad had multiple affairs and was a drinker, and he had been drinking at the time of his accident. He was thirty-six years old.

And he was also a church minister for a while.

I know . . . all of this is rather unbelievable. Mom told me that she didn't find out about her father's death for days because authorities were unable to find her mother. She had apparently run off after being beaten up by my grandfather and was staying with friends . . . again. My mother found out when a next-door neighbor read about his death in the newspaper. Hearing the awful news, she fainted on the spot. She had no idea!

My maternal grandmother, Lee Slaughter, was also a big drinker. She liked blended concoctions, and her preferred drink was the Brandy Alexander, a sweet, brandy-based cocktail consisting of cognac and crème de cacao. My enduring image of her is arriving at her place while she was stirring a big pitcher of Brandy Alexander's.

Grandma Lee was ahead of her time back in the 1960s. She lived with several men and was married four or five times. You didn't do that unless you were Elizabeth Taylor back then. I didn't see Grandma Lee nearly as much as Grandma Clare, however.

Throughout my teenage years, I frustrated Dad because he was always trying to teach me how to fix things or build stuff, but I was never interested in working with my hands. Always sarcastic with his family, we didn't speak much, and a long conversation between us would be ten words. He made me "work" alongside him in the summers or on Saturdays in his budding heating and air conditioning business, which I greatly resented. I wanted to be with my friends, which was a natural reaction.

Growing up, the one thing I always heard him gripe about was Chicago's brutal winters. Maybe it's because Dad spent many of his days in freezing basements and underneath houses trying to repair a broken-down heating system, but at the dinner table, he was always saying stuff like, "We gotta do something about this" or "We gotta get outta here. I just can't take these winters anymore."

Another thing working on my dad's mind was the jealousy he felt about his younger brother's success. Fred had attended and graduated from Wright State University on a basketball and tennis scholarship. He later earned a master's degree and eventually his Ph.D. in Psychology. He married a stunning blonde-haired, blue-eyed model and moved to an upscale Chicago suburb, where he became a successful psychologist and real estate developer. He was well on his way toward financial and personal success.

Dad? He was bumping along through life, and I would categorize our family as lower-middle class. While his brother had a cushy job and a thriving private practice as a psychologist, Dad griped about middle-of-the-night emergency calls to get the heat on at someone's dilapidated walk-up. For my father, there had to be a better day.

One summer evening, after the dinner dishes were cleared away, he unfolded a map of the United States. "If we could live anywhere, where should we live?" he asked my sisters and me.

I was dumbfounded. I knew Dad wasn't happy with his job, but I didn't think things were *that* bad that we had to move. I was ten years old, about to enter the fourth grade. I had plenty of good friends, and Chicago was all that I had known.

Dad didn't wait for suggestions. He punched his right forefinger in the middle of the state of Georgia. "Atlanta! That's where we should go. I hear it's growing like crazy, and the weather is great."

I looked closer at the map. The distance from Chicago to Atlanta looked like a million miles. We're talking the northern end of the continental United States to the southern end.

Dad smiled. I could tell that he liked his idea. "Tell you what," he said. "I'm gonna go down there, and I'm gonna get work. Then I'm gonna send for you guys, and you can come down there."

And that's exactly what happened.

The year was 1969, and Atlanta had experienced rapid growth in the city's population and economy during the 1960s, so much so that this semi-capital of the Deep South was called "the city too busy to hate." In sports, the city had recently become major league: the Milwaukee Braves moved to Atlanta in 1966; the NFL expanded to Atlanta in the same year with the addition of the Falcons; and the NBA's St. Louis Hawks moved to Atlanta in 1968 to become the Atlanta Hawks.

I can't say that I cared very much about this at the age of ten. All I knew was that Atlanta was much smaller than Chicago, and in my young mind, smaller meant not as good.

Dad packed up, climbed into his old Ford Econoline work van, and drove by himself to Atlanta that summer. He dropped into restaurants to drum up business for his new company, which he called Atlanta Refrigeration. He was able to get enough repair work to lease space for a workshop and office in the Buckhead area of Atlanta.

Then Dad put his old Fuller Brush days to good use by printing up a flyer and going door-to-door selling central air conditioning units.

"Morning, ma'am," he'd say. "You're cooling your house, right?"

The woman of the home would usually say they did have air conditioning.

"I see it's one of those window units for the living room," Dad would say. "That's better than nothing, but you can have central air conditioning for a very affordable price, and can I install it in only three days."

And that's how Dad got his foot into the door in Atlanta.

Soon, Dad was hiring guys to help him out, even though they didn't know a thing about installing and repairing air conditioning or heating units. Dad had his hands full keeping on top of all his jobs.

He didn't have time to move us to Atlanta until Christmas break, when he returned to Chicago to pack us up during the middle of my fourth-grade year.

Dad became successful in Atlanta, though not as successful as he could have been. I believe it's because he never had the vision to take his HVAC—heating, ventilation, and air conditioning—business to the next level. That's too bad because Atlanta's suburbs would grow like colorful wildflowers following a spring rain during the 1970s and 1980s. Dad could have made a mint putting in central air conditioning in thousands and thousands of new homes. Years later, Dad would sell his company to one of his employees who *did* have the vision to expand. Today Atlanta Refrigeration works with over 6,000 restaurant, hotel, and retail clients.

At the time, though, his modest success led to a lot of other things. Turns out that my dad was a big drinker as well as a big womanizer, and I saw it all happen at an impressionable age.

I would say that's a bad combination, given what happened to me during my childhood.

3

COMING OF AGE

Mike

Our move to Atlanta was reminiscent of the lyrics to one of my favorite television shows growing up in the 1960s, *The Beverly Hillbillies*. Dad's work van and Mom's green Ford station wagon with sporty wood grain paneling were jammed and piled high with all our furniture and worldly belongings. The way we rolled into Georgia, we must have looked like Jed Clampett and the rest of his kin—wide-eyed and uncertain about what lay ahead.

We arrived at our new home—a small three-bedroom apartment in Sandy Springs, a suburb north of Atlanta—after fourteen grueling hours on the road. Sandy Springs was bisected by Georgia 400 and Interstate 285, whose construction in the 1960s initiated a housing boom north of downtown that included thousands of tract homes and apartment complexes. Compared to the small lots in Chicago with houses so close you had to turn sideways to walk between them, I discovered plenty of big backyards and manicured parks in which to play underneath a sprawling canopy of hickory and pine trees that earned Atlanta the nickname "The City in a Forest."

Atlanta had another nickname—"Hotlanta"—which certainly didn't hurt Dad's fledgling air conditioning business. I didn't see him a lot after we moved because he was working all the time. With Atlanta so spread out, Dad had to drive lengthy distances to many of his jobs. His long workdays created a lot of stress and lonely times around our house.

After a couple of years, Dad had a great idea when he decided that Atlanta Refrigeration would become one of the first businesses to offer 24-hour service in the early 1970s. To make that happen, Dad installed a business phone in the family room of our home, dedicated to receiving incoming calls twenty-four hours a day, seven days a week.

It wasn't unusual for my father to be rousted out of bed by the loud ringing of his business phone. Those post-midnight service calls woke the entire house but never bothered him. To Dad, the *brrr-ing* sounded more like *cha-ching*—since he would be charging nearly double his normal hourly rate. For Dad, it was *all* about the money.

To pad the bottom line even further, I saw him cut a few corners . . . like the times he'd go out on a service call and determine that the customer needed a new motor, fan, or compressor for his air conditioning unit. Those types of jobs weren't uncommon, especially in a part of the country where the air conditioning units were on 24/7 for months at a time.

He'd remove the defective part and tell the homeowner it had to be replaced with a brand new piece of equipment. He would act as if he was leaving to procure the part from a local supplier, but he'd drive back to his shop instead. From there he'd call the customer, and with great regret, announce that he needed a couple of hours to locate the new part for their air conditioning unit.

By now, the wife and kiddies were broiling and everyone was miserable. They would pay anything to get their air conditioning working again quickly. Dad always promised to hurry.

After hanging up the phone, Dad would search the back of his shop, where he kept a pile of used parts all in running condition. He'd polish one up, get it nice and clean, and then install it as new at a much higher price.

He showed the same sort of deceitful behavior in his personal life. I'll never forget the time when he called the police and said an expensive ring had been stolen from the house: *You see, officer, we were having a party last weekend, and the house was filled up with friends and people we didn't know . . . and now Lois' diamond ring is missing . . . it's worth at least $10,000!*

Dad would file the police report and then submit a claim on his home insurance policy. His dishonesty and those kinds of things bothered me, even when I was young. But if Dad saw a way to beat the system and make a buck, he'd grab it.

Dad justified his actions by telling himself that he was taking care of his family. The ends justified the means. If he had to screw somebody over by selling them old used parts or telling a lie to the insurance company to get ahead in life, then that's what he was going to do. If he had to tell the sweet and trusting little old lady two doors down the street from our house on Lake Forrest Drive that she needed to downsize into an apartment—and then convince her to sell him her house for *way* under market value— then that was okay, too. Dad was just being a savvy businessman. It didn't matter who he hurt in the process.

I knew what he was doing was dishonest because I learned right and wrong from my mother. She did a good job teaching me some fundamental values, and throughout my childhood, Mom was always there for me, loving and supportive.

I think I know why Mom and I enjoyed such a special bond. During the first year of my life in Norfolk, Virginia, Dad was out to sea with the U.S. Navy, and I only saw him once or twice before my first birthday. When he left the Navy and rejoined the family, the closeness between Mom and me was firmly established. This became a huge source of conflict between them as I was growing up. In his eyes, she treated me better than she treated him, which made my father jealous and insecure.

Dad took out his frustration on my mother whenever they argued about something, which was a regular occurrence around our house. I often heard them yelling and screaming at each other in the middle of the night. I heard doors slamming. Threats made. I would shake with fear as I lay in my twin bed, listening to the thundering sound of Dad's voice.

Ugly things were shouted: "What the &#%$ do you do around here all day while I'm out working my ass off? How hard can it be taking care of three kids? You're a worthless slut! Is Mike even my son, that lazy son of a bitch! He's good for nothing!"

I didn't understand any of this growing up, nor did I have any idea what precipitated their knockdown, drag-out fights. If I had to hazard a guess, their squabbles usually had something to do with money—or lack of it. Everything in our house was about money. They were always just getting by, even with the "creative" repairs my father foisted on his unwitting customers.

Their quarrels often started in the master bedroom and would spill out into the hallway and into our den before finally reaching the kitchen. They would slap and hit each other as Mom would return fire. "I hate you, you asshole!" was a typical response from Mom.

One time when I was in the eighth grade, they came storming out of their bedroom screaming at each other. He was furious, and I feared for her life for some reason. I thought Dad meant it when he said, "I wish you were out of my life for good!"

I stepped between them. "Dad, stop! Leave her alone!"

"Are you @#$%-ing stupid? I oughta knock the &%$# out of you!"

He made a threatening gesture with his fist, but I didn't care. I was almost wishing he would hit me. Instead, he aimed more verbal fire in my direction. "You're so @#$%-ing ungrateful! After everything I've given you," he said, pointing in the direction of our swimming pool in the backyard. "All I do is work my ass off for you. I wish you had never been born. You're worthless and will never amount to anything!"

And so it went. Mom would rush to my defense, telling my father to leave me alone, but each verbal blow wounded my heart. I grew up thinking there was nothing I could do to win my dad's approval or his love.

It's no wonder why I was embarrassed to be seen with my father in front of my peers. I hated those occasions when he picked me up from school in his dented work van with *Atlanta Refrigeration* boldly scripted across the side of his truck. He'd always have his work uniform on—dark gray pants and a light gray shirt with the name "Jim" embroidered on the left breast pocket. He looked like a blue-collar auto mechanic who'd been under a car hood for the last eight hours, working on oily engine parts and wiping his hands on his clothes to get clean.

Whenever he rolled into the school pick-up zone, I wanted to disappear into a sinkhole. We lived in an affluent part of town, and I knew that the kids would make fun of me, calling my dad a "grease monkey" and asking me why he looked so dirty.

My dad gave my classmates another reason to ridicule me the time he drove my oldest sister Debbie and me to school one morning. On this occasion, we didn't have to ride in his grungy work van. Instead, he drove us in the family Lincoln Continental— dark gray and a long boat of a car. Our '68 Lincoln was the same model that President Kennedy was riding in when he got shot in Dallas—the kind with the four doors hinged on the outside. The rear doors were called "suicide doors" because they tended to fly open if they were caught by the wind, resulting in crashes or an occupant being thrown out of the car.

Well, my sister and I weren't thrown out of the car on the way to school that day, but it felt like it after Dad deposited us in the school driveway and sped off—while Debbie still had one foot inside the car. She fell, and Dad ran over her foot.

Debbie screamed, which prompted Dad to slam on the breaks. I ran to Debbie's side, but she didn't appear to be seriously injured with a broken ankle or shattered leg—just a glancing blow. We were lucky.

Dad seemed annoyed by the entire incident. He jumped out of the car with a perturbed look to check on Debbie.

"How could you do that—run over Debbie?" I demanded.

"It's all your fault!" he roared.

Of course it was my fault. I was driving the car. But I knew better than to wise off to Dad, so I let it go.

Seeing Debbie was going to be okay, Dad jumped into the long Lincoln and peeled out of the school parking lot, burning rubber and leaving both of us with our mouths wide open. The sound of the fast acceleration prompted more stares from my classmates. Now they'd have another club with which to strike me at school that day.

I could have overlooked his misdeeds and mistreatment if he had given me any reason to be proud of him—or shown his support for me. I played football and baseball throughout my youth, but he rarely came to any of my games. And if he did, I never heard him say anything encouraging like, "You had a great game out there today—way to go." Instead, he'd remind me about the ball that bounced through my legs or the tackle I missed. That's if he spoke to me at all.

The only time my father was nice to me was when he gave me things—like a new baseball mitt, a shiny bike, or a gas-powered mini-bike. He surprised me in that way every now and then, but I learned from an early age that gifts from Dad came with strings attached. Shortly after he gave me a big present, he'd ask me to work with him at the shop on Saturdays or go on repair calls during my summer break. I can remember being paid $3 a day to lug tools and broken motors back and forth from the truck, which I didn't think was very much money. Instead of building a work ethic within me, Dad squashed any desire to learn a trade and work with my hands.

If I moaned about wanting to see my friends instead of losing a Saturday working for him, I knew what was coming: "Is this all the thanks I get? Look at what a great father I am. I just gave you—" and then he'd list the item he recently purchased for me.

I'd stop complaining and thank him, but I always felt like it was more out of a sense of guilt than a sense of gratitude. Sooner or later, though, he'd revert to form and tell me what a crappy son I was—even though I was giving up my Saturdays and summers for him. No matter what I did, I couldn't win.

Neither could my poor mother. I haven't forgotten the time when Mom was pregnant with my youngest sister, Patty. I was twelve years old, and one day, Mom, my two younger sisters, and I went to Kmart to pick up some things. Mom wasn't feeling well that day so she decided not to put on any makeup or fix her hair just to run a couple of errands. For some reason, Dad happened to step inside the same Kmart that sweltering summer afternoon.

When he saw Mom in the store, he unloaded on her. "You look terrible. I'm embarrassed to be seen with you. I can't believe you left the house looking like that, you miserable excuse for a woman!" Dad spoke in a raised voice that had other shoppers averting their eyes and pushing their carts to another aisle as quickly as they could.

I grieved for Mom, having to endure that verbal abuse late in her pregnancy. Think about it: she was just thirty years old at the time and was still a wonderful looking woman. Yet my dad saw another opportunity to crush her spirit.

I was reminded that day why I hated my father. He was mean to the person I was closest to in life, and there was nothing I could ever do to win his approval. He didn't love me, so I didn't love him.

This all happened as I was going through adolescence. At the age of thirteen, I determined that when I grew up, I would blaze my own trail in life and not treat those I loved in the same manner.

Little did I know that I would follow in his footsteps.

When I enrolled at Liberty Guinn Elementary School after moving from Chicago, I brought home a form to fill out the first week.

"Mom, they're asking me what religion I am. What should I write?"

The last time we had been to church was in Chicago the previous Easter when we attended a Catholic service. Both sides of the family had been Catholics for generations, but my parents were Christmas-and-Easter Catholics at best. I was about to ask Mom how do you spell *Catholic* when—

"Tell 'em you're Protestant."

Protestant? I didn't know what that meant, but it sounded good to me. I think Mom wanted me to write in "Protestant" because we weren't practicing Catholics and everyone in the Deep South seemed to attend a Protestant denomination— Baptist, Lutheran, Methodist, or Presbyterian, to name a few. Saying we were Protestant would give us cover until we could get this religion thing figured out.

We did try a few Protestant churches, including the time a family across the street invited us to their church. My parents weren't impressed by any of the congregations we visited. I hated the experience. It seemed like every church we visited had trough-like baptismals where people of all ages, dressed in white robes, were baptized under water midway through the service. I thought the whole baptism scene was really weird.

Sometimes I had to sit and squirm in Sunday school class, where the teacher had the attitude of *You're going straight to hell if you don't get saved.* Saved from what? That was my question. Maybe they were talking about being saved from church because I hated wasting my Sundays in this fashion. I also hated church because the people in the pews weren't as nice to the visitors as they were to the regulars. It was like they were part of some club and we didn't belong.

Church frightened me, and so did church people. Because they scared me to death, I didn't want anything to do with them. The Bible stories I heard in Sunday school seemed like fairy tales. If you asked me when I was twelve years old what I believed, I would declare that I really didn't believe in God and knew nothing about Jesus Christ. I certainly didn't know anything about having a relationship with the God who created the universe.

I think I felt that way because my parents never talked about God, religion, or what the Bible said when I was growing up. I do remember Mom telling my sisters and me several Bible stories when we were much younger, but she didn't do a good job explaining why Noah's ark had to be built or why Jesus had to be crucified.

Dad never talked about religion and didn't like to get personal about anything. The time he tried to talk about the birds and the bees wasn't helpful either.

One hot summer day when I was thirteen, I was helping Dad for the usual $3 a day. What I could never understand was why someone who installed and repaired air conditioning units didn't have any air conditioning in his van, but that was my father. Then again, there were plenty of vehicles that didn't have A/C in the early 1970s. Maybe he was just trying to save a few bucks when he bought his work van.

On this particular day, it was 102 degrees in the shade. We were driving around Atlanta with the windows rolled down and getting all sweaty and greasy. The last place I wanted to be was in that van on a sticky day, but that's where I found myself.

We were driving along the freeway when Dad coughed. I looked over, and his face was redder than it normally was in the searing heat.

"Uh, Mike, do you know anything about sex?" he inquired.

"Hmmm, well Dad, not really . . ."

"Do you, you know, how to do it?"

I had no idea what Dad was talking about. He had never spoken to me in this way, so I was curious what he was going to say.

"Do what?" I managed.

Dad coughed again and then plunged ahead. "Women have, uh, you know, this place between their legs . . . it's called a vagina, and there's an opening there. And uh, you know, you get excited and get hard, and then you get on top of them, and it feels really, really good, and you just, you know, move around, and then you cum and it really feels good. That's how you have babies."

And that's how he ended his "talk" with me. There was no discussion about love being associated with this act or that sex was something reserved for married couples. But whatever he was talking about sure sounded like fun, especially to my maturing body swirling with tons of testosterone.

I spoke to my friend David about what Dad had said, and he showed me a book that his parents had purchased. It was called *The Joy of Sex*, and there were drawings of all sorts of sexual positions and information on how to stimulate a woman and make her have an orgasm. My buddy and I would thumb though *The Joy of Sex* every afternoon after school.

When the school year ended, David let me take the book home for several weeks. I read and reread that volume over and over. The illustrations of men and women in full, frank detail of having sex formed an indelible imprint in my mind. I felt like I had earned my bachelor's degree in the mechanics of making love that summer.

As I started the teen years, I saw Dad less and less in the evenings. He preferred to hang out at his new shop on Defoor Avenue with a couple of guys who worked for him. When quitting time arrived, they'd break open the Jack Daniels and a pack of playing cards. They'd drink and play poker half the night and even longer on weekends. There were times when Dad wouldn't come home at all, preferring to sleep on the grease-stained carpet. I guess he favored gambling and drinking to seeing his family. At least, that's how I interpreted his actions.

I don't know why he didn't come home because we had moved out of the dumpy apartment on Roswell Road when my parents bought a nice brick ranch house on an acre-and-a-half with a pool and basketball court in the big backyard. (All for $40,000, I might add.) Maybe Dad felt like he had to work more to pay the mortgage, but it seemed like he was happiest when working and not with his family.

Mom got fed up, never knowing when or if he would come home. One night, while he was still at the office drinking and playing poker with his buddies, she locked up the house. He came home around 4 a.m. and couldn't get inside. I don't know how that happened, but I think he lost his house key. Not wanting us to know how late he got home, he decided against banging on the front door. He looked around for the nearest place to lay his head and decided he'd sack out in the back of Mom's car.

The back seat was covered with a pair of curtains. *Perfect*, Dad thought. *They'll keep me warm.* But the curtains were made of a fiberglass material, and for the next couple of days, Dad couldn't stop scratching himself. He was miserable after sleeping in the back of Mom's station wagon.

Mom and I thought it was hysterical, the way he itched and scratched himself. We laughed our heads off behind his back.

I didn't play much organized sports in the early 1970s—baseball, basketball, and football—because Dad never had time to play catch with me or shoot baskets in the backyard. The only reason I played Little League baseball was because I happened to spend the night with my friend Keith, and when we woke up the next morning, his mother took the both of us to Morgan Falls Park so that Keith could sign up and try out for upcoming baseball season.

I hadn't played much sandlot baseball before, but everyone looked to be having fun, so I found a pay phone and called Mom to ask if I could sign up, too. I was thrilled when she said yes. I turned out to be a pretty good baseball player. I pitched, I caught,

I played third base—I did whatever the coach told me to do.

When I got to Ridgeview High School as a freshman, Keith said he was going to sign up to be the equipment manager of the football team. That sounded like a lot of fun to me because I figured being equipment manager would be a good way to learn about how football was played. At that time, I didn't know the difference between a linebacker and a quarterback.

I walked into the office of the eighth-grade football coach, Hershel Robinson. He was a big, handsome African-American with a winning smile and beach ball Afro who looked like he knew his way around a football field.

"I'd like to be an equipment manager," I said one afternoon as summer practice was starting.

"No," he replied in a gravelly voice, "there's no way you're gonna be an equipment manager. You're gonna play football."

"But I don't know how to play."

"I'll teach you everything you need to know. Are you fast?"

"I think so."

"Good."

At my first practice, Coach Robinson told me to line up at the halfback position. "After the quarterback pitches you the ball, I want you to run down the field and don't stop until you get to the end zone."

And that's what I did. No one could catch me once I had the ball. I was bigger and faster than everybody, and when they did try to tackle me, I had enough size to swat them away like flies or carry them on my back into the end zone. Kind of like what Forrest Gump did when he was told to run in a certain direction.

Coach Robinson then asked me if I wanted to play defense. I was up for that, so he showed me how to play middle linebacker, but I didn't think I was very good on the defensive side of the football. Meanwhile, I kept growing and adding weight, and by my sophomore year, I was over 200 pounds and better suited for playing on the offensive and defensive lines. Eventually, I settled into the center position, and by my senior year, I made the All-County team.

But sports were not my passion in high school—girls were. By tenth grade, I had read *The Joy of Sex* cover to cover twenty times, and I was ready to find out what having sex was all about. I was determined to touch all four bases: kissing a girl (first base); fondling her breasts (second base); touching her vagina (third base); and experiencing intercourse (home plate). At the age of fifteen, I was ready to hit a home run.

Toward the end of my sophomore year, I was attracted to a really cute girl who had aspirations of being an actress. I'll call her Jennifer. Ironically, we met in a biology class as lab partners at a time when my hormones were raging out of control. We also had a gym class together, and there was a curtain in the gymnasium that we could jump behind when no one was looking. We kissed, touching first base. Then she let me fondle her breasts. Now that I had reached second base, I could see home plate. But we both knew nothing more was going to happen while we had our gym clothes on and a volleyball game was being played just outside the curtain.

Jennifer was being raised by a single mom who worked during the day. Her strict mother had a standing rule: No boys in the house. Never, ever, ever.

Jennifer had a little brother, an eight-year-old twerp who reminded me of the fish in *Cat in the Hat*: *He should not be here, he should not be about, he should not be here, when your mother is out!*

I wasn't going to let him—or her mom's edicts—stop me. One

afternoon, I gave him money to go to the movies with a friend so that Jennifer and I could have the house to ourselves. Once her brother had left, we got down to business in her bedroom as I smoothly rounded third base and headed for home. We both lost our virginity on an ordinary summer afternoon in her bed.

I was hooked—and couldn't wait to have sex with her again . . . and again. I would ride over to her house on my mini-bike each day that summer, stopping at a gas station along the way to buy condoms—we called them rubbers back then—in a men's bathroom vending machine.

We got bolder as time went on, even taking showers together with her little brother in the house. One day, after Jennifer got into an argument with her younger sibling, the little nerd ratted us out. Jennifer's mom confronted her, and when she learned the truth, she beat Jennifer within an inch of her life and sent her off to an all-girls' boarding school in Gainesville, Georgia.

I never saw Jennifer again. I never even talked to her. The way I found out that she wasn't returning to Ridgeview High School for her junior year was through a letter I received through a mutual friend. Jennifer's note said she never wanted to see me again, and I had ruined her life forever.

That would not be the last time I would hear a woman say that to me.

I was crushed to receive Jennifer's letter. Not because I felt bad for her or that our relationship had to come to an abrupt end. I felt bad for me. I was losing out on having sex. Now I had to start all over again with someone else.

You may be wondering: *Didn't your parents wonder where*

you were day after day that summer or concerned when you arrived home late at night?

They never inquired as to my whereabouts. Dad was more interested in doing his cards-and-drinking thing, and Mom . . . she trusted her baby boy. But she was also starting to drink heavily, too. This was her way to cope with loneliness and Dad's verbal abuse, I would imagine. She was more discreet than my father was, however. In fact, she hid her drinking problem rather well, even though there were times I'd come home from school and find her on the couch, fast asleep and the house a big mess.

By the time my junior year rolled around, I felt like I could do anything I wanted. No adults in my life really cared where I was or how I was doing in school. When the weekends came around and I heard about the next kegger, I'd show up to drink as much beer as I could—short of passing out before driving home. When joints were passed around, I'd smoke a little pot here and there, but not on a regular basis. I didn't like smoking dope because it didn't do anything for me, unlike the buzz I got from alcohol.

Even though I wasn't a pothead, you could call me a slacker when it came to getting good grades in high school. I wasn't a very good student because I had chosen to focus on girls instead. I skated through with a solid 2.0 grade-point average because I *never* did any homework. I failed American History my sophomore year because I refused to write a paper, even when I was told that I would have to repeat the class the following year if I didn't hand in the assignment.

I didn't care and hated being told what to do. They could fail me.

So there I was the following September, the only junior in a class full of sophomores taking American History. I was a young junior, however, having just turned sixteen at the end of August, but I was still ahead of my classmates in many ways.

My dad got me a car when I turned sixteen. Remember, he enjoyed giving me things—his way of showing love, I suppose—so he purchased a 1972 beige Volkswagen Beetle for me. The fun four-cylinder, two-door came with a four-speed stick shift. In coming years, I would teach all my girlfriends how to shift the gears from their passenger seat. How was I expected to use my right hand to shift when I had my right arm around their shoulders—or elsewhere?

With wheels, I was dangerous. Not as a driver, but as someone mobile and unaccountable. There was a sophomore girl in American History who was cute as a button. Olivia was a sweet, good girl who thought I was a good guy. I had her fooled. She loved the attention I showed her and fell for every line. Her parents weren't happy that I would keep her out late, but that wasn't going to stop me from taking her virginity that first time her parents were out of town. Poor girl, but she was the next in line.

Olivia and I were an item for most of the school year, but she never knew I was fooling around behind her back. If she was busy some weekend, I'd find some other girl and take her out for some sexual mischief. Or if my parents were out of town, I'd invite another girl over and drink with her and eventually take her to bed. I didn't see anything wrong with what I was doing, nor did I feel bad. I thought having sex was normal and fun.

I deceived so many girls, and perhaps that's because I was comfortable around females—a friendly face who showed a knack for being a good listener. I wasn't some smooth operator but someone who related well to the fairer sex. Let's face it: guys mature later and are often socially awkward in high school, but nobody could say that about me. You could say that gave me a competitive advantage, if you will.

For whatever reason, all my friends in high school were females. I didn't have any guy friends. I'm not sure if it was because I felt that I had something to prove, but I took some measure of pride in my ability to engage young women at many different levels, especially the attractive ones I was interested in.

Some were attractive, and some were smart. Not too many were good-looking *and* smart, but that was their problem and not mine. There were times when I made sure there was no alcohol in my drink but plenty in theirs. I knew that if they drank enough, they would lose their inhibitions about getting naked with me, and I was almost always right.

If you're thinking I was getting pretty smart at this love-'em-and-leave-'em game, then think again. I can't believe how many times I did not use protection, which only illustrates how invincible I felt. But all teen guys think they're bullet-proof, right?

When my junior year ended, Dad was in a giving mood again. This time he gave me a 1972 majestic blue Porsche 914, a mid-engine, Targa-topped roadster that was quite a chick magnet.

But there was one girl who caught my eye, and she was different than the rest.

Stephanie Johnson and I had met on a triple date back in my freshman year. She wasn't my date that night at Friendly's, an East Coast restaurant chain best known for its ice cream sundaes, but we remained friendly with each other while I was sowing some serious wild oats with other girls.

When the rose fell off the bloom with Olivia at Christmastime of my junior year, I started hanging out with Stephanie, who was captain of the drill team. We had been friendly ever since her brother, Eddie, played on the same Pony League baseball team with me. Even back then, I'd see her in the stands and would imagine she came to the game just to watch me.

We liked each other and went everywhere together . . . as friends. Our relationship was like the characters portrayed by Billy Crystal and Meg Ryan in *When Harry Met Sally*. We would go to movies, ball games, the local park, but *nothing* ever happened. She was easy to talk to and had long, pretty blonde hair with a beautiful white smile. She was hot too . . . very sexy and very well endowed, which was a big deal to me. But something told me that it was better that we remain good friends for the time being.

That would change in the spring of my junior year of high school.

4

Just a Formality

Mike

You'd think that making the varsity baseball team my junior year would be just a formality. After all, I was a good enough player to be the only sophomore from my class to make the varsity team the year before. You'd think that I could skip a couple of days of tryouts because everyone, including the coach, knew how good I was.

That was my thinking, which explains why I didn't bother showing up for baseball tryouts on a Friday after school and early Saturday afternoon in late February. You see, Mom and Dad had driven my sisters to a mountain hamlet in North Georgia for the weekend, leaving me a rare opportunity to enjoy an empty house. Accordingly, I made plans to have a good time, and that didn't include attending the baseball tryouts.

I partied with my good buddy Mac at my house on Friday night as a warm-up for my day date on Saturday with a beautiful young sophomore that I'll call Erica. She was a stunner with a great body who would later be crowned a beauty queen in many pageants.

We had my parents' house all to ourselves that afternoon. Using my tried-and-true seduction method of spiking her drink with rum while there was nothing but Coke in my glass, she got tipsy pretty quickly. She was putty in my hands, and within the hour, we were making love in my parents' king-size bed.

I didn't think twice about violating the sanctity of my parents' bedroom. Nor was I worried that Mom and Dad would come home early and discover us in their bed. I had no fear of consequences because there weren't any.

Several hours after I kissed Erica goodbye, Stephanie Johnson dropped by the house. I wasn't expecting her, so it was a nice surprise when she came through the carport and knocked on the kitchen door. I welcomed her inside, and we caught up about what was happening in our lives. I mentioned that I had seen Erica that afternoon but refrained from giving her the blow-by-blow details. I was a gentleman, after all, but I'm sure Stephanie figured that I didn't have Erica over for milk and cookies.

Seeing Stephanie that evening was wonderful. She sure looked good to me. Think about it. The house was still empty, it had been a whole six hours since I had sex, and I could feel my motors revving up again. We sat on the couch in our small wood-paneled den as I leaned over to kiss her, but she blanched.

"No, we can't do this," she said. "We're friends."

"I know we're friends, but you're really special to me," I replied.

"I think I better go now."

"But—"

Stephanie would hear none of it. "Goodbye," she announced. With a flourish, she picked up her bag and stormed out of the front door. I barely had time to stand up.

Stephanie, I decided, would be a long-term project. She stood out from the pack, and something told me that she would be worth the wait.

I dropped by the boys' locker room on Monday afternoon to tell the baseball coach why I wasn't at the tryouts on Friday or Saturday. Coach Bill Thompson was fresh out of college with bushy, blond hair sticking out from underneath his Ridgeview High ball cap. He sported gold wire-rimmed glasses and a thin, wispy moustache. The young coach wore dark blue polyester shorts, a blue windbreaker, and a cocky son-of-a-gun attitude on the sleeve of his shirt.

"Where were you, Reis?" he demanded. "You could have called."

"I was sick—too sick to make it to a phone," I said.

"You're cut from the team. You're gone."

"What do you mean I'm gone?"

"You missed the tryouts, so you're not on the team. It's that simple."

"But I was sick—"

"Doesn't matter."

"That's fine. I don't care. I'm too good to play on your crummy baseball team anyway."

Deep down, though, I was relieved to be cut from varsity baseball. Now I had the opportunity to pursue what I was really passionate about: girls, drinking, and sex, although not necessarily in that order.

You see, I was working on my Ph.D. degree in sex, even though I was still a high school student. I had mastered the Intro 101 classes found in the pages of *The Joy of Sex*, but now I had found a new syllabus: the *Penthouse Forum*. This tablet-sized spinoff from *Penthouse* magazine was billed as the ultimate publication for individuals interested in erotic fiction and filled with a variety of explicit letters about the kinkiest sexual behavior.

Within the pages of *Penthouse Forum*, I was transported to

a world of deviant sexual practices: couples having sex in public places where they could get caught, watching your girlfriend having sex with others, role-playing, threesomes, orgies, and swapping partners.

After reading a few issues, I latched on to the idea that any and all of these topics were perfectly normal sexual behavior, which meant that it was healthy to fantasize about these sexual activities and even talk about them with your partner.

At the time, I had no idea I was passing through a red door marked Deviancy. The more I read, the more I thought this stuff was *normal.* I derived great enjoyment from fantasizing about doing some of those things described in alluring detail on the pages of the soft-core porn magazine.

Doing graduate study in *Penthouse Forum* was the culmination of an education that began when I was eleven years old. Back then, I would accompany my father to the barbershop. While we waited for chairs to open up, Dad would thumb through the glossy pages of *Playboy*, always turning the centerfold sideways to get a full look. He would let me take a peak at Miss May or Miss October, and when he was done, he'd hand me the magazine so that I could sample the rest of the enticing pictures.

I can still recall the jolt my young body received when taking in the unbelievable images of the air-brushed nudes. The men in the barbershop would tease my dad about the "little shaver" staring at the pages of *Playboy*, and I can distinctly remember several of them saying that they didn't read *Playboy* for the pictures but for the articles, which seemed a curious statement at the time. I thought ogling the pictures was enough, but as I would learn in the pages of *Penthouse Forum,* words can create tremendous fantasies in the theater of your mind—the brain.

My sex education continued when I reached high school and

Dad asked me to accompany him on repair calls to . . . strip clubs. Apparently, he had cornered the market when it came to repairing air conditioning units at a series of strip clubs on Peachtree Street in downtown Atlanta.

So there I was, no more than fifteen years old, walking into strip clubs with a toolbox in my left hand and a handful of curiosity in the other. Even in the middle of the day, buxom girls would be on a small stage working the pole and stripping off their tops and bottoms. I was usually backstage, assisting Dad as young women cavorted around in various stages of undress. My eyes popped out from viewing all the flesh.

When I got my driver's license a year later, I had the freedom to go on field trips for further study. Sure, I liked to party, hook up with girls, and drink a lot, but then a brilliant thought hit me—I could go to a strip club! After getting wasted at a party one Saturday night, I hopped into the car and drove myself to downtown Atlanta, where I found the same strip club Dad and I had worked in the year before. Looking older because of my size, the bouncer waved me in without asking for my ID.

I stepped inside to the dank environment, which reeked of alcohol, smoke, and bodily fluids. I was drunk and horny with $25 bucks in my pocket. Not a good combination for making it out of there with any money for the twenty-mile drive home.

I sat down at a stage-side table. Suddenly, five or six strippers materialized out of nowhere and descended upon me like honey bees. "You wanna party?" they kept asking. "You wanna party?"

A black stripper named Cinnamon took a chair next to me. "I bet you know how to show a girl a good time. My, you are handsome," she said. She touched me in a few places just so I knew that she meant what she said. I was sure that she was in love with me, and when she suggested that I buy a bottle of champagne for the table, I replied that I only had $25.

Apparently, that was the magic number because she said, "That'll be enough." I gave her all the money I had and drank the entire bottle of champagne with her while we watched the show. Somehow when the champagne ran out, so did she.

Most sixteen-year-olds don't develop a taste for champagne until they're much older, but I was working on an advanced degree in drinking as well. Even though I had been allowed sips of beer and mixed drinks when I sat on a barstool in Chicago next to my grandfather, I didn't start seriously drinking until I was thirteen years old. That's when some buddies and I would grab a couple of six-packs of Pabst Blue Ribbon (purchased by a friend or older brother) to drink in the woods behind the elementary school. At first I didn't care for the taste, but I loved how drinking beer made me feel.

When high school came around, it was a rare weekend when I wasn't at a friend's house when his or her parents were away for the night or the weekend. I'd knock down some brew, one red cup after another. I discovered that when I was under the influence, I was more attractive, smarter, funnier, and more social. My friends liked me more. Why shouldn't they? That's what I loved about drinking, the way I lost my inhibitions and could be the real me.

My drink of choice during high school became a cherry or lime Mr. Misty from Dairy Queen, which I would spike with rum or vodka. The slushy Mr. Misty drink was a knockoff of the Slurpees found at 7-Eleven convenience stores. I found a liquor store near Chastain Park that never asked for my ID when I'd buy a pint of hard spirits.

I'd exit the lobby of Dairy Queen, sip the first inch to create some head room, and top off my Mr. Misty with rum or vodka in my car. Then I'd swirl the concoction around with my straw. The Dairy Queen paper cup and the neon-colored crushed-ice drink were the perfect cover. Nobody would suspect a thing while I sipped my Mr. Misty as I drove around town.

I can't remember who taught me to spike Mr. Mistys this way, which were cloyingly sweet. Although I couldn't really taste the alcohol, I did get a buzz on. Two Mr. Mistys would knock me for a loop.

If you're wondering how or why I did all this drinking and driving, it's because DUIs weren't a big deal in the mid-1970s. The drinking age in Georgia had been lowered to eighteen in 1972, so there was a certain permissiveness in the air. Cops didn't set up roadblocks like they do now, and there was no talk about the dangers of drinking and driving. (The state of Georgia would change its mind and raise the drinking age to nineteen in 1980 and to twenty-one in 1986.)

Now that I was no longer playing baseball, I had more free time on my hands. I found myself hanging out with Stephanie every chance I got. We met every day for lunch at school, went to the movies together, bowling, and even went out to dinner, even though we were "just friends" and not dating. At the same time, we looked like brother and sister because we shared blond hair and blue eyes.

We would have fascinating conversations. I'd tell her about some of my past relationships, and she'd tell me about guys she was interested in. Sharing closely held details of your personal life, I would later learn, was a form of intimacy. I was feeling very close to Stephanie throughout the spring of our junior year.

The next time I tried to kiss her, she allowed me to touch first base. It didn't take long for me to swing for the fences. Once I introduced Stephanie to the "joy of sex"—her first time, by the way—an open highway of love was set before us. We didn't want to stop or slow down. The brakes had been removed, our hormones were *en fuego*, and we enjoyed each other immensely. We became *very* sexually active and took every opportunity to "do it."

After we became an item, we enjoyed spending every free moment together for the next eight months. We were foolish and took a lot of reckless chances, as nearly all teens do at that age. I learned that having sex was a lot more fun while under the influence of alcohol and fantasizing about things I had read in *Penthouse Forum*.

Suddenly, out of nowhere and at the end of our senior year, Stephanie broke up with me. She had heard I had been with another girl, but I tried to explain to her that it was nothing serious. Stephanie had been out of town, so I certainly couldn't be expected to go an entire weekend without sex. I followed the Stephen Stills song from the 1970s to the hilt: *If you can't be with the one you love, love the one you're with.*

See how warped my compass of morality was? But I felt such low self-esteem that I needed a warm body next to me to validate that I was worth something. It wasn't necessarily about the sex, either. I just wanted to know that an attractive girl would want me. I knew that if I told my side of the story to the editors of *Penthouse Forum*, they would totally agree with my actions.

Stephanie, however, didn't see things in the same light. She said we were finished. I begged and pleaded for her to take me back, but she stuck to her guns. She knew my history *before* we became a couple, so she knew I couldn't be trusted.

Things might have ended right there but for a twist of fate.

There was no expectation that I would go to college in my house. I didn't think I would be able to get into the University of Georgia, the big state school in Athens, as a ho-hum C-average student. But when I heard that Stephanie—a straight-A student with excellent SAT results—was accepted, I thought I'd give it a shot anyway. To my great surprise, the University of Georgia accepted my fair-to-middling 2.0 GPA and SAT test scores. (That wouldn't happen today.)

If Georgia hadn't accepted me, I would have probably gone into the Army or Navy—a totally different direction. But when the University of Georgia said yes, I saw this as my last opportunity to win back Stephanie.

The reason I wanted her back in my life didn't have anything to do with the sex part. It had more to do with issues of my self-esteem. Up until this time, I had fallen into a familiar pattern: no matter which girl I dated or which young woman I thought I was in love with, I still had to prove to myself that she wanted me. Winning Stephanie back into my arms would validate my worth.

Stephanie settled into Creswell Hall, the woman's dorm for freshmen. I was bivouacked in Russell Hall, the men's dorm conveniently across the street from Creswell Hall. As someone used to getting what he wanted, I set myself on a course to get together again. I charmed her. I stayed attentive, reminding her time after time that I loved her.

Although she was hesitant at first, Stephanie came around soon enough, and we picked up where we left off. We never went home on the weekends like our roommates did, which meant we had either dorm room to ourselves. I found a recipe in *Playboy* for a punch spiked with Southern Comfort that we started drinking before Bulldog football games. Soon we were drinking our special punch before going out to the movies, before having dinner, and always before having sex.

College life our freshmen year was all about getting horizontal with each other. Sex was certainly all around us on the Georgia campus. Remember, this was the mid-1970s when streaking was still the rage. Women whipped off their T-shirts from their dorm rooms as hundreds of men gathered beneath them. Every bar on Baxter Street sponsored a wet T-shirt contest. Two drive-in movie theaters in Athens showed a continuous fare of X-rated movies, which spurred a lot of sex in the parking lot.

As much fun as everyone was having, life was no day at the beach for our parents. I would return home to find that nothing had changed between Mom and Dad. They were still fighting, still calling each other names. They had been in a loveless marriage ever since I was in elementary school, which explains why my father didn't come home on many evenings.

Dad had hired a young woman that I'll call Janine—she was no more than seventeen or eighteen years old at the time—as his office assistant. Janine came from a low-income family living in Cartersville, a more rural city in the north side of metro Atlanta. She became very impressed with my father, and Dad, liking the attention, started a torrid affair with her. Eventually, he put Janine up in a nearby apartment. Mom discovered this subterfuge and kicked him out of the house, so Dad went to live with his new girlfriend who, it must be noted, was a year *younger* than me. At the time, Dad was in his early forties. The whole thing was weird and awkward.

This was all coming to a head during my freshman year at Georgia, which is another reason I didn't go home on weekends.

Things weren't much better at the Johnson house either. Her father, Bobby, was a builder who constructed several expensive spec homes that sat on the market and didn't sell. The cost of carrying them plowed under his business. Johnson Builders lost everything, and Stephanie's father had to file for bankruptcy protection. Her mom, Kathy, went to work to support the family, which included three younger brothers at home.

What turmoil swirling around our dysfunctional families! I couldn't handle the upheaval. I had to escape the insanity, but where could I go?

Stephanie and I looked to each other for support and talked about our options. We agreed that our families were disintegrating around us. Neither of us wanted to go back to that. I told her that we should get married, start a family, and do it the right way. We weren't going to have a messed-up family or issues with drinking, I said. Remember, I didn't think I had a problem with alcohol. I was just doing what I thought teenagers did back then.

Like my mother and father nearly twenty years earlier, we hatched a plan—a plan to get married while we were still teenagers.

I know. We were only eighteen years old and lacked a lot of things—like maturity, money, and life experiences. Our job prospects weren't stellar. But we had each other, and with a pioneer spirit, we believed that anything we faced in the future had to be better than what we were leaving behind.

When I asked Stephanie to marry me in August 1977, she said yes. We decided to quit school and get jobs, which was the equivalent of burning your ships in the harbor upon arrival at a new land. There was no turning back now.

Stephanie got a job waitressing at a HoJo's—a Howard Johnson restaurant in Sandy Springs. I emptied my bank account and paid the Snelling & Snelling employment agency the princely sum of $750 to find me a $10,000 manager trainee job at Arthur Treacher's Fish & Chips, a seafood-and-chips fast food restaurant chain.

After we started working, we knew it was time to announce the engagement to our families. The thought of asking Bobby

Johnson for his daughter's hand never occurred to me. I recall going over to Stephanie's house to break the news on a Sunday afternoon around the backyard pool. Bobby nursed his usual beer, and Kathy was holding one of those yellow plastic baseball bats, playing with it.

When I announced our plans to marry, I thought Kathy was going to beat me over the head with that plastic bat.

"You're way too young to get married!" she bellowed. "How are you going to support yourselves? What about school?"

Bobby took a long swig of beer before speaking his piece. "There's no damn way I'm going to let you two get married."

But like my mom's parents more than twenty years earlier, Stephanie's mother and father knew they couldn't stop us. I promised that we would both work until the wedding, and once we came back from the honeymoon, I would make sure that Stephanie would go back to school and earn her teaching degree.

The worried look on their faces told me that they didn't believe me, but they knew there was no way they could turn back the tide.

When I informed my parents about our plans, they expressed reservations and reminded me that I was making my own bed and would have to lie in it. But that was the extent of their input; they were distracted by their own problems. They were in the throes of a messy and sometimes violent separation that would ultimately end in divorce—a split that screwed Mom over. She would receive a small amount of cash every now and then, but Dad eventually stopped paying child support for my younger sisters.

My parent's problems were the least of my worries—I had a wedding to plan. Since her parents were going through rocky financial times, Stephanie and I would pay for most of the wedding from the money we were earning.

I chose Gregg Costin to be my best man. I had met him at Dekalb College that summer when I took a few classes before deciding to get married. Gregg, a couple of years older than me, was a native of Toms River, New Jersey, and had a strong *Joisey* accent to prove it. He sounded like Tony Manero, the character played by John Travolta in *Saturday Night Fever*, which came out in 1977.

When hitting the discos on Saturday nights, Gregg dressed like Tony, wearing silk shirts, gold chains, and tight bell bottom pants while adopting his confident, cocky on-screen persona. As we talked about the wedding, Gregg convinced me that we should both wear four-inch platform shoes instead of the standard issue shiny black patent-leather shoes that came with the tux rental.

Years later, I can only laugh looking at our wedding pictures. I teetered on the platform shoes, standing six feet, three inches, while Gregg towered over me at six feet, seven inches. We wore gray pinstripe tuxes with long tails and gray-stripped ascots. Our ruffled shirts had plenty of lace and frills.

We were married at St. Jude the Apostle Catholic Church in Sandy Springs before a hundred family members and friends. The reception at the church was punch and cake, no alcohol. That's all we could afford. My parents had their own reception at the house afterward, where there was *plenty* of alcohol.

Stephanie and I enjoyed ourselves, but we were itching to get to the honeymoon suite at the Peachtree Plaza Hotel downtown. You see, it had been a whole two weeks since we had made love. We originally decided to remain celibate throughout our six-month engagement—it seemed like the right thing to do at the time—but that vow lasted two weeks. We'd pledge to wait all over again . . . but that proved impossible. We did manage to keep our hands off each other the final two weeks before the wedding.

When it came to choosing a honeymoon locale, we could have gone anywhere—the Caribbean, the beaches of Florida, or some posh resort. We had options because Dad offered to pay for the honeymoon. He always came through with the big gift.

I was thumbing through some of Stephanie's bridal magazines, and I saw these seductive ads for honeymooning in the Poconos, a woodsy hill area in eastern Pennsylvania. The brochures I received in the mail showed pictures of round beds, mirrors all around, heart-shaped bathtubs, and log-burning fireplaces. If these honeymoon hotels were selling a tantalizing setting for great sex, they had me sold.

"Look at how much fun we'd have," I said to Stephanie.

I convinced her that this was the best place for us to honeymoon. I remember selecting this destination as an opportunity to have great sex. In other words, I picked the Poconos out of lust, not out of love.

After spending our wedding night in downtown Atlanta—and nearly missing the plane because of so little sleep—we flew to Pennsylvania. Our honeymoon suite was just like the brochure photos: the round bed with the crimson red slipcover; mirrors on every wall as well as the ceiling; and a heart-shaped tub also surrounded by mirrors. I enjoyed being able to watch us make love; that fed into my voyeuristic tendencies championed in *Penthouse Forum*.

We never left the cabin during our honeymoon. After five days of room service and sex, we returned to Atlanta satisfied and ready to tackle married life.

I had no idea that the sins of my father would be visited upon me.

5

SEEDS OF DESTRUCTION

Mike

After we got engaged, I started my manager trainee job with Arthur Treacher's Fish & Chips, a fast food seafood restaurant chain. You don't see many of them around now in the South, but they're like Long John Silver's. Deep-fried battered cod and French fries were their calling cards.

I didn't have to stand over a fryer very long as I moved up the managerial ranks. Before too long, I was running an Arthur Treacher's in Marietta near KFC's "Big Chicken" restaurant—a local landmark. As I promised her parents, Stephanie enrolled at Kennesaw State to begin working on a teaching degree while she took a part-time job in the deli department at a nearby Kroger supermarket.

Unfortunately, the Arthur Treacher's restaurant went under only two months after our honeymoon, so I jumped over to a company called General Finance, located in Buckhead. General Finance made loans, so my job was to qualify borrowers and make collections. The best thing about my new loan officer position was that I went to work in a three-piece suit and tie and didn't have to wear that embarrassing restaurant uniform and paper hat anymore. I felt like an adult going to work, and while the $750 monthly pay was nothing great, at least it was a start. I had grasped the bottom rung of the corporate ladder.

Working in the upscale glamour of Buckhead came with other perks. For instance, the office secretary at General Finance was a shapely knockout with big brown eyes and an unbelievable hour-glass figure. All the young guys in the company wanted a piece of Kim, and she was the hot topic of water cooler conversations. Being around her all day certainly revved up my jets, and I still can't believe Kim would regularly meet me in the storage room for some heavy-duty make-out sessions. We never had sex, but this was the first time I stepped in the direction of being unfaithful.

On the home front, Stephanie and I hated apartment living. Mom, bless her heart, pulled money from an account she had saved on her own and gave us $4,000 to assume the mortgage on a modest starter home in Kennesaw. Now we were under the weight of a $327 mortgage payment each month. (Yes, times have changed.)

To help us cover that nut, Stephanie quit her $5.25 an hour job at Kroger to become a waitress at Momma's Café, located in an industrial section of Atlanta not far from where I-75 enters downtown. Surrounded by warehouses, manufacturing plants, and distribution companies, Momma's customers were typically blue-collar plant workers and trucker types, sprinkled with a few middle-management white-collar supervisors, which explains why the eatery was open for breakfast and lunch only, 6 a.m. to 2 p.m., from Monday through Friday.

Stephanie waited tables and made great tips serving up grits and gravy for breakfast and country-fried steak with fried okra to the lunch crowd. She also had a great boss . . . my mother. You see, a couple of years earlier, my parents had bought this restaurant for Mom to run. I'm not sure why Mom wanted to get into the restaurant business with three daughters still at home, but I suspect she needed to get out of the house while my sisters were in school.

Mom always needed good help, which is where Stephanie fit in, but the restaurant was a good thirty miles from Kennesaw. Dad seized the opportunity to come up with an over-the-top gift again—and something to hold over our heads—when he gave Stephanie an Atlanta Refrigeration credit card to pay for the gas. When her shift was over, she was off to class at Kennesaw State.

No matter how much we hustled, though, we were slowly sinking. Like my father, I found out how difficult it was to make it to the end of the month with any money left in the till. We were barely scraping by and a car repair away from disaster.

On the personal front, I was eating like a sumo wrestler in training. I started each day with a couple of chocolate donuts followed by a big fast food lunch with dessert—usually some type of ice cream or frozen yogurt. Then I'd go out for drinks and snacks with the guys after work and finish strong by chowing down on the less-than-healthy special-of-the-day from Momma's Café that Stephanie brought home each night.

Maybe it was all this eating plus the chips and Lemon Luv pies I consumed when I was working at Arthur Treacher's, but I ballooned to 270 pounds during our first two years of marriage. I needed a turnaround, which meant working out, shedding weight, and going back to school. If I was to get anywhere in life, I needed to look good and get a college degree.

I enrolled at Georgia State University and took a night job in the credit collections department of Rich's, a department store chain that would later become Macy's. Since the George State campus was downtown and so was Rich's, I could attend class during the day and then walk over to Rich's, where I phoned deadbeats behind on their store credit cards and asked them when they were going to pay up. I had a lot of practice doing that at General Finance.

A typical day was really long: I left our house in Kennesaw at 4 a.m. to make the thirty-three mile commute to the Georgia State campus, where I lifted weights and worked out at the athletic center before attending a full slate of classes. Any free hours were spent studying in the library prior to reporting to Rich's at dinner time. I wouldn't get home before 11 p.m., which meant I was operating on four or five hours of sleep.

But life can't be all work and no play, right? Back in the late '70s, disco and the Bee Gees were the big thing, so I would relax on weekends by going to a nightclub called The Limelight—the Studio 54 of Atlanta. Stephanie, who wasn't interested in driving to a downtown disco late at night, said it was fine when I told her my best man Gregg Costin would accompany me. She trusted me. She really did.

Now I had the physique to shake my booty inside a flashy discotheque: I had lost a ton of weight—close to 100 pounds—and was hovering at 175 pounds. I dressed like Gregg—and his alter ego Tony Manero in *Saturday Night Fever*—when I wore really tight gray bellbottom pants with a wide white belt and a silky long-sleeved white shirt unbuttoned to my navel. I even donned a gold chain around my neck to complete the look. The only thing missing was a nest of hair on my chest.

So imagine the scene. It was after midnight on the crowded dance floor of The Limelight. Hundreds of sweaty bodies were gyrating to synthesized disco music set in a 4/4 rhythm. A mirror ball reflected dazzling bits of light. Colored lights flashed, and smoke rose up from the floor. You had to shout to make yourself heard.

Gregg and I watched from our perches next to a long wooden bar. We had downed a half-dozen drinks up to this point, nodding our heads with the boom-beat of the dance music. Part of the fun was spotting celebrities, and we saw a few actors who looked familiar, plus a couple of NBA players who stood head and shoulders above the crowd. Gregg was from the metro New York area, so he was in his element.

"Are you ready to make a move?" he screamed over the music.

"Move where?" I asked.

Gregg looked at me. I hadn't understood what he was driving at. "Make a move!" he yelled.

I still didn't comprehend where he wanted to go.

"Follow me!" he commanded. Gregg finished his drink and set his sights on several clusters of women who weren't dancing. I followed in his trail as he marched toward two sexy-looking women.

He made eye contact with both and began his spiel. "Look," he said without preamble. "We both don't want to waste a lot of time. There are two of you, and two of us. We both know what we are here for, so let's not waste any more time. Do you want to have sex with us or not?"

I'm surprised that we didn't get drinks tossed in our faces after uttering his bold request. One of the women laughed because she thought we were kidding. Both turned their backs on us, which I interpreted as a no.

On to the next set of girls. And the next set. And the next.

After a tally of stone-faced rejections, Gregg was unbowed. "You see, Mike, it's a numbers game. The law of averages says sooner or later we'll get a yes."

My best man was right. Toward the end of the evening, two young women were dumb enough to say yes. There were "private" rooms at the disco in which you could pay top dollar to have sex or blow through some lines of cocaine, but we didn't have that kind of money. We ended up in Gregg's car, kissing and petting—but no sex—or at least how former President Bill Clinton would later define it.

One night Gregg used his direct pitch on a young woman whose boyfriend was in the vicinity. Next thing I knew, a burly guy was raining blows on my drinking buddy, and several other guys joined the fracas. This was one time I was glad to be thrown out of a disco.

Some women, after hearing the "Do you want to have sex or not?" line, thought it was part of a really funny joke. They weren't about to indulge our fantasy, but they were willing to engage us, which made for some interesting conversations.

At twenty-one years of age, it was all about having fun. A feeling was creeping into my consciousness, and it was this: *You're entitled to let loose. You're going to school, working hard, and you're providing for Stephanie. You're allowed to have some fun.*

Let the justifications begin.

I stayed in school year-round, and during my last year at Georgia State University, I began making plans for nailing down that first, full-time corporate job after graduation that would jump-start my career. I envisioned myself as Ward Cleaver coming home to pearl-wearing June/Stephanie and a couple of rambunctious boys with a white picket fence around our doll-like house.

I was thinking this way because we had just learned that Stephanie was pregnant. I was about to become a parent, serious stuff to be sure, but I was confident about becoming a wonderful father and doing a better job than my dad did.

A recruiter at Georgia State told me that Hallmark Cards was looking to hire account managers. Hallmark Cards? Everyone had heard of them. Hallmark stores were everywhere. They were a huge billion-dollar company, and I envisioned myself zooming up the corporate ladder once upper management caught wind of my leadership and business acumen.

First, though, I had to get hired by Hallmark, but I knew my résumé looked a little thin. I didn't think frying breaded fish at Arthur Treacher's Fish & Chips or collecting debts from the boiler room of General Finance and Rich's were wow factors.

I desperately needed this job with Hallmark Cards. Since Stephanie had stopped working because she was late in her pregnancy, we were on the verge of going under. Having this income as soon as I graduated could save the day. That's why I needed a little résumé enhancement, so I added a second job: home improvement estimator for Johnson Builders—the bankrupt company that belonged to Stephanie's father.

The job was totally bogus, but I told my father-in-law what I was doing. "Sometimes you have to get creative," I explained. Bobby Johnson smiled and said he was on board.

I was asked about Johnson Builders during my interview with a Hallmark's Human Resources manager. The conversation went something like this:

HR person (a male): "Tell me about this job you had as a home improvement estimator. What were your responsibilities?"

Me (after shifting in my seat to give me a moment longer to think): "Well, I would make the appointment, and then it was my responsibility to go to the client's home, where I would take measurements and prepare an estimate for the cost of doing the remodel, whether it was a kitchen, bathroom, or additional bedroom. Then I would take all the measurements back to the home office, where we would come up with a firm bid. Then I would present the quote to the client. It was my responsibility to sell them on the idea of doing the remodel."

HR person: "What kind of rejections would you get?"

Me (still making it up): "I remember one time when I presented a quote to re-do a bathroom. New shower and tile, new toilet—the works. The client said it was higher than the other quote they had received, so why was that? 'We're higher than some other companies because we stand behind what we do,' I said. 'We have great service with great terms, and we use only the finest materials.' Then I listed several more benefits.

HR person: "Did you close the sale?"

Me (trying to think what would be the best answer): "Actually, on this occasion we did get the job. My manager was pleased."

HR person: "How often would you close a sale?"

Me (feeling more confident): "I'd say 70 percent of the time. I think that's pretty good in this business."

HR person: "I see you left a phone number for Johnson Builders, and your manager was Bobby Johnson. Can we give him a call?"

Me (feeling nervous again): "Sure. Can I tell him when he should expect to hear from you?"

HR person: "Sometime tomorrow afternoon."

Perfect, I thought. That gave me enough time to call my father-in-law and warn him that he would be receiving a phone call.

Sure enough, when someone from Hallmark phoned the next day, my father-in-law was ready.

"Mike has been one of our best employees," Bobby said. "A great guy. He'd have a real future in our business, but I know he's excited about this opportunity with Hallmark."

After a series of more grueling interviews over the next three months, I landed the job, which was welcome news since Stephanie had already given birth to our first son, Mike, whom we named after me. I started a twelve-week training program with Hallmark Cards in March 1982. When the three-month course was over, I was assigned to a territory based out of Canton, Ohio.

Even though our young family would be leaving our home and families behind, Stephanie and I were very excited about making the move. We figured this would be the first of many relocations as I climbed the ladder of success, as well as a chance for me to finally get away from the madness swirling around my parents. We settled in North Canton, a suburb.

My first sales meeting with Hallmark was back in Atlanta, of all places. I had a great time playing host to my fellow account executives since downtown Atlanta was my old stomping grounds. When the daylong meetings were over, we gathered in the hotel lobby, and I led them to my favorite downtown bars and strip clubs. That first night we stayed up all night drinking, really tearing it up. When the first inkling of dawn arrived, we shot back to the hotel to shower and freshen up just in time for the first meeting of the day at 7:30 a.m.

We were burning the candle at both ends.

One night, I ran into a hot girl I knew from high school at the trendy disco Park Place across the street from Perimeter Mall. Kristen had been a fantastic swimmer, so she had that broad-shouldered tight-body build with blonde hair and blue eyes to match. My new work buddies teased me about this "old flame," but I insisted she was just a good friend back in my homeroom at Ridgeview, which was true.

All the guys wanted her and wanted to take a shot at her, but I got there first and she ended up in my hotel room. We had sex, and this was the first time I crossed—make that jumped—over the line in the sand of my marriage. Honestly, I didn't think I did anything wrong because I didn't love her. I was just having a little fun on a road trip. My only concern was that I would get some kind of disease, but that wasn't enough to stop me from getting under the sheets with her that night.

Meanwhile, back on the home front, Stephanie was pregnant again and enjoying life in North Canton. I was thrilled to hear that she was expecting, which only goes to show how well I could "compartmentalize" my behavior. Two years and one day after Mike's birth on September 18, 1981, Stephanie gave birth on September 19, 1983, to a second son that we named Chris.

Stephanie had her hands full being a stay-at-home mom with two boys two and under, and I had my hands full at work. I continued to turn to alcohol and other women to relieve the pressure I was under.

You see, I was the first young father in the history of mankind to have a wife and two young children to provide for, keep a mortgage paid, and cut the grass in the backyard. I had a lot on my plate.

What I'm trying to say is that as long as I held up my end of the bargain financially, I was entitled to do what I wanted to do.

One of the first things I learned about Corporate America was that it was a smart idea to become involved with the community. One of the main ways to do that was to belong to a service organization like the Rotary or Lions Club. A friend at work suggested I join the Jaycees—short for the United States Junior Chamber of Commerce. The Jaycees were a leadership development organization for those under thirty-five years of age that used community service projects as a training ground for bigger and better things. For instance, the Canton Jaycees put on Easter egg hunts, Fourth of July fireworks shows, and Oktoberfest weekends.

Monthly meetings were held on Tuesday nights. Afterward, a bunch of the guys and I would go to a local restaurant/bar with live music. I liked hanging out there with a newfound drinking buddy and Hallmark colleague based up the road in Akron. I'll call him Sam. He was married as well and was making plans to start a family with his new wife.

Let me explain something. When you're two married guys hanging out in a bar, pounding down drink after drink with your friends, stupid stuff can happen. It's a lethal combination. And if you didn't have any kind of moral compass—which was my situation—then *really really* stupid stuff can happen.

I think we were on our fourth drink of the evening, listening to live music, when Sam leaned over. "Watch this," he said.

He left his drink at the bar and walked over to a good-looking woman in her mid-twenties. She was thin and looked like a flower child of the '60s with straight shoulder-length dark hair and dark brown eyes. Naturally attractive, she had a few freckles on her face with a touch of make-up.

"Hi, I'm Sam," he said as a way of introduction. "I think you're pretty cute. Would you like to dance?"

"No, not really," she replied. "But I like your friend over there." She nodded in my direction.

Sam made a beeline back to me as he took on the role of

wingman. "I struck out, but she's interested in you," he said.

I shrugged my shoulders. I wasn't all that interested, but it never hurt to have my ego stroked. "Tell you what, Sam. I'm not going to do anything, but I'll go over there and talk to her."

And that's what I did. I introduced myself and said, "My friend said you thought I was kind of cute. You're cute, too. What are you doing here?"

"Well, to be honest, I'm with a guy in the band. He's the lead singer."

"Cool. Are you married?" I didn't want to waste my time talking with someone who required too much work to land.

Donna Jennings looked at me. "No. We're just dating. Are you married?"

I was prepared for this question. "No," I declared without hesitation. "I'm just out with the guys tonight."

My wedding ring was safely tucked away in my left pants pocket. I always took my wedding ring off before I went into a bar. If you're wondering if there was a telltale indentation on my skin from wearing a wedding ring, the answer would be no. The band was loose enough around my left ring finger so as not to leave an impression. In fact, the ring was a bit big for my finger. I could put my left hand in my pocket and take the ring off quite easily with just the thumb and little finger of my left hand.

Donna set her drink down. "Do you want to dance?"

I didn't see any harm in that. She was with the lead singer in the band, right? Her boyfriend would be keeping an eye on us from the stage.

"Sure," I replied, and like a lamb led to slaughter, I followed her onto the crammed dance floor filled with dancing couples.

The band played a combination of oldies music and Top 40 covers, but the tempo didn't matter—we danced as if each number was a slow song. We held each other close as I nuzzled her neck, talking and flirting the night away. Just before the bar was about to close, she smiled and said, "Let's exchange phone numbers."

I didn't see any harm in that, but I made sure I gave Donna the number to my office phone in the basement of my house. She wrote her phone number on a piece of paper, and I distinctly remember leaving the bar and wadding her piece of paper and tossing it aside as I walked to the car. You see, the game at that point was to see how many women I could get attracted to me. It wasn't how many I could take to bed. The sex wasn't as important as the thrill of someone desiring me.

Two weeks passed, and I received a phone call while I was doing some after-dinner work downstairs in the basement. I picked up the office phone, wondering who would be calling me at work at that hour.

"Hi, this is Donna," the voice said. "I just came across your number and wanted to see if you wanted to get together for a drink."

"Sure," I replied. I wish I had thought longer than one second before agreeing to a clandestine meeting with a woman who was not my wife, but I didn't. Actually, a feeling of relief came over me. Here I was, twenty-five years old with two kids and big responsibilities, plus all the baggage I brought to the marriage with my father and family history. I was feeling overwhelmed. This was a chance to blow off steam and have some harmless fun.

I could tell Stephanie that I was going out with Sam again . . . she would never suspect a thing. Sam and I hung out together all the time.

"How about we meet in the bar at the Holiday Inn for a drink tomorrow night at 7 o'clock?" I asked.

"That'll be fine."

The last time I saw Donna, I was so wasted that I was concerned that my beer goggles may have deceived me once again. The Holiday Inn seemed like a safe option to meet in case I needed to make a quick getaway.

After hanging up, I remembered that Stephanie was taking Mike and Chris to Atlanta in a couple of weeks to visit her parents. If Donna looked as good as I remembered, the timing could be perfect to have a lot more fun with her.

Donna passed my little sight test, so I asked her to meet me at the Geisen Haus, a beer garden in downtown Canton, after Stephanie and the boys left for Atlanta. The Geisen Haus was a rollicking place, loud and reeking of stale beer. I didn't mind. This was an escape for me.

We drank several pitchers and laughed nonstop. As usual, I became funnier as the night went on. By the time we started on our fourth pitcher, I let her do most of the talking. She was twenty-seven years old, almost two years older than me. She had grown up in a St. Louis suburb. She had attended a nearby college for a year, but dropped out and moved to Golden, Colorado, for a change of scenery. Now she found herself in Canton, waitressing at the same bar and grill that we had met at that night and helping a friend with some interior house painting.

Turns out she wasn't single; Donna said she was in the process of getting a divorce, so even though she was separated and lived apart from her husband, technically she was still married. The guy she was splitting from worked for his dad's company, a landscaping firm, but he was stoned most of the time. Donna insisted she never loved him but married him out of pressure from her parents when she hit the ripe old age of twenty-three.

I nodded my head in sympathy and said all the right things. This was all part of my plan. I didn't say too much toward the end because I was getting really drunk, and so was she. When it came time to leave, she didn't pull any punches. "Do you want to go back to my place?" she asked.

I knew what she meant: *Do you wanna have sex?*

I followed her to an old two-bedroom house she shared with another girl in Massillon. The preliminaries were quickly dispatched, and we got naked and jumped into bed. Ironically our first sexual encounter was a complete failure. We were both too drunk to officially do the deed.

After that, we went out on a few more dates before getting away to the resort town of Put-in-Bay on Lake Erie for a weekend of wine and sex. From that point on, we began our love affair in earnest. This type of behavior continued the entire time Stephanie and the boys were in Atlanta—a good two-and-a-half weeks.

Right before my family returned, the guilt was eating me up. After having sex one morning at Donna's, I finally told her the truth.

"I'm married. I wanted to tell you all along, but I fell in love with you. It's not right though, and we have to end this," I said.

Donna looked devastated. "I knew it was too good to be true, but I'm in love with you now."

"I'm sorry, but I really don't have a choice."

Donna was hurt, angry, and tearful. "I understand, but we have three more days before your family comes home. Let's make the most of it." And that's exactly what we did.

When we finally said our goodbyes that should have been the end of the affair, but a week later I succumbed to the feelings that I had developed for her. I didn't bother to call her. Instead, I dropped by her house one afternoon, where we fell into each other's arms and kissed each other passionately upon seeing each other. It was like a scene from one of those romantic movies where the couple reunites after a long separation.

Like a moth drawn to a flickering flame, I couldn't stay away from her. With her dark hair and eyes, Donna looked very different from most of my previous conquests who were blonde and buxom. She was a great drinking buddy and a lot of fun in and out of bed.

Part of my subconscious had to do a bit of rationalizing. After all, I was married with two sons, and on some level, I understood the commitments I had made when I got married. But I explained away my behavior by reminding myself that I got married young and had tied myself down. I never got a chance to have fun, as if all those girls I bedded in high school didn't count.

I didn't see the relationship with Donna having a long shelf life. But our sexual relationship—which was getting heavier and more intense with each passing week—changed how I felt. I was developing strong feelings for Donna and would daydream about what it would be like to be with her all the time. At the same time, I didn't want to give up my family, so I was a torn soul.

There were many evenings when I'd meet Donna in a bar, go to her place and sleep with her, and come home around midnight. I would slip into bed, and Stephanie never said anything about my whereabouts. She figured that I had gone out with the guys.

This was the culture we each subscribed to in North Canton: the women would stay home and take care of the kids, and the guys would work hard all week long to provide for the family. Because we labored long hours, we were entitled to go out and have some fun. My nocturnal behavior was acceptable, and visiting the local strip clubs with my drinking buddies became a weekly occurrence.

I was also an enlightened guy who understood my wife's need

to get out of the house, so there were evenings when she and the gal friend next door would go out to the bars while I stayed home and babysat the kids. So we saw eye to eye on the need to get out of the house sometimes.

But then my midnight returns slipped to one in the morning. Then 2 a.m. One night, I came home at four o'clock in the morning, but this time Stephanie was not fast asleep. She was sitting up in bed, holding a pillow against her stomach, when I tiptoed in.

"You're having an affair!" she proclaimed.

I didn't hesitate or equivocate. "Yes, I am."

How come I was so truthful after being so deceitful?

I've wondered why as well, but I think it was because I had already made up my mind that our marriage was over. I had swung in a different direction.

My affirmative answer unleashed a volley of swings and accusations. "How could you do this to me? What were you thinking? What's going to happen to the kids?" she cried. Tears of sadness flowed down her cheeks.

I was moved and felt remorse. "I'm going to break it off," I promised. "I've made a terrible mistake. I don't know what I was thinking, but I only love you."

Eventually, Stephanie agreed to stay with me, bless her soul, but she had to see change in me. The first thing I did was tell Donna we were done. She did not take the news well and went on a drinking binge that got so bad that her parents had to put her in an alcoholic rehab facility back in Missouri.

I needed outside intervention as well for my "issues." At Stephanie's urging, I agreed to see a psychologist who could help me understand why I felt compelled to cheat on my wife.

As I was feebly trying to put our marriage back together, we got some good news: Hallmark was offering me a promotion that would also necessitate a move from Canton to Columbus, Ohio, a distance of 125 miles.

Stephanie was relieved to hear of my advancement in the company. A move to a new city—and a healthy distance from the other woman—would give our marriage a fighting chance of survival.

Too bad she was wrong.

6

THE RAZOR'S EDGE

Mike

Sometimes a family move is like hitting the reset button—a chance to start all over again.

That wasn't happening for Stephanie and me, however. Even though I had earned a promotion from Hallmark, it was apparent our marriage was hanging by a thread. I know because it was me who decided to take up with Donna again after she got out of a treatment center.

I couldn't stay away from her because I didn't think I could live without Donna. I was deriving all my self-worth from her. Remember, I needed to be desired, and I could tell Donna desired me greatly. I didn't think anyone else would ever love me or make me happy like her again, so how could I live without her? This was the start of yet another addiction for me: codependency.

This is essentially why I decided to walk away from my marriage, even though I had promised Stephanie that I wanted to form a family that was better than the ones we were leaving behind. On one of the darkest days of my life, I informed Stephanie that I was leaving her and moving into an apartment with Donna. It was the culmination of yet another one of my plans hatched weeks earlier for Donna and me to finally be together in Columbus.

As tears streamed down her face, Stephanie asked, "How could you do this to me? I did everything for you. The house was always clean and perfect just the way you like it. I made dinner every night, paid the bills, and our love life was fantastic. What did I do to deserve this?"

Stephanie didn't do anything to deserve this fate. I justified my actions by routing my mind through a series of checkpoints:

- *You married too young.*
- *You were handed too much responsibility too early in your life.*
- *You married her to escape from your family.*
- *You were never really "in love" with her.*
- *You married her because she was a safe and secure person.*
- *At the end of the day, it was her fault. If she had been a better wife, paid more attention to you than the boys, you'd be happy, but you're not. Besides, all the couples you know are getting divorced. That's what you do when you're not happy . . . you split up. Life is too short.*

I don't like remembering this part because it was so painful, but physical distress gripped my heart when I backed a U-Haul truck into the driveway and pulled out the loading ramp. My composure melted when four-year-old Mike and two-year-old Chris ran out of the house and started playing on the ramp—running up and down from the garage to the empty storage hold.

Mike was devastated and couldn't comprehend why Daddy was leaving. Chris, a toddler, didn't understand what was happening.

Inside the garage, I crouched and looked both boys in the eyes. "Daddy won't be living here anymore, but I'm going to come see you all the time," I promised. "I'm not leaving you. I'm just going to live somewhere else."

"Daddy, why are you leaving?" Mike asked.

My son's question ripped my heart into little pieces. I didn't know what to say. I worshipped Mike and Chris. They were innocent little boys with big smiles, bright blond hair and personalities to match. They looked perfect, and I would get compliments all the time about how cute they looked.

Some of the simplest things in life—like cuddling up on the floor in front of the TV with Mike and Chris and watching a Braves' game on the Superstation wasn't going to happen anymore—at least at their home. If we did watch an Atlanta baseball game, it would have to be at my place, but our family life would never be the same.

And now my oldest son was asking me why I was leaving. How could I explain to a four-year-old child the desire to please myself *first* ahead of others? How could he or his brother Chris understand what drove me to leave them while I followed a path that I thought would make me happy?

I didn't know what else to say to Mike except for, "I'm sorry. I love you more than anything in this world. I'll always be there for you. Always."

I packed up a few boxes of clothes, loaded up my home office furniture, and moved out of their lives and into a new one with Donna. Her divorce had been finalized just a couple of months earlier, and it didn't make any difference that I was still married.

My family back in Atlanta knew nothing about this radical turn in my life. Hiding things from my family would be a skill that I mastered throughout my life. Ever since we moved away from Georgia, I had distanced myself from my father, my mother, and my three sisters. By this time, three years after we moved, they had no idea how to contact me. It was like I had disappeared off the face of the Earth.

Whatever path I chose in life, I didn't need them. Nor did I want to be looking over my shoulder at my past.

Chris

I don't remember the day Dad left us. I was two years old when my parents separated, so I can't remember Mom and Dad ever being together. My older brother, Mike, was crushed because he knew what it was like to have both parents in the home, but not me.

Growing up, I thought every dad came in and out of your life. That's normal, right? I had no idea that a father was supposed to live with you. I thought it was perfectly acceptable that Mike and I would see our father on weekends.

Mike

Stephanie wasn't in as big of a hurry as I was to get divorced, but she agreed we could work things out by seeing see a lawyer together. As dissolutions of marriage go, this one proceeded forward without too much drama. We sat down with an attorney and drew up terms, which basically boiled down to this: from then until the boys turned eighteen, I would pay $850 a month as a combination of alimony and child support. After filing, the courts issued the final divorce decree in June 1986.

At the time, $850 was exactly the take-home amount of one of my twice-monthly paychecks, meaning half my pay was earmarked to support Mike and Chris, and half of my pay would have to provide for Donna and myself. Even though our marriage was over, I believe Stephanie held out hope that I would come to my senses, leave Donna, and reconcile with her.

The strain of leaving my family and living on a meager

income, though, would take its toll on my relationship with Donna. I had a hair-trigger temper to begin with, so it didn't take much for me to unleash verbal venom in Donna's direction whenever things didn't go exactly as I wanted.

One time, I arrived at our apartment in a bad mood. I found Donna on the couch, watching a stupid show on TV. Something snapped when I saw her unhappy face.

"What in the hell are you upset about?" I demanded. "I'm the one who left my wife and kids, not you! I have two little boys. You have nothing. You came from nothing. If it wasn't for me, you'd be living in some trailer somewhere."

The fact that she had never graduated from college or held an important job was something I used against her time and time again.

I continued to pile on. "You are such a loser. You're as dumb as a box of rocks, you have no education, you have nothing going for you, and you've lived with a succession of worthless guys, so you're lucky to be with me," was another familiar refrain from the portals of my mind.

Those were fighting words, of course. "Go @#$% yourself," she'd fire back. "I hate your guts."

I felt so guilty leaving my family, yet I couldn't go back. I was angry at myself for what I had done, which I took out on Donna every chance I could. I blamed her for my actions every chance I got.

Shortly after I moved in with Donna, Stephanie called and said Mike and Chris had each developed bad cases of chicken pox, so I dropped everything and rushed to be with them—day and night—for the next two days because the boys were both so sick. They also came down with salmonella poisoning, which was worrisome.

When I returned a couple of days later, Donna did not look particularly pleased to see me. As I demonstrated before, the miserable look on her face was enough for me to uncork more pent-up fury.

"What the hell is wrong with you?" I said in a raised voice. "You got what you want. You got me. And you broke up my family. Only a slut would do that. That's what you were when we met. I hate you . . . you bitch. I can't believe how you ruined my life."

Once again, Donna wasn't going to take that lying down, although I knew my nasty tirade had sliced-and-diced her heart. "I can't believe you would even say that. You're such an asshole. Go @#$% yourself."

"Really? You've slept with every man on the face of the Earth! I'm sure while I was gone you were @#$%-ing somebody else."

Donna glared at me. "I can't stand you. I'm out of here."

She ran to the bedroom. When she attempted to gather some belongings, I took a dark turn toward violence. I grabbed and shook her, and then she ran into the living room. Frustrated that I wasn't getting through to her, I threw a chair against the wall, which did a number on the chair and the wall. Then I balled my fist and punched a hole in the wall in frustration.

Upon seeing I crossed that breach, Donna seized a framed picture off the wall and heaved it across the living room, striking another wall and shattering the glass. That really set me off, and I started throwing anything I could get my hands on, smashing household items as I stalked the house.

Fed up, Donna gathered her purse and ran out the front door in tears. I knew where she was going. She had a cousin living in the German Village area of Columbus, and this wouldn't be the first time she sought refuge at her relative's place.

This time, though, I thought she was gone for good. How

could I not think so? I left the house and drove like a madman to a nearby liquor store, where I purchased several bottles of vodka. Then I returned and drank myself into oblivion. In my stupor, I decided life was not worth living. I had really @#$%-ed up.

I flew off the couch in a rage. This was it! I tossed every bit of furniture I could lift against the walls. I tore open kitchen cabinets and flung dishes to the floor, where they exploded into tiny pieces. Glasses, pots, boxes of food—everything was destroyed.

And now it was time to destroy myself. I stumbled into the bathroom, where I found a razor blade. I didn't hesitate. I watched myself—as if in a trance—as I placed the razor's edge against my skin and slit my wrists—two meaty slices on each wrist. Bright red blood spurt to the surface, but I knew that I had not sliced deep enough into the skin to kill myself. I was just trying to get Donna's attention. I wanted her to come back from her cousin's place and discover me in this suicidal condition.

Slicing my wrists would show Donna how much I loved her. How much I needed her. How empty I was. I used to have a wife who loved me, but for some messed-up reason, I decided that wasn't enough. I had to have somebody else, and that somebody was Donna.

I looked around, but I wasn't able to focus clearly. I was starting to get a little light-headed. I stumbled into the living room and saw the mass of destruction. I wiped my bleeding wrists on the wall. I smeared blood on the couch in a fit of desperation. And I then I felt myself losing strength.

I fell on the floor of my home office and reached up for the phone sitting on my desk. I dialed Sam, my old drinking buddy from Akron.

"Hey, Sam, it's Mike," I whispered.

"Mike, what's wrong? You sound—"

"I just want to die. I don't want to live anymore. All the stuff I have done . . . it's just not worth it."

"Where are you?"

I could hear the concern in Sam's voice. "Home."

"Just keep talking to me. We're going to get you through this. Just stay on the phone with me."

That's the last thing I remember saying to Sam. The next thing I recall was when paramedics broke down the front door. They rushed in, strapped me to a gurney, and rushed me to a nearby emergency room.

When I came to, Stephanie was looking into my eyes, dabbing away tears. She looked as somber as I had ever seen her.

What raced through my mind was, *Where's Donna?* Then I did the unthinkable and asked Stephanie to phone Donna to let her know about my condition . . . and she did. At the time, though, Stephanie told me she couldn't reach her. Years later, I learned that Donna actually said to Stephanie, "I don't care. That's not my problem."

I can only imagine what Stephanie was thinking: *This isn't the guy I knew in high school. This isn't the guy I married. The Mike I knew would never try to take his life.*

I was humiliated to be in her presence. I had gone off the deep end, and she must have thought I was crazy.

Once I got sewn up, I was stabilized and wheeled to a hospital room for "observation." The next morning, nurses checked me into the psychiatric ward. I was expecting that. Stephanie was by my side when I was wheeled into the new ward and got settled into my room.

"We're going to get through this," Stephanie said. "You're going to be all right."

I appreciated her support, but when she left, I remember

being all alone in a quiet room, a prisoner of my thoughts.

I remained in the psych ward for a week. The only thing I learned there was what they wanted me to say so that I could get out. For instance, I discovered that they wanted me to play the victim card. I remember having a discussion with a therapist, and I was telling her what happened: *I had this girlfriend, and she left, and with the pressure of losing my family, I tried to kill myself . . .*

She looked up from her note-taking. "I think you have an assertiveness issue," she began. "You are not being assertive enough. You are not setting the right boundaries, so people are crossing them."

I latched on to those thoughts and ran with them. What happened was not my fault. I should have had boundaries in place, but because I didn't I was a victim of whatever had happened to me before. I had come from a dysfunctional family with an abusive background. I had married too young. *Yada yada yada.*

I talked to the therapist about the negative effects that these "issues" had in my life. What happened wasn't my fault, I said. It's what others did to me while I was growing up. I started to believe the lies I told myself.

The therapist placed me on the anti-depressant medicine Tofranil, which helped feed my victimhood. I was told that I had a chemical imbalance, and that's the reason I acted out the way I did.

The anti-depressant seemed to work pretty well. Now I was ready to win Donna back into my life. I was dependent on her to move on. Within a week, I was released from the psych ward.

The first thing I did when I reached Donna was beg her to come back. I described how I had received therapy, and for the first time in my life, I understood why I had acted so erratically. I had a chemical imbalance, I said, but now I was taking anti-depressant medicine to balance things out. There was a light at the end of the long, dark tunnel. I was moving forward with life and wanted her with me.

Personally, I thought the chemical imbalance was total crap, but I was serious about wanting Donna back. "Look, I love you," I said, "and this kind of thing is never going to happen again. It wasn't you—it was all me. This is about all my problems. I really needed to get some help, and now I'm taking care of this."

I showed her the bottle containing the anti-depressant drugs. "See? Here's what I'm taking. Come back to me. Things are going to be different."

Donna did come back, and we worked together to put the apartment back together. That was quite a chore and a sobering one as well, but I needed her—and she needed me. That's why we were perfect for each other.

I think we went a whole week before the next big blowout.

A vicious cycle of fighting and making up marked our relation-ship for the next few months. We fought hard and we loved hard.

We would have the greatest sex after our fights. At least we still had that common bond and great mutual interest. My ex-pectations in this area were still high—very high. Besides want-ing her available every night, I would expect her to be wearing a negligee—or even surprise me by being naked—when I got home from work. Sex was the glue that held our relationship together.

Whenever our yelling and screaming reached a crescendo, I would apologize for what I said and reiterate that I didn't mean it. "I just got angry," I'd say. "You can understand, right? I mean, leaving my wife and kids hasn't been easy."

Not exactly the most magnanimous expression of regret on

my part, but it was often good enough. "I know you are under a lot of pressure and miss the boys," she'd say. "I just want us to be together and happy."

"And we will." I assured her. "Once we get married, all of our problems will be solved."

"Yeah, I know, I know."

Toward the end of 1986, after our relationship survived six months of violent fighting, I felt like I needed to propose to Donna so I wouldn't lose her. I shopped for the biggest ring I thought I could afford but really couldn't. The ring came with a eye-popping full carat and a $3,000 price tag, which was a lot of money twenty-five years ago.

Donna said yes to my proposal. Putting an engagement ring on her finger seemed to calm the waters that November, but as Christmas neared, we had *another* major blowout. We stuck to our scripts and yelled the usual accusations—I said she was a @#$%-ing whore who broke up my home, and she retaliated by reminding me that I was selfish son of a bitch who used her as I saw fit.

I stormed out of our apartment that afternoon and hit the state liquor store, where I picked up a bottle of Smirnoff before heading to Stephanie's house. I knew I'd have her place to myself since Stephanie and the boys were visiting her parents for the holidays in Atlanta.

I popped in the pornographic video that I picked up at a no-name video store and proceeded to drink the entire bottle until I passed out. Four hours later, I woke up, but my phone calls to Donna went unanswered. After having said yes to my marriage proposal a week earlier, it never dawned on me she would leave now.

I drove like a maniac back to our apartment, still under the influence. The car she drove wasn't in its usual parking spot. Actually, she was driving *my* car—a sporty Pontiac Fiero. Donna didn't own a vehicle, so I let her drive the Pontiac. I also had a company car at the time, a Ford Taurus.

I found the gaudy diamond ring perched on my desk in my home office and the closet empty of her clothes.

I took the company car to search for her. The only place she could go were some of our favorite bars, so I looked inside those watering holes. She wasn't there.

One day passed, then two and three days. I had no idea where she'd gone, but I knew she wouldn't leave town in my car. On a hunch, I drove to the Columbus airport and rode around the main parking lot. Sure enough, I found my Pontiac. That could only mean one thing: she had flown to St. Louis, where her parents lived.

The message was clear: It was over. We were done.

I was devastated. I had walked away from my marriage to be with Donna, and it was all for naught. The only bright spot was that I was able to return the engagement ring and get my money back. I moved out of the apartment and into a crummy dive of a townhouse that was smaller and cheaper. At least my rent was cut in half.

Now I didn't have Stephanie and the boys, and I didn't have Donna. I had made a mess of my interpersonal relationships, but there was no way to back up on the freeway of life. I had recently taken a new job with Dr Pepper/Seven Up as an account sales manager, so I threw myself into my new work to distract myself from my woes. Most evenings I would return to my low-class apartment with a bagful of White Castle burgers and fries, which I'd eat in my waterbed and then fall asleep. Before long, I would munch on fast food and stay in bed all day as I became more and more depressed. The antidepressants I took to win Donna back were gone long ago.

I couldn't go on like this forever. No man could stay sane otherwise. Sooner or later I had to go out, get back in circulation. I started returning to my old haunts and drinking a ton. Every weekend I had a different girl in my bed. Some were terrible looking, but it really didn't matter. "Coyote ugly," I called them, but I needed their validation that I was worthy.

Almost three months after Donna left, my office phone rang in the dead of night. I had no idea who could be calling me, but I figured it had to be important so I dragged myself out of bed.

A glance at my alarm clock told me that it was just after 4 a.m.

"Hello?"

"Uh, hi, it's me."

"Oh, hi, Donna. Do you know what time it is?"

"I do."

"What do you want?"

"There is something I need to tell you."

"I'm listening."

"I'm pregnant."

I was suddenly a lot more awake. Her pronouncement momentarily stunned me, but I quickly caught my footing. "So? What does that have to do with me?"

"You're the father."

Once again, my world was rocked. "You've been gone for three months and you're just coming around to tell me? How long have you known?"

"I found out right after I left."

I didn't trust Donna, I'm afraid to say. The only trustworthy women in my life were my mother and Stephanie.

"Is there a possibility that I'm not the father?"

"Well, I'm three months pregnant, so you obviously got me pregnant before we broke up."

"So why are you calling me now, at four in the morning?"

"I just thought you should know."

"Why now? Why not two months ago?"

"I wasn't strong enough. I needed time to sort things out."

"What do you want me to do about it? Are you going to keep it?"

"Yes."

"Maybe we need to talk about this. We should get together. Why don't you come here to Columbus?"

"I'll have to call you back."

Donna followed through a day later. "My parents said they would pay for a ticket to fly me to Columbus. We can spend a few days together and talk about what we want to do."

"That'll be great."

I remember going to the Columbus Airport, and those were the days when visitors could get past security to greet passengers as they exited the plane. When Donna came out of the jet bridge, she definitely looked pregnant at four months along. I felt sorry for her. My first thought was *I have to rescue her. She needs me.* Some kind of 1950s sensibility kicked in, meaning I had to marry her because it was the right thing to do.

The thought of having another child, however, was not one I welcomed. When Donna and I were together, she wasn't sure she wanted kids. That was perfect for me since that meant I could remain the center of attention. Besides, when Stephanie and I were still married, we decided that the only kids we were going to have were Mike and Chris.

But now I had been dealt a new hand.

I drove Donna to my dumpy townhouse, sparsely furnished with my oversized fabric couch, two small wooden end tables and a lumpy old side chair. After spending a few hours together, I said that we should consider getting married so I could take care of her and our child. At the same time though, I expressed reservations about whether our marriage would really work given our past history.

"Maybe we need to spend some time together and make sure this is the right thing to do before we get married," I said.

Donna agreed to my great relief. "Yeah, we don't have to get married right away. I think we should wait."

By the time I took her back to the airport, the die had been cast: Donna would return to Columbus, and we would give our combative relationship a chance.

We had to give our love a second chance.

It's all we had left . . . actually, it's all I had left.

7

LONG-DISTANCE DAD

Mike

Once we agreed to get back together, Donna flew back to St. Louis, where her father took pity on the situation and bought her a used compact car. Within a week, Donna drove out from the Gateway City to Columbus.

I remember asking Donna to marry me again while sitting at the small dinette table in the kitchen where I gave her a second engagement ring. This time around, I was smart about things; I bought her a modest ring for $500. We agreed that we needed to see a counselor to give us the best chance to make it. The counselor, a woman, advised us to have a "solid" prenuptial agreement in place before we moved forward and got married.

That sounded like wise advice to me. I told Donna that I would not marry her unless she signed an agreement that basically stipulated that whatever assets I brought into the marriage were mine if things didn't work out. I wanted to make sure that she wasn't marrying me for my money, which wasn't much but was more than she had.

She signed the prenup quickly and without question.

Donna returned to St. Louis to prepare for the marriage ceremony, which was as modest as my engagement band. We were joined together in the bonds of matrimony on June 6, 1987, in a tacky wedding chapel before three witnesses: her father, mother, and brother. She did not wear a wedding dress because she was six months along and had a big stomach. Someone's Kodak Instamatic camera took a few shots.

After the ceremony, her parents took us out to eat at the downtown men's club her father belonged to. Then we settled into our room at a downtown St. Louis hotel near the Arch. The next day, we drove to her parent's lake house in Bonne Terre, Missouri, sixty miles south of the city, for a short honeymoon.

I had told Stephanie just before my departure that I was getting married. I can't remember exactly what I said, but most likely I mentioned that I was marrying Donna because she was pregnant.

Our son, Jack, was born three months after the honeymoon on August 26, 1987. Stephanie and the boys were still living in Columbus, so Mike and Chris saw their new half-brother every other weekend. They loved Jack and were great with him. I always tried to make out like nothing was wrong, but there was always a lot of tension and stress when Mike and Chris were around because everything had to be perfect. I never wanted to waste any time I had with them.

And then this alternate universe I had constructed blew up. It happened during a business trip to Cleveland, while working for Dr Pepper/Seven Up, when I got a call from my ex-wife.

"I want to let you know that I'm moving back to Atlanta and taking the boys with me," she began. "We don't have family here, and I need help with the boys to get a good job. We're going to move down there and live with my parents until I can find a teaching position." Years later, Stephanie confessed that her primary reason for leaving was to escape the pain of living so close to my new family.

Stephanie was trying to be civil, but what she said set me off. "There's no @#$%-ing way you're taking my kids away from me," I said. "Atlanta is a thousand @#$%-ing miles away. How am I supposed to see Mike and Chris on a regular basis if you've taken them that far away?"

I was furious, but despite my verbal blasts, Stephanie didn't budge. "Well, I'm sure we can work out some sort of revised visitation plan," she said.

"The hell we are!" I called her every name in the book and threatened to get a lawyer. I was so upset that she was taking the boys from me that I *did* contact a lawyer and file a lawsuit.

At the end of the legal day, though, I couldn't stop her from moving to Atlanta, but I was able to negotiate how long and how often I would get to see them during the holidays and summer months, when they were out of school.

I loved those boys and wanted to be with them as often as I could. In the back of my mind, I formulated a plan: If there were any jobs out there that would either take me back to Atlanta or get me closer to the Peach State, then I would move my second family closer to them.

Chris

While we were still in Columbus, Mom had a part-time job doing some kind of data entry at night to help pay a mortgage she couldn't afford. We had friends down the street who would come and watch Mike and me, and then Mom would look after their kids as a babysitting exchange.

Early one morning, while coming home from a long night of work, Mom fell asleep at the wheel. She ran off the road, hitting a metal guard rail. Thank God she wasn't injured. I don't believe she was going very fast, and luckily damage to the car was minimal. The experience, however, frightened her more than anything else. Mom said afterward she couldn't go on anymore without help. We had to move back to Atlanta, where we could get much-needed family support from my grandparents.

I was only three at the time, but I recall that we were in dire straights when we arrived in Atlanta. We didn't have much money, so we moved into Grandpa and Grandma's basement and shared one bedroom and a bathroom. There were two single beds flanking each side of the small room, and I was sandwiched between my mom and brother on a tiny cot. The three of us bunked it, but we didn't mind because we were all together. As a kid, I didn't know anything different. I thought this was how everyone lived.

I knew nothing about the behind-the-scenes custody battle between Mom and Dad. All I knew was that Dad would come down from Ohio once a month to see us.

Mike

Less than six months after Stephanie took the boys to Atlanta, I made our first move closer to Atlanta: I accepted a job with the Pepsi Bottling Group (PBG) in Indianapolis, Indiana, as a district sales manager. Indianapolis was only a couple of hours closer to Atlanta, but at least it was a step in the right direction.

Being a long-distance dad tore at my heart. I certainly felt guilty for not being there for Mike and Chris, which is why I made a big effort to drive to Atlanta every three or four weeks and have them at Thanksgiving or Christmas. As part of my agreement with Stephanie, the boys would also stay with us for three weeks during the summer break.

Neither of us had the money to put the boys on a plane, so Stephanie and I worked things out for holidays and the summer to meet at a McDonald's restaurant on Highway 41 south of Chattanooga, about two hours from Atlanta. I would drive seven hours from Indianapolis, a lot longer distance, but I never complained, mostly out of guilt. I was always excited to see the boys, but the exchange was always awkward.

My resolve to see the boys at least every three or four weeks during the school year meant a marathon weekend of driving. I would stop working at 6 p.m. on a Friday afternoon and get into the car and start driving to Atlanta—a trip every bit of nine hours.

Around 10 p.m. or so, it wasn't uncommon for me to start dozing off, but I was bound and determined to spend all day Saturday with Mike and Chris, so I wasn't about to get a motel room for the night. Instead, I would pull into rest stops and sleep for thirty minutes, maybe an hour in the car. Then I'd wake back up and get back on the road.

Sometimes I had to take three or four naps on the way. I usually rolled into Sandy Springs, the suburb where Stephanie's parents lived, around six or seven in the morning. I'd get pancakes with sausage at McDonalds and then pick up the boys.

Chris

I have somewhat good memories of the times Dad dropped in for the weekend. He was the *fun dad* who took us to do cool things whenever he was around. Most of the time, we would go to the movies, fish, play in the park, go to the arcade, or get some ice cream. One of the things I liked was when Dad took us hiking inside the Chattahoochee River National Recreation Area. We loved running ahead of Dad, up and down the trails, along the river, exploring as we went. Being outdoors with my dad and older brother was a special for me. It was our time together— "guy time." I treasured those little moments.

We would spend the night at a Hampton Inn or something like that, the three of us crammed into one room. My brother and I slept in one bed while Dad would take the other bed. Sometimes there was just one king-sized bed in the room, so the three of us would sleep in the same bed. Dad tried not to waste any precious minutes during these weekend visits, so he always seemed to be in a hurry to try to do as much as possible.

Mike
I'd start my return trip to Indianapolis right after lunch around 2 or 3 p.m. on Sunday afternoon. I would make this long, back-and-forth trip at least once a month, which exhausted me, but I didn't want Mike and Chris to grow up without knowing their dad.

Chris
Looking back, I could tell that he was feeling guilty about leaving us. I never asked him why he and Mom broke up. Maybe I didn't want to look at my dad in a bad way. Life's complicated when you're a kid.

Soon after we were settled, Mom got a job teaching at John Hope Elementary School in downtown Atlanta. Teaching in the inner city paid more, which is why Mom took the job. Mike was enrolled in kindergarten and I was in preschool, but we weren't on the same campus, so Mom and Grandma worked things out to get us where we needed to be. Mom would drop me off at preschool in the morning and pick me up in the later afternoon, while Grandma would take Mike to his elementary school and pick him up when the school day was over. It was a collaborative effort—it takes a village to raise a child and all that.

We lived in my grandparents' basement for two years until Mom started shopping for a house in Roswell, north of downtown Atlanta.

Mike

I felt sorry that my boys were growing up in a basement, sharing a bedroom and a bathroom with their mother. As usual, I was tortured by guilt.

I decided to give Stephanie all the equity that we got out of our Columbus house, even though I was legally entitled to half. The amount was a little more than $15,000, which was enough for Stephanie to purchase a small two-story home with white aluminum siding and black shutters that sat on a large corner lot in the Park Bridge subdivision of Roswell. One of the best features of the home was that it was within walking distance of Roswell Area Park, where there were football and baseball fields and basketball courts.

The house had three bedrooms and two-and-a-half baths. Roswell was in a great school district, and North Roswell Elementary School was just a block away. Stephanie shrewdly negotiated a good price for the house, but that wasn't her first priority. Location, location, location was more important to her.

Chris

I was starting kindergarten at the time, so it certainly made life a lot easier when my brother and I could attend nearby North Roswell. Since Mom had to leave for work at 5:30 a.m., she didn't have any choice but to have us walk to school.

Every afternoon, we were latchkey kids with strict instructions to stay inside the house until Mom came home. She didn't like hearing about the times we were outside, but two rambunctious boys couldn't stay cooped up in the house every afternoon.

I remember Mom taking my brother and me to her school several times. At five and six years of age, it was a culture shock traveling from white suburban Roswell to inner-city black Atlanta.

Mom was the only white teacher in the entire school, so she had to be tough as nails in an environment where it wasn't unusual for homeless people to be camped outside the steps of her portable classroom each morning, where gang bangers sold drugs on campus, or where kids brought guns to school. She never took crap from anybody, and that made an impression on me.

Mom was also determined that we would go to church every Sunday. She returned to her roots in the Catholic faith and insisted that we go to Mass every Saturday night or Sunday morning. Mike and I would try to give her every excuse in the book so that we didn't have to go, but she didn't take any crap from us either, even when we made fun of the altar boys and the strange vestments they had to wear—the floor-length black cassocks with white surplices.

I didn't like catechism classes at all. I remember the teacher telling us that Halloween was Satan's day to play and that Halloween should not be celebrated. What—no trick or treating? I didn't get that. Basically, I found the Catholic Church difficult to understand and boring: stand up, sit down, kneel . . . stand up, sit down, kneel . . . chant, chant, chant. We fought Mom every time we had to go.

Since Mike and I were relatively close in age, we were best friends. We always celebrated our birthdays together since Mike was born on September 18 and I arrived September 19. This meant less work for Mom with baking a cake and throwing a neighborhood birthday party.

Mom had to economize everywhere she could and weigh every purchase. A single mom raising two growing boys on a teacher's salary was really, really tough. I always wore hand-me-downs from Mike, and we shopped at garage sales for clothes and toys.

Mike and I learned to look out for each other since there was no parent in the home before or after school. We were fortunate to live in our own home and not in a crammed apartment with no backyard, but Mom racked up a lot of credit card debt over the years to make that happen. But she never let on to the financial struggles weighing her down, or about the stress of living from paycheck to paycheck and wondering if there would be enough money to keep us fed and a roof over our heads.

I remember an occasion in first grade when the refrigerator was empty, except for a little milk, a half-bottle of ketchup, and some mayo. The only thing in the cupboard was a blue box of Kraft Mac & Cheese. That night, she cooked the macaroni and cheese and served Mike and me the entire skillet.

"Aren't you going to eat, Mom?" I asked.

"No, that's okay," she replied. "I'm not hungry."

As a young boy, I accepted Mom's explanation, but years later, it was evident that she was going to feed us before she ate herself.

There were other occasions when I came home from school and searched the pantry for a snack, but there wasn't much to choose from. Mom would say, "We don't have the money right now to buy food, so we have to wait for my next paycheck."

That was our reality. At times, a big treat was ordering a large cheese pizza from Little Caesars' because they had great coupons in the Sunday newspaper. On Friday nights, the three of us would sit on the couch, bundle up under a blanket, and watch shows like *Family Matters*, *Step by Step*, and *Boy Meets World* while we munched on our pizza. Those nights are some of my best memories growing up.

I was one of those kids who were always happy. I felt the most carefree when I was outside running around the neighborhood with friends or playing football in the yard. Mom put me in youth soccer in first grade, but like nearly all kids at that age, I didn't know what I was doing out there. We played "bunch ball"—a flock of miniature players following the ball around the field like a swarm of bees.

The first time I played organized football I was eight years old and in third grade. This was a league where all the kids couldn't weigh more than ninety pounds. We called it "pound ball." With this being my first season of football, Coach DeShane put me on the offensive line at right guard. I didn't mind because I got to wear forearm pads, and that was a big deal to me at the time.

When the defense needed practice, Coach would move me to running back on the scout team. Even though I didn't really know what I was doing, I loved being handed the football and tearing up field, making defenders miss me time after time.

Halfway through the season, Mom came home to the following message on her answering machine: "Hi, Stephanie. This is Coach DeShane. We've been watching Chris, and we don't think he should play right guard anymore. We think he's a pretty good athlete because he's been killing our defense. We want to move him to running back and quarterback, but I just wanted to make sure that's okay with you."

I loved hearing that message. Every kid wants to play those positions. So I was moved into the backfield, and that's when I really started to like football.

I was always happy to see Dad, and I got used to shuffling back and forth between two households. My older brother, however, saw things differently. Whenever we got in the car for the drive to the McDonald's outside Chattanooga, Mike would become really emotional in the car. I would see tears roll down his face. I couldn't understand why my brother was crying, but it was probably because he understood the family dynamics better than I did.

I put up an emotional wall and tried to roll with the tide, while Mike internalized our broken home situation and felt emotional whiplashes. I think it's because he had witnessed the break-up, while I was too young to remember anything—or understand what was going on.

All I knew was that I went to this guy's house and called him Dad, and he had a whole other family. By this time, I had another half-sibling: Katy had been born eighteen months after Jack on December 12, 1988. This was a lot to take in, but then again, I was a kindergartner. I thought every kid's dad had another family.

One time, Dad had driven to Chattanooga to pick us up for Christmas, and we ran into a blizzard on the way back to Indiana. Dad drove a Ford Aerostar minivan, and I was curled up on the backseat trying to get some sleep, but I couldn't. I remember the blowing snow building up on the front windshield. The snowstorm got so bad that we had to pull into a roadside motel and wait out the terrible weather. We eventually got to Dad's place, and the next day he took my brother and me to a Christmas tree farm. Jack came along as well.

Mike

Jack was about two-and-a-half at the time and quite a handful, fussing all the time.

Chris

After we cut down a tree and tied it onto the roof of the minivan, Dad took the three of us to Burger King. When our meal arrived,

Jack opened up the wrapping around his hamburger and threw a fit.

Why? Because the hamburger patty and top half of the bun were not put on straight. He was very particular about having his hamburger exactly right for some reason, so he made a big scene in the restaurant, kicking and screaming, turning beet red as everyone around us looked to see what all the commotion was about. Mike and I thought that it was crazy to get all amped up about something as silly a Burger King hamburger.

Mike

Jack was a difficult preschooler, and with our second daughter, Katy, having just celebrated her first birthday, I would say that Donna and I were in over our heads on the parenting front.

Drinking helped me deal with my troubles. I kept a lid on things by only tossing back a few whenever I went out after work or with Donna on weekends. During this particular Christmas when I picked up the boys during a blizzard, the chaos inside my home over the next few days was enough to drive any man to drink.

On Christmas Eve morning, I found a quart of holiday eggnog in the refrigerator, and I took a bottle of rum stashed away in a pantry cabinet and made my own holiday mixer—eggnog and rum. The taste was sweet and pleasant, and I must have finished off a quart of yuletide cheer in record time as we finished bundling up the kids to brave the snow for a family outing that day.

I remember becoming frustrated with my lot in life, which all started with the woman who was now my second wife. Jack was crying as we tried to leave. Donna was screaming in his direction and looked miserable. I felt like this special day—Christmas Eve—was being ruined. "I'm totally sick of this @#$%," I complained. "This is all your fault."

Donna was holding Katy in her arms. When she defended herself, our fight escalated into another skirmish from the *War of the Roses.*

This time I had had it. In an alcohol-fueled tirade, with insults flying back and forth, I had reached my limit. I pushed her around and invaded her private space. I slapped Donna on the side of her face with an open hand.

Chris

I remember Dad rushing my brother and me to the front door and saying, "Get in the car." Actually, he yelled at us, so I could tell he meant business. Mike and I did as we were told and stormed into the minivan. I didn't know what was happening except that we sped out of that neighborhood way too fast for the snow and ice on the road. I was definitely scared.

Mike

I stopped at a convenience store and found a pay phone. I called Stephanie and reached her. "Listen, something has happened," I began. "Donna and I got into a big fight and things got out of control."

"How are the boys doing? Is everything all right?" Stephanie asked.

"I'm not sure. Actually, there's one thing I'm sure of: I can't go back to the house."

Even though I had been drinking, I sobered up rather quickly. Stephanie had an idea.

"Listen, Indianapolis isn't too far from Terre Haute. Take them to Grandma Beck's house. I'll get there tonight."

Terre Haute was just a couple of hours away, so Stephanie's idea was a good one. After leaving the boys with Stephanie's grandmother, I found a cheap motel and spent Christmas Day and the rest of the holiday week with Stephanie and the boys at Grandma Beck's.

By the time I returned home a week later, I discovered that Donna, along with half of our household furniture, were gone. She told her parents that I had hit her, which is all the Jenningses needed to hear as they dropped everything and drove to Indianapolis to rescue their only daughter. They loaded up a U-Haul trailer with the living room couch, a full-size bed, a crib, an assortment of baby things, and luggage filled with clothes. Then they drove Donna, Jack, and Katy back to the safe refuge of St. Louis.

Déjà vu all over again. Only this time it came with a restraining order.

Over the next couple of weeks, I would call her parents' home, and her mother would take the phone and inform me that Donna didn't want to talk. I would repeat what I said on previous phone calls: that I was sorry about everything that had happened and wanted to make amends.

"Yes, but you slapped her," her mom said.

"I know, and I'm profoundly sorry for that. Things got out of control, and things were said that shouldn't have been said. I want you to know that I did not beat her up. I slapped her—with an open hand. That doesn't make it any better, but I just want you to know what happened. I'm begging for another chance to take care of my family."

Those phone calls got me nowhere for a couple of months. I was convinced it was over with us. Once again, I was alone in our house, which meant I had to go find entertainment beyond my four walls. Fortunately, I had had some practice, like the way I took up with a cute secretary in the office, Monica. She happened to tell me one afternoon that she had recently broken up with her boyfriend. That's all the opening I needed.

"My marriage is over," I said. "Why don't we go out for drinks tonight? How about Friday's?"

Sounded like a great idea to her. "Yeah, I would love to."

That evening, we knocked down one drink after another at T.G.I. Friday's—we drank and drank and drank until we were sozzled. We ended up at my house that night, where the sanctity of my marital bed was violated. A couple of days later, we spent the weekend at her place, where we had sex ten or twelve times that weekend. She was very complimentary of my skills and made me feel better about myself.

Once again, it never dawned on me that I was doing something wrong. I had all the justifications in the world: since Donna had left me, I was entitled. I could do as I wished. The affair didn't last, but it sure boosted my self-esteem and took the edge off a trying time.

Trying time understates the turmoil that spun me around like hurricane-force winds. With a divorce, a separation, and four kids from two wives, what else could go wrong?

Try filing for bankruptcy.

8

The Slippery Slope

Mike

As I've mentioned, a huge chunk of my salary was going toward child support for Mike and Chris—$850 a month—about 40 percent of my take-home pay when I was with the Pepsi Bottling Group.

By the time Donna took the kids and headed to St. Louis, we had accumulated just over $10,000 in credit card debt. Ten grand seems like a piddling amount today; in 2012, the average American household carried $16,000 in credit card debt. But twenty-five years ago, I thought $10,000 was a massive amount. Besides our mortgage, the other outstanding obligation included $15,000 owed on the minivan.

Overwhelmed and underwater, I had to take drastic measures. I unloaded the Aerostar minivan and bought a cheap 1983 Buick station wagon from a "Buy Here, Pay Here" car lot located in a bad part of town. I put our modest ranch-style home on the market. Then I filed for Chapter 7 bankruptcy protection, which wiped out our debt overnight. Once the decree was finalized, my credit rating was ruined.

I thought my life was ruined anyway. The only bright spot was that Donna was accepting my phone calls, so at least we were talking. Each time I expressed remorse and asked that she give me another chance, she said she would think about it.

Once again, I was alone—and it was all my fault. Or largely my fault. Or partially my fault. My mind tormented me regarding the shades of culpability. Even though I accepted responsibility for my actions, part of me still blamed Donna. She must have said something that day to set me off, so really, her actions caused me to act that way. Besides, I never connected my drinking with the way I would behave when I *did* drink.

The only bit of good news was that Pepsi promoted me to sales operation manager and put me in charge of developing a new bulk delivery system. One of my first business trips took me to St. Louis, so I contacted Donna. She agreed to come to my hotel, the downtown Marriott, and bring along Jack and Katy.

When they entered the lobby, I was crushed because Katy was starting to walk and Jack was older and cuter than ever.

"Please take me back," I pleaded. "Please give me another chance. I've changed. Things will be different. I promise."

This time I noticed softness in Donna's eyes. Maybe she had looked around and saw that her prospects for a bright future had dimmed considerably since she was a single-parent mom with two children under the age of four. Maybe she had done the math and realized that I couldn't afford to pay child support for *two* families. Whatever the reason, she decided to come back to Indianapolis and see if we could get our family turned around. I was grateful for the opportunity.

Things were relatively quiet for a couple of years as we moved into a low-rent, three-bedroom townhouse with ugly shag carpeting near the bottling plant, but nothing about my behavior really changed. To stretch my paycheck, I would substitute my usual vodka with cheap brew here and there so I could continue enjoying the Indy bar scene a couple of times each week after work. I'd literally charm the pants off many of the attractive woman I met while on the prowl.

Donna and I still feuded and spouted nasty comments to each other, but I suppose we were getting used to this version of reality. Our fights usually blew over quickly. I guess you could say *quiet* was a relative term with us.

One of the best things, though, about Donna was how she was sexually adventurous and open to doing everything and anything with me. We were exactly on the same page—the *Penthouse Forum* page.

When Jack and Katy came along, Donna and I couldn't go out as much as we liked, so we were left to entertain each other in our master bedroom. We looked for ways to have better and better sex. Talking about lovers from the past was a great way to get turned on. I would become extremely aroused each time she embellished a lurid story from the past. Of course, the more excited I got, the more she seemed to want to do it.

Later, when I proposed watching porn movies to "have some fun," she would accompany me to porn stores and help me pick out a couple of *Debbie Does Dallas*-type titles for the evening. We'd watch them together in bed and enjoy talking about and mimicking what we saw on the small screen.

Things did not stop there—far from it. When we did have the chance to get an evening away, I put forward the idea of going to a strip club together for something more "live." Donna was all for it. We found one particular strip club in Indianapolis that featured both men and women strippers, complete with a velvet-curtained stage and golden poles. The performers would step out before the boisterous audience and proceed to take all their clothes off, leaving themselves completely naked.

When the show was over, they'd slip their skimpy outfits back on and make the rounds with audience members, who could pay for a "lap dance," which I won't describe in detail here. When Donna had a lap dance with a guy, I got very excited watching that happen. When I tipped a female stripper to give me the same treatment, Donna was titillated. Then we'd go home and use these memories to have mind-blowing sex.

I was becoming more and more addicted to anything having to do with the flesh, and my addictions were starting to pile up at this point in my life.

⁂

In early 1992, I heard about an in-house corporate position opening up with Pepsi that involved a relocation from Indianapolis to Nashville.

Nashville . . . that would put me about four hours from Mike and Chris in Atlanta. No more long Friday night drives. This opportunity fit my desire that each time I climbed a rung of the corporate ladder, I would be one step closer to Atlanta.

I aggressively sought the position of franchise manager for Pepsi, meaning that I would become the corporate liaison between the bottlers and corporate PepsiCo in New York. I got the job, which was a big break. As I assumed my new duties, I started calling on the tenth-largest Pepsi bottler at the time, Beamen Bottling, with production plants located throughout central Tennessee and south to Rome, Georgia.

I had to make sure that they represented the entire line of Pepsi products and that we had proper distribution for all the retail stores as well as the "fountain accounts"—fast food restaurants, convenience stores, and the like. I didn't like country music at the time or know Nashville very well prior to the move, but I was pleased to learn that "Music City" teemed with bars, honky tonks, and juke joints. Here was a town that appreciated a good, stiff drink. Everything was perfect. My promotion fueled a desire for even *more* on the sexual front.

For Donna's birthday one time, I had the bright idea of hiring a male stripper to come to our house. What about the kids? They were young and in bed, but I was so consumed by sex that I really did not think through the implications of bringing a male stripper into our home.

Late that evening, toward midnight, I sat on the couch and observed the two interact as his little show began. When he approached her, she looked at me for approval, which I granted with a nod and a smile. I watched my wife touch this young hard body, fondling him in the process, but they didn't go further on this evening. When the male stripper left, Donna and I continued things to their logical conclusion and had a great time.

I wanted to do that again, so I called the same male stripper for a return engagement. The next time he came to our home, I quietly observed while he had sex with my wife in front of the fireplace in our family room. I allowed that to happen, believing it was a turn-on.

I didn't think this was bizarre behavior at all, which is an important point I want to get across to readers. Remember, the pages of *Penthouse Forum* reinforced the idea over and over that you could do anything and everything when it came to sex. Any and all sexual practices were normal, even healthy.

In addition, there was reinforcement all around me: I lived in a sexualized culture where there were no boundaries and no consequences regarding any form of sex, where watching others have sex in Hollywood movies was a form of voyeurism, where sitcoms broke down our defenses by building humorous situations around sex, and where sexy models with deep cleavage were featured in advertisements for everything from new car sales to lingerie spreads.

We only lived in Nashville a little over a year, but while we were there, Donna and I discovered a new "spectator sport": going to bars where I watched men attempt to pick her up.

I don't know if there's a name for this voyeuristic activity, but it sure got our jets revved up. We'd start the evening by dropping into a local bar that featured live music. Nothing unusual about that: every drinking establishment on Music Row featured aspiring musicians trying to break into the recording business. Once we stepped inside the bar or honky-tonk, we'd go our separate ways. She would go do her thing, and I would do mine.

I liked to take a seat at the bar, order my usual vodka on the rocks, and observe her getting hit on by men. I found that to be a fascinating study in human interaction. Donna always kept on her wedding ring because single guys—and married ones—liked meeting married women in a bar. A wedding ring meant she wasn't interested in a serious relationship and was merely looking for some excitement to spice up a dull marriage. A married woman was safe, and guys could count on no emotional attachment.

Single women, however, didn't want anything to do with married guys. The thought of striking up a flirty conversation with a married guy on the make wasn't part of their nature. That's why I made sure my wedding ring was tucked safely away in my pants pocket.

Sometimes I chatted up women, but I wasn't out to make a Saturday night hook-up with another woman. What I liked about the whole scene was looking around the smoke-filled bar and trying to guess who would make a move on Donna—and then watching the guy's body language as he swooped in for a "party pick-up."

I'm sure this sounds weird to the average reader, and looking back today, it *was* weird. But back then, I was in the throes of sexual addiction that always demanded something different, something more, and something new.

We'd leave the bar at quitting time, and Donna would give me a play-by-play of what the guys said or intimated. Hearing her descriptions turned me on. The more she told me, the more I wanted to hear, and the more I heard, the more I got excited. It was like being addicted to a drug. And if I had anything interesting to talk about from the girls I met, I would relate what our conversations entailed. When Donna and I got home and into bed, we would have the most incredible lovemaking sessions.

All this talking about sex, reading about sex, watching movies about sex, and participating in various sexual practices steered us down paths that took us to unexpected places. That unexpected place for Donna and me was group sex.

Here's how we got there.

After a while, even going into bars and watching Donna get hit on got old. We needed something even newer, something we hadn't done before. Donna and I talked about what sexual frontiers we hadn't crossed. Our discussions progressed to the point when I said, "Wouldn't it be fun if we had sex with another couple?"

The problem with voicing something like that is that sooner or later, the mind finds ways to rationalize such behavior. (*It's not cheating since we're doing it together . . . it's just for fun . . . it's among consenting adults.*)

While Donna and I talked tantalizingly about exploring this area of mutual interest, she didn't know about the young, attractive woman I was having an affair with in Chattanooga. She was married too, but like me, she was purely into the affair for the drinking and sex. I'll call her Marie.

At any rate, I told Donna that I had met someone on one of my frequent business trips to Chattanooga and had been cheating on her for some time. Donna was hurt, but I didn't notice. "Marie's married, too," I said, "and after talking to her, I think she and her husband would be a good couple for us to have some fun with. They are open to exchanging partners."

I thought this was the greatest idea in the world. We would all get what we wanted, but Marie had to convince her husband to go along with this *ménage à quatre* arrangement. Don't ask me how or why, but she was able to do that.

Some people call this "swinging" or "playing." Donna and I quickly learned that there was a whole subculture out there that was into swapping spouses. Swingers' parties would be held monthly at a Holiday Inn or a Ramada, where couples would rent rooms for group sex. Donna and I got into that scene for a while. We'd check into our room and go downstairs to a ballroom complete with music and several bars, where we'd meet like-minded folks. Let the partying begin.

The adrenaline rush was always amazing . . . even addicting, but I had to do a lot of internal rationalizing—and drink a lot of alcohol—to get me to the point where I would readily do these things. The rationalizing went like this:

I love my wife so much that I want her to have as much fun as possible by having sex with other men. Giving her the freedom to be with these men will only make her love and want me more. What other man would let her do that? It makes our relationship more honest, open, and secure than most couples.

We knew that society frowned upon swinging, but for us personally, we had no moral compass saying that it was wrong. After a while, it seemed perfectly normal to participate in this type of sexual activity.

Sometimes it was difficult to meet couples—imagine that— or find a couple where we were both attracted to the opposite sex partner. When that happened, we'd spice things up by going "solo" and having sex with other people in full knowledge of the other partner. It was just easier, more practical to do it apart from each other. Besides, we would talk about our "nights out" while we had sex anyway. It was just like being there.

See how slippery the slope had become?

In 1993, after living a year in Nashville, I heard internally that Pepsi had a business development manager position open in Atlanta.

Atlanta was the Promised Land—the shining city where Mike and Chris lived. There was no way I wasn't going to get this job. I threw myself into the interview process and won the position. I was on Cloud 9.

Donna was probably starting to feel like a military wife, having to move every couple of years to the next posting, but she didn't mind when I promised her that this would be our last move. We rolled into Alpharetta, just six miles north of Roswell. While it made sense to live relatively close to the boys, I didn't want to put Stephanie in the uncomfortable position of running into Donna and the kids at school or the grocery store by living in the same suburb of Atlanta.

The greatest thing about living in the same geographic area was that I could coach Mike and Chris in sports or see a lot more of their games. The danger, though, was that someone who knew Stephanie and the boys would discover our secret lives.

Chris

Having a mom who was a schoolteacher certainly helped when it came to getting my homework done, but Mom's school day usually wasn't finished when she got home from the afternoon commute. She'd have tests to grade and papers to correct, so we would all tackle our "homework" around the dinner table. What kept me going was that Mom always had a knack for being a great encourager.

"Chris, I will never be disappointed in you as long as you try your hardest," she would say. "I know if you try your hardest and put all your effort into it, then that is all I can ask of you." I always thought that was cool to hear and relieved some of the pressure to perform. I became a good student even though I wasn't the smartest kid in the class. I think I did well in school because I wanted to succeed and didn't mind working hard to achieve good grades. I'm not entirely sure where that passion and drive came from, but I wanted to do my best and win at everything.

Let me tell you: I wasn't a good loser. One time, Dad took Mike and me bowling and brought a video camera along. When I noticed that he was filming us, I looked toward the camcorder with an irritated glare and said, "Get that out of my face."

"What's wrong, Chris?" my dad said in the background.

"Get the camera out of my face."

I was upset because I had just lost a bowling game to Mike. I don't care if we were playing checkers or one-on-one basketball, I hated to lose to Mike or anyone else. Back in elementary school, I would start crying if I lost because I wanted to win so badly. I was super competitive from a young age. I hated to lose in the worst way.

Mike and my father would never ease up and let me win either, whatever the game or the sport we were playing. But I didn't want it any other way. Competition had a way of lighting a fire underneath me, and when I did win, I knew it was real. Competition always had me coming back for more.

Mike and I were best friends and pretty much did everything together during our elementary school years, but things changed drastically when he was in middle school. Mike was in seventh grade and I was still a fifth-grader when he made a startling announcement one evening at the dinner table: "I want to change bedrooms so I can have my own space."

Mom and I looked at him. We had always shared a bedroom. Even now, when we lived in a three-bedroom house, Mike and I slept in the same bedroom. We kept the extra bedroom ready as a guest room.

Mom tried to stall him. "Okay, in the summer, when school is over, we'll think about moving you to the guest room."

"No, I want to move tonight."

He was adamant and stubborn. Despite Mom's protestations, his feet were dug in. He wanted his own room—now.

Mom sensed he wouldn't budge. "Okay. You can move, but you're going to have to do it by yourself."

That night, I watched as Mike took apart our bunk bed and moved his bed to the extra bedroom. Then he grabbed his clothes by the armful and carried them to the new closet and dresser. This was the beginning of the end of our childhood friendship. Overnight, we went from being best buds to *I don't want to hang out with you any longer. I want my freedom.*

Mike was thirteen at the time, going through puberty. The swirling hormones must have done something because I noticed that he was getting into a lot more trouble at school. This wasn't the Mike that I had known.

It all hit the fan when Mike ended up getting expelled and

was ordered to attend Haynes Bridge Middle School in Alpharetta, which made the logistics of getting him to school a nightmare for Mom. She would have to get up super early in the morning and drive him to my dad's house, where Donna would then take him to his new school.

This was the start of a dark period in our home. From then on, Mike was flat-out hostile to Mom and me. I couldn't understand it. He would scream obscenities at the top of his lungs, punch holes in the drywall in a fit of rage, and always seemed to be mad at the world, taking it out on the people who loved him the most.

Most weekdays, Mom and I could never tell what kind of mood Mike would be in when he got home from school. We walked on eggshells, and many afternoons I'd grab a basketball and make a beeline for the rusty hoop just off our driveway. I'd shoot hoops for hours, praying that it would stay light out just a little longer so I didn't have to go inside. I hated being fearful that I'd say something wrong or do something to make him go off. I felt like I had lost my brother and best friend, but I guess he was in the throes of teenage rebellion.

He had a short fuse, just like Dad. One night at the dinner table, something set him off. He grabbed a ketchup bottle and smashed it on the table, splattering the red sauce all over of the place. Mom and I sat there covered in ketchup, silent and stunned by what had taken place.

Looking over, I could see tears fall down my mom's face as she quietly said, "I'm sorry, Chris."

"It's not your fault, Mom." Then I wiped the sauce off my face.

"I know. But I'm still sorry. You don't deserve this."

I finished the rest of my meal doused in ketchup and staring into my plate of food, wondering how someone could act like this.

There were many nights like that. I was the collateral damage to Mike's rage, and Mom would always apologize to me after each big blowout. I knew it wasn't her fault—and that was the worst part. It was difficult to sit back and watch my mom being tormented emotionally by my brother.

Often times when I was in my bedroom, I could hear him screaming at Mom in the kitchen, the yelling working its way upstairs and into the hall right outside my bedroom. A sick feeling would come over me as if someone was punching me in the stomach. Then I'd hear the screaming get more intense. A pillow over my head was my only refuge as I tried to drown out the noise that went on for hours.

Sometimes I'd have enough and try to be my mom's savior, hoping my bravado would cause my brother to back down. I'd yank open the door to give him a piece of my mind. "Why are you screaming at Mom?" I'd ask. "She's trying to do the best she can to provide for the family, and you know she would do anything for us."

Mike didn't like being challenged, especially by a younger brother. My outbursts often resulted in physical retaliation. I'm not talking about brotherly roughhousing but Mike smacking me with his fists while I struggled to land a punch or two.

These "fight club" kind of brawls were a fairly common occurrence during this time. I only wanted to help Mom out, although most of the time I probably made things worse. At least Mike wasn't screaming at Mom anymore. That's all I cared about.

In a quieter moment, after one of the usual scream fests, I walked into Mom's room and found her sitting on the bed, tissue in hand. Her face was red from crying. It broke my heart to see Mom like this. No one should be treated this way.

She looked at me and said, "Are you okay?"

"I'm fine, Mom." I stared at the carpet, not wanting to see the pain in her eyes.

"I'm sorry about all this." She buried her face in her hands and began to cry.

The helplessness I felt as I watched Mom defeated and broken took its toll on me. I looked at her with tears filling my eyes and said, "Mom, you don't have to worry about me. I'm going to be somebody some day, and this will all go away. I'll never be like Mike."

Those words changed my life and shaped every decision I made from that moment on. For some reason, I thought that if I just made my mother proud and never disappointed her, then that would make everything better. And if Mike's actions and words could destroy our family, then surely my behavior could help make everything right again . . . or at least better.

I hated my brother for the longest time because I felt like he wrecked our family. So I put the weight of the world on my shoulders and let his actions fuel me to do the opposite of whatever my brother did. If he was yelling at Mom, I would be nice to Mom. If he got bad grades, I would get good grades. If he was always stirring things up, I would be the peacemaker. I felt like I had to stand up for Mom because Mike was beating her down emotionally.

Mom only had one weapon—"I'm going to call your dad." I can't blame her. My brother was a five-foot, ten-inch, 200-pound raging teenager. It's not like Mom was weak, but my brother was afraid of Dad because he had a temper as well. For some reason though, I was never as scared of my father as he was.

Mike

It wasn't unusual for Stephanie to call during the evening or on weekends when she was having trouble with Mike. I didn't mind at all, and I would drop whatever I was doing with Donna and the kids and go running over to Stephanie's house.

I'm not sure if my appearance helped, but it made me feel better to be involved, which helped compensate for the guilt I still felt. I would try to reason with Mike at first, but it wasn't long before my face would turn red, and I would start yelling and screaming at him as my body shook with anger. Like father, like son I suppose. At least he was still afraid of me, and that's all I had left.

Chris

The crushing blow, however, came when I was thirteen and a water pipe burst in our front yard. Water leaked everywhere and made our front yard a grassy swimming pool.

Mom got an estimate from a plumber, who said it would cost $3,000 to replace the pipe and get everything fixed. Mom said, "I don't have three thousand bucks to do this." I could tell she was worried.

She had a friend who offered to help out, but we needed more free labor. Mike and I were enlisted to help out. Mom had to count on us, and I was cool with that.

I distinctly remember Mom saying to us, "Make sure that you guys are here after school and bring some friends with you who can help out." I had already recruited two of my buddies to help us dig a trench in the yard to lay the new pipe. My brother promised he'd be there.

My friends and I started working our shovels after school, but there was no Mike in sight. *Maybe he's just running late*, I thought to myself. Fortunately, it had rained earlier that day so the ground was really soft. That made the trenching part easier, and it was kind of fun getting as dirty as we wanted.

We kept digging as the time passed—one hour, two hours, and three hours. After four hours in a knee-deep trench, my brother still hadn't shown up. By then, there was a long gaping trench in the yard with piles of dirt all around us. The hard part was done. Then Mom's friend dropped by and helped us replace the broken pipe and get the trench filled back in. It was quite a job, but we saved $3,000 dollars that we didn't have.

It was dark when Mike finally showed up. Mom got in his face. "We are a family, and we're supposed to stick together and help each other out," she said firmly. "We asked you to do this one thing for us, but you couldn't be bothered to show up?"

Covered in mud and sweat, I watched as he walked right past me without a single sign of remorse on his face. Mom's face painted a different picture—one of disappointment.

I was so furious that I couldn't even bring myself to say anything to him. The damage that was done crushed my trust in what I thought our family was supposed to be like. *It's just Mom and me now,* I said to myself. I couldn't count on anyone else.

I was mystified by his behavior. Years later, I came to understand why he was lashing out in the worst way and doing really dumb things even though he was super smart. It seems that one day he did the math and figured out that Jack was born three months after Dad and Donna got married. Mike put on his poker face and tried to bluff Mom, using the little facts he knew.

"I know why you and Dad got a divorce," he said one evening to Mom. "Dad told me that he left us for Donna because he got her pregnant."

"I can't believe your father told you!" Mom said irritatingly. She took a deep breath. "Well, honey, I'm not mad at Dad or Donna. It happened and it's over. I'm not bitter about it."

"I knew it!" Mike yelled.

Mom's jaw dropped as she realized Mike had pulled a fast one on her. Now he had a more complete answer, but that didn't change the feelings of abandonment that were always just under the surface.

Mike

Mike and I had shared a special bond at the time when I walked out on Stephanie and the boys, even though he was only four years old. As he grew older, it was obvious from his behavior at home that he was deeply wounded, but he never told me what he knew or how he felt about my marriage to Donna. We still had a great relationship whenever we spent time together, but I wondered how much damage I had caused.

Chris

It sure seemed like there was a lot of turmoil growing up. When I was eight years old, I started playing "pound ball" at the Roswell Area Park—peewee football. Dad was one of our coaches, and I was an asset on the team. At the time, though, I was a "dramatic" kid who wanted to be the center of attention, so I would exaggerate my "injuries," whining and complaining about being hurt.

At one practice, I played drama queen one too many times for Dad's liking, so he yanked me off the ground and cussed me out. I don't remember what he said, but he embarrassed me. Before I reached the sidelines, I ripped off my helmet and threw it toward the bench.

Dad tried to explain why he had taken action, but I was through for the day. I was embarrassed and upset that my dad would cuss at me, so I turned and started to walk toward the parking lot where Mom was waiting.

"Where do you think you're going?" Dad said.

I didn't answer. I always gave him the silent treatment when he made me mad. He grabbed my arm and spun me around so that I would look at him.

"Why are you so upset with me?"

"You cussed at me," I replied.

Our conversation stopped after that as I stormed off. When I hopped into Mom's SUV, she could tell something had happened, but I didn't want to get into it.

That was my way of coping with things—shutting people off. My mom always warned my dad, "Be careful with Chris. He'll turn away from you and never talk to you again. And he won't think twice about it either."

Dad tried to call me several times over the next few days, but I didn't want to listen to him. I was still upset.

"Chris, you've got to talk to your dad," Mom said.

Eventually, I did, and he apologized for his actions. "I'm sorry I lost my temper," he said. "I shouldn't have cussed at you."

I accepted his apology, but he never coached me again.

Mike

I saw how frustrated Chris was getting with my behavior. And to be honest, I didn't enjoy coaching anyway. I was just doing it for Chris because I thought that would make him happy. It was my way to make things more "normal" between us, but I took coaching way too seriously. I thought I was the second coming of Vince Lombardi.

Chris

Or maybe the second coming of Bill Parcells, the crusty and often profane head coach who won two Super Bowl rings. Dad screamed at referees all the time in Pop Warner, saying embarrassing things like:

- "What the hell is wrong with you?"
- "How did you miss that play? You're killing us, ref."
- "Get your @#$%-ing head out of your ass."

He got on the refs pretty hard and was warned to watch his language.

Mike

I never wanted to embarrass Chris, which is why I stopped coaching him. I also made sure I didn't get drunk with other parents on the team. I couldn't let parents see that side of me.

The exception was one of the parents I coached with—I'll call him Randy—who loved to drink as much as I did. We'd go out after the game to Hooters and get wings and beer.

Chris

Coach Randy drank a ton, and the reason I know that is because I would spend the night at his house, and his son and I would laugh when his mom had to push him up the stairs because he was too drunk to put one foot in front of another. Even though I knew my dad liked to have a few cocktails, I never saw him act this way.

Since Dad had moved close to us in Alpharetta, Mike and I would stay at his place every other weekend. Packing up every two weeks became a chore I hated and is the reason I'm the biggest procrastinator when it comes to packing today. I'd pull a duffel bag out of the closet and sit there and think about it for a half hour.

Packing was a constant reminder that my parents were divorced and made me think, *Why can't I just have a normal family like all my other friends so I don't have to keep moving every other weekend?* It just never felt like home at Dad's house, so spending the week with Mom and then moving in with Dad and his household for the weekend wasn't easy. I loved seeing my father, but it seemed like I was being forced to spend time with a second family.

Mike

I knew it wasn't easy going back and forth, but Chris never complained to me about coming over every other weekend. He was always a joy to have around, and I loved having him with me as often as I could. I never felt like we were a real family unless Mike and Chris were with us.

Chris

In eighth grade, I went through my growth spurt and shot up to six feet. I was a beanpole at 180 pounds—skinny and fast. The growth spurt helped catapult me athletically as I became a pretty good football player. I was excited to go to the next level of competition at Roswell High and see what I could do.

I wouldn't be going to the same high school as my older brother, though. Since Mike went to a different middle school, he was fed into Milton High School north of Roswell. That meant we would be enrolled in rival high schools.

Mike was playing football on Milton's varsity team, and since we were two years apart, the likelihood that we would go head-to-head was almost nonexistent. Mom and Dad never thought I'd make the varsity football team my freshman or sophomore year. Few high school athletes did.

But then I surprised everyone—even myself.

9

Pressure to Perform

Chris

One of the things I had to overcome in middle school was how I got labeled as a troublemaker from teachers or coaches who had Mike. They knew my brother's history of acting out.

I remember a certain P.E. coach who never liked me even though I always did what was expected of me. Sure, I had an outgoing personality and could be loud at times—but hey, I was in middle school!

One time I was goofing off in gym class, and this P.E. teacher glared at me. "You're going to be just like your brother—a nobody," she said. "And you're never going to make it in high school. You'll be a nobody there, too."

Her biting comments stung, but I would use them as fuel to prove her and others wrong.

I was looking forward to high school, where I wouldn't have to follow in Mike's footsteps since he was at Milton High in Alpharetta. I wanted to blaze my own trail at Roswell High.

Mike, by his junior year, had settled down some. The discipline of playing on the Eagles football team certainly helped. Even though Mike and I were enrolled in rival high schools, my parents never thought we'd play against each other since we were two grades apart. They assumed I wouldn't make the varsity football team until my junior year—after Mike had graduated and gone on to college.

That was my thinking too when I showed up for spring try-outs for the Roswell varsity team while I was still in *eighth* grade. They take their football seriously in the South—so serious that my high school included eighth-graders during spring practice for the coming fall season.

I really wanted to make a good impression, but not because I thought I could win a spot on the varsity team at one of the largest schools in the Fulton County School System. With 2,500 students in four grades, Roswell was a 5A school known for its athletic prowess. (Georgia's biggest high schools played in Class AAAAA.)

One afternoon, we did a series of drills, including one where a running back rushed toward you and tried to mow you over—a one-on-one drill, runner versus tackler. The point of the exercise was to see if you—the tackler—could take down a running back moving straight ahead with a full head of steam.

I couldn't wait for my chance in the tackling box. I had been performing well during the week of drills, and I could hear the coaches asking themselves why an eighth-grader was looking so good against sophomores and juniors.

Coach Pete Poulos, the linebacker coach, blew his whistle. "Gather around, men," he bellowed, his voice raspy from years of screaming at high school football players. "We're going to do Oklahoma now."

Some of the players groaned. "Oklahoma" was the toughest one-on-one tackle drill there was. Then Coach looked toward me with his typical bulldog stare. "Chris, if you knock this guy on his butt, we'll all go in and take a water break. If you don't, we're staying out here for more drills."

Coach Poulos was testing me. He wanted to see how an eighth-grader responded to a challenge. Would I rise to the occasion? Or would I let the pressure get the better of me? The stakes were sky high. My teammates were depending on me to win them a water break. The one thing I had confidence in, however, was throwing my body around like a crazy person.

So imagine the scene—my teammates surrounding me and the upperclassman ball carrier, every one yelling at me to knock him off his feet and nail him to the ground like a hammer to a stake.

My burly adversary lined up at the 30-yard line and I took a spot fifteen yards away on the 15-yard line. About forty guys were whooping and hollering as Coach Poulos readied his whistle. With a tweet, the runner took off straight for me.

With adrenaline pumping and my heart pounding, I exploded from my crouched stance and closed the gap quickly. At full speed, I lowered my shoulder and drove myself into the ball-carrier's midsection. Even though he outweighed me, my strong momentum lifted him off the ground. In one sweeping motion, I laid him down flat on his back. There was a big thump as his body bounced off the ground. I stood over him, taunting him by staring into his grimaced face just to make sure he never forgot that a fourteen-year-old had just knocked him flat.

Coach Poulos blew his whistle. "Take five, gentlemen," he said in shock. My teammates went crazy with joy, slapping me on the helmet since this meant we all got a water break. I was suddenly everyone's best friend and gained instant respect from my teammates.

I took off my helmet and wiped the grass and sweat from my eyes. Several coaches had clustered into a circle as I jogged off the field to get some water. I heard one say, "This kid has some skill. I'm impressed."

"You don't see plays like that from a kid at that age," said another.

As I was walking off the field, Coach Tim McFarlin, the head varsity coach, called me over. "The other coaches and I were talking, and we're thinking we have enough linebackers for next season. Let's move you to defensive back. You're fast, you're smart, and we think that would be a better fit."

You mean I've made the team as a freshman? I knew I couldn't ask Coach that, but my hopes were high. Coach also said I had impressed the coaching staff with my pass-catching ability, so there was a good chance I'd be going both ways and playing wide receiver on offense.

"That'll be great, Coach." Just like that, I practiced with the varsity the rest of spring and made the varsity football team as a freshman, which didn't happen very often at a big city school like Roswell High. The crazy thing was that I wasn't the only freshman on the squad. My good buddy Sedrick Cook, a running back, made the team as well. People were surprised when they learned that not just one but two freshmen were playing varsity football.

Could two fourteen-year-olds hold their own against seventeen- and eighteen-year-old young men? That question quickly disappeared when the 1998 football season rolled around and Sedrick and I became a dynamic freshmen duo. Besides starting on both sides of the ball, Sedrick and I excelled at running back punts on special teams.

Opponents looking up and seeing two freshman back deep to receive the punt actually worked to our advantage because our coaches came up with great plays for us. We would both stand back deep with Sedrick on one side and me on the other. Then one of us would catch the ball and start running toward the other. The player with the ball would either fake or give the ball to the other runner, depending on which side the return was called to.

A wall of blockers would form as the ball carrier would try to get behind the wall and run toward the end zone. We kept a lot of the coverage teams guessing and often made big yardage at key moments of the game.

That year we ended up being average, winning six of ten games in the regular season before being knocked out of the first round of the playoffs. But all the talk around town was about how Sedrick and me, the two freshman, led the team to a playoff appearance.

As you can understand, there was grumbling because the seniors didn't like the coaches constantly praising the young players like Sedrick and me, but we made a majority of the big plays that year—if not all the plays. The highlight reel at the end-of-the-year football banquet could've been likened to ESPN's "Top Ten Plays" of Sedrick and me making big hits and running for long touchdowns. Needless to say, the upperclassmen and their parents weren't too fond of the video and the awards we collected that night.

No sooner had I put my fork down after the football banquet than I moved on to basketball season. I had always loved basketball. We had a basketball goal in the driveway, and I could shoot hoops for hours—especially if I was trying to escape Mike for a while. Naturally, I became pretty good at playing the game.

Once again, I raised a few eyebrows when I made the varsity team as a freshman. Not so much with skill but more with my tenacity and hustle around the ball. I could tell I impressed the coaches, especially with the way I ran the suicide drill in practice. The entire team would line up at the baseline, and then upon the coach's whistle, we would run to the free throw line, then back to the baseline, then to the half-court line, back to the baseline, then the free throw line on the other side and back, and finally full court and back. I almost always beat everyone.

My coaches saw me gut things out and push myself to the limit on every drill. It didn't hurt that I was a tenacious defender, strong rebounder, and overall scrapper whenever I was on the court. I was kind of like the NBA's Dennis Rodman without all the theatrical flamboyancy.

Mike

It was really amazing for Chris to make the varsity basketball team as a freshman because Roswell High was a big school consistently in the hunt for the state championship.

His coach, Vince Alexandri, rarely smiled as he paced up and down the sideline in front of the bench. With arms folded and an intense look on his face, he shouted offensive plays and defensive alignments with a scratchy voice. He did his best to look like NBA coaching legend Pat Riley with his slick-backed hair.

During time-outs, he peppered his speech with profanity if the team was performing poorly. I heard stories of him berating his team in fits of rage, throwing chairs and turning over benches in the locker room. Coach Alexandri came from a college basketball coaching background up north, so he took things a little too seriously, but he won a lot of games, so nobody ever questioned him about his methods.

I loved going to every game, but Chris never got to play early in the season unless the team was getting ahead or behind by fifteen points at the end the game. It's hard to impress coaches with thirty seconds of garbage time at the end of the game, but I'll tell you something: he would play harder in those thirty seconds than anyone else on the court, and he never complained about his lack of playing time.

During his freshman year, Chris' team was playing a tournament between Christmas and New Year's. They were winning a lot of games, but on the day before New Year's Eve, the team tanked against an opponent they were supposed to beat. Chris got his usual thirty seconds of play at the end of a blow-out loss.

Coach Alexandri was fit to be tied. He decided to punish the team with a 6 a.m. practice the following morning—New Year's Eve.

Chris was staying with me that New Year's weekend, and I knew how upset he was that he had to get up that early to practice even though he wasn't to blame for the team's poor performance. But he didn't complain. He never did. I admired how Chris, who had turned fifteen in September, got on with his business and kept working hard in practice, even though he wasn't getting to play much.

Slowly but surely, he started seeing more PT—playing time. By the time the state tournament rolled around in March, he was part of the starting five. He played basketball the way he played football—intelligently and all-out. His defense was off the charts.

What impressed me the most during this time was the way he took a tough situation and made the best of it.

Chris

Having strong freshman seasons on the varsity football and basketball teams brought me notoriety and press coverage, which I think Mike resented. It was a tough situation because he battled Mom on everything. When Mike turned sixteen, Mom bought a new car for herself and gave him the old used car so she wouldn't have to drive him to Dad's house at the crack of dawn every morning before school.

One time, Mom knocked on both of our bedroom doors before she left the house. "Time to wake up."

"Yeah, Mom, I'm up," I replied.

"Will you go wake up your brother?" Even though Mom had given Mike's door a good bang, she knew he was still dozing.

Me? I had no problem getting out of bed right after Mom woke me up. I actually liked the routine of putting on my school clothes, brushing my teeth and splashing some water on my face, going downstairs and having a bowl of Cinnamon Toast Crunch cereal, stuffing my backpack with books and homework, and leaving the house on time for school. The routine made me feel a sense of normality and control.

Mike? He couldn't be bothered to get out of bed.

After Mom left, I knocked on his door. "Mike, get up," I said.

"I will," was his muffled reply.

Ten minutes later, Mom called the house from the car. (We didn't have our own cell phones back then.) When I answered, Mom asked, "Is Mike up yet?"

"No. Not yet." From past experience, I knew the dance we were about to do.

"Well, I'm going to call back. Let it ring," Mom said.

I let the phone ring so my brother could pick it up, but he couldn't be bothered to lift the irritatingly jangling phone off the hook.

"Mike! Pick up the phone! It's Mom! She wants to talk to you," I hollered from downstairs.

On something like the tenth or fifteen ring, he groggily picked up the phone and heard Mom say, "Mike, time to get up. You need to get to school."

And yet he still didn't get out of bed.

Five minutes later, Mom called back to check on him, but this time he didn't answer the phone. I took the call.

"Would you wake him up?" I could hear the exasperation in

Mom's voice.

"Mom, I've tried a million times."

By this time, I was aggravated because I'd been pulled into the situation and the job had fallen on me to get him to school on time. But always the dutiful son, I banged on his door in desperation and said one more time, "Mike, you need to get up. Mom's getting upset with you, and you're going to be late . . . again."

I was part of a carpool, so I had to go when the horn blew. Mike, however, had his own car, so he showed up late for first period that day. Sometimes he blew off school entirely. This impacted his grades, which could have been good because he was a smart guy, but he didn't try and didn't care. This only added extra headaches for Mom.

People around us noticed that we were like night and day, which made it rough on both of us. Teachers, parents, coaches, and even some of my classmates considered me "perfect"—the straight arrow, all-American athlete who made straight A's and made all the right choices all the time. The pressure to keep up with that image overwhelmed me at times.

Mike

I faced certain pressures as well after being promoted to national account sales manager in the Southeast Region and switched to a new product category at Pepsi in Atlanta—the Fountain Beverage Division (FBD).

The soft drink business is competitive enough in retail stores, but at least you share shelf space with your competition. Not the FBD. National restaurant chains sold either Coke or Pepsi but never both. That meant a lot of hustling and keeping customers happy, which I was good at. In my business, it was all about making the numbers, and I performed so well that my sales reports practically glowed in the dark.

As I joked to my friends and customers, "Do you know how good you have to be to sell Pepsi in a Coke town?" My bravado always elicited laughs because Atlanta is where a local pharmacist, Dr. John Pemberton, concocted the Coca-Cola Cola formula back in 19th century. These days, one of Atlanta's biggest tourist attractions is the World of Coke, the museum that welcomes more than 1 million visitors a year.

One of the best things about working for Pepsi was the opportunity to travel to my favorite city, Chicago, for the National Restaurant Association Show at McCormick Place. The annual NRA trade show drew more than 1,800 exhibitors and tens of thousands of attendees. The event was nothing more than a huge party, and I was like a kid in a candy shop.

Trade shows are always about making connections, and I was looking to make a few in the crowded bars along Rush Street following a long day working in our corporate booth. After a few warm-up stops, I landed at one of my favorite martini bars, Sinatra's, around nine o'clock and started to do some serious drinking and interacting. Let's just say it was a hopping bar scene.

I've done my fair share of cocktailing, but being the astute student of human nature that I am, I've learned something over the years: you don't start telling your whopper stories until later in the evening, when everyone is fairly inebriated.

I was knocking down my eighth or ninth round around midnight when my drinking buddy from California spotted a couple of gorgeous girls. Before you could say "It's getting hot in here," I was standing beside these beguiling ladies, flashing my killer smile.

Maybe it was my reddish blond hair and fair skin or my genial nice-guy demeanor, but I heard this pick-up line from one of the ladies: "You sure look familiar. Have I seen you before?"

That was my cue to roll the tape.

"Don't you know who I am?" I said.

"No, who are you?" asked one of the cute but tipsy account reps.

"I'm Brett Hull. I play for the Blackhawks, the hockey team here in town."

I received a lot of "wows" and instant respect impersonating an NHL professional hockey player. I bore a faint resemblance to the stocky five-foot, ten-inch, 200-pound right-winger who was the son of Bobby Hull, a longtime professional hockey player who played for the Chicago Blackhawks. But Brett Hull didn't play for Chicago. He was with the St. Louis Blues at the time, but that bit of information was beyond the lovely heads of the sports-challenged young ladies.

"Who'd like a drink?" I asked. Suddenly, I was the most popular guy around since I was doing the buying. I had learned long ago that my Grandpa Ben was right when he said, "If you've got a buck, you've got a friend." Let's put it this way: I had discovered that ordering a round was always a worthwhile investment. I never went back to the hotel room empty-handed.

In those pre-TMZ days, I could get away with murder. There were times when I said I played football for the Indianapolis Colts or Atlanta Falcons, always careful to pass myself off as a special teams player. During baseball's off-season, I was a second baseman or utility player for the Atlanta Braves. Women fell for my shtick every time. I would roll off some obscure name and say something like, "You probably haven't heard of me because I'm not a starter," but their worshipful eyes would be as big as saucers.

When I met total strangers in a bar, I never used my real

name. I liked to introduce myself as "Rock" or "Pete." I thought those were cool names. Besides, I could throw out a corny joke when introducing my wingman: "Hi, I'm Pete and this is my friend Repeat." I really thought I was funny, but that's because I had usually consumed more than a half-dozen vodkas on the rocks by this time.

I had no competition when it came to entertaining customers and making new ones through a haze of alcohol. My first few years in the new division, I would take existing and potential customers to NFL Super Bowls, college basketball Final Fours, and Major League Baseball All-Star Games, sparing no expense to make sure they had a great time. They loved me!

After a while though, I learned that I could expand my scope of influence by throwing over-the-top Super Bowl parties over a three-day weekend at a posh resort. I would bring in sports celebrities like former Cincinnati Bengals and New York Jets quarterback Boomer Esiason to glad-hand twenty-five or thirty of our most important customers.

Of course, I became known as the "fun guy" that everyone wanted to be around and do business with. I worked hard for my customers and played even harder. My accounts expected an open bar at every event—an invitation to get trashed, and I always drank like a fish at these events. No one ever noticed though because they were just as smashed as I was. Again, I thought to myself, I was *entitled* to party because I work so hard. I rationalized my behavior as being a requirement of my job to provide for my family.

There just aren't enough pages in this book to share all of my drinking stories, but one late night in particular sticks out. I call this my Studio 54 story. I was in Las Vegas, hosting a meeting that included a customer named Rick. We moseyed over to the

MGM Grand one evening, going through tumblers of vodka on the rocks (for me) and scotch (for him), when we got the bright idea to check out the frenetic action inside the Vegas version of the historic '70s disco, Studio 54. The line behind the velvet rope was still a mile long after midnight. We were waiting our turn when we saw the doorman wave the entertainer Seal through.

"Hold our place," Rick said. I watched him approach the maitre d' and slip three Benjamin Franklins into his hand—$300—and just like that, the velvet rope was released. The place was jamming, the music was deafening, and we started mixing our drinks by chasing beer with Grand Marnier shots.

The place was so packed that Rick and I would get separated at times. Studio 54 was a multi-level club, and I remember watching Rick dancing from the third level. Who he was dancing with, I have no idea, and I don't think he did either. Actually, I wouldn't call what he was doing dancing. It was more like he was trying not to fall down.

It was getting late—three or four in the morning—when I yelled into Rick's ear that we should probably think about heading out.

"No way!" he yelled over the loud music. "We're having a great time!" Next thing I know, he was ordering two more rounds of shots before heading out on his own again. When I finally found Rick, he was leaning against a bar. His eyes were glazed over, and he was weaving back and forth. He looked like he was going to pass out any second.

We really needed to go. Then, to my alarm, Rick performed a scene from *The Exorcist* and shot a stream of vomit at least four feet long onto the bar. Horrified patrons scattered, and barkeeps rushed to wipe up the mess with white towels. At this point, I knew we had overstayed our welcome.

I closed the distance and caught Rick before he keeled over, but not before he spewed more projectile vomit. I had to get him out of there quick and to his room, but we weren't staying at the MGM Grand; we were booked at the Luxor down the Strip. That meant I had to get us to the taxi stand ASAP.

I wrapped one of Rick's arms around me and dragged him through the casino—his toes scuffing the carpet. He was talking gibberish and being obnoxious to people along the way. When we arrived at the taxi stand, he spotted a nearby phone and reached for it, looking as though he was about to hurl again!

The cab line guests stared and began to point fingers in his direction, but nothing phased Rick. He tucked the phone next to his ear. "Hello? Room service? I'm hungry. I need something to eat."

I grabbed the phone from his hands and hung up. "Rick, let's go."

Valet attendants waved us to the first cab. When we arrived at the Luxor, Rick was in worse shape. Fortunately, he was smaller than me, so I threw him over my shoulders and schlepped him up to his room. I unceremoniously dropped him on his bed, but I wasn't about to take his clothes off. I turned the lights off and left him in the room, passed out on his bed.

The next day, Rick had a big smile on his face. It was almost like nothing ever happened. "I owe you one, Mike, but I'm feeling great. What are we doing tonight?"

Rick, to this day, almost fifteen years later, fondly tells that story over and over again, saying it was one of the funnest nights of his life. It seems like all my drinking stories were a variation of that Vegas one since I could really hold my liquor. *They* were the ones throwing up. *They* were the ones who I dragged back to their rooms in the wee hours. *They* were the ones who thought my idea to visit just one more bar at 3 a.m. after a long evening of bar hopping was brilliant. And *they* were the ones who passed out in the parking lot.

Since it was me doing the corporate entertaining, I was supposed to be the responsible adult, which was absurd. I was completely dependent on alcohol to make me sociable and the life of the party because in many ways I was still that worthless fat, shy kid who would never amount to anything and who no one would ever like. But the name of the game in my business was building relationships with corporate customers, and in that respect, becoming everyone's best drinking buddy and a down-to-earth guy who could relate to anyone at any level helped me become a "Top Gun" in the division . . . the best of the best. It was hard for my superiors to argue with success some times.

Now, you may be wondering: *How could you afford to do all this drinking, especially since money was tight supporting two households?*

It was easy. I drank, whenever I could, on the company nickel throughout my career. I had an expense account, and if I was out with customers or meeting a "potential" customer—a loose term, I know—then my bar tabs went straight to my monthly expense report. I was careful not to abuse this privilege, and the companies I worked for received a great return on their investment, but that's how I could afford to support my drinking.

I was never questioned about these expensive bar charges—even if I ran up tabs at places like the Pussycat Lounge, Pink Pony, Doll House, or the Gold Club.

Chris

I didn't know about this side of Dad growing up. He kept a tight lock on his drinking exploits whenever he was around Mike or me.

Mike

There was a lot that Chris didn't know, like the time I got my first DUI shortly after we moved to Atlanta. Back then, I was working at the Pepsi office attached to a Marriott hotel in Marietta. I enjoyed going into the hotel bar after work several nights a week for a few drinks.

My excuse—and it was a valid one—was to avoid the famous Atlanta rush hour traffic before making the twenty-six mile commute home to Alpharetta. One rainy Friday night, they were doing karaoke in the bar, so I decided to stay longer than normal. I must have had four or five vodkas while singing the night away. Around 10 p.m., I decided it was time for a change in scenery. I got in my car and drove to Studebaker's, a 1950s-themed nightclub down the street.

Once there, I started flirting with a nice-looking blonde who looked to be about my age. I knew her from somewhere, but since I was on my third vodka since arriving, I couldn't quite place her in the foggy recesses of my brain. Meanwhile, I continued hitting on her until I realized—I coached her son on Chris' peewee basketball team!

You'd think that would stop me in my tracks, but I kept right on plowing ahead and caroused with her until 2 a.m. in the morning. To say I had quite a bit to drink that evening would be an understatement.

I got into my car and headed home. As I was passing through Roswell, I decided *What the heck, I'm going to change lanes without putting on my turn signal.* That's when a blue light flashed in my rearview mirror.

I was pulled over and promptly failed the field sobriety test, which landed me in a holding cell at the City of Roswell jailhouse. My alcohol count turned out to be .012 percent, a bit over the legal limit of .008. I was certain, though, that I was just fine to drive.

Donna had to get up in the middle of the night to bail me out—with the kids in tow—after I called her around 4 a.m. I kept saying, "I'm sorry, I'm really sorry," but I wasn't sorry that I got arrested. I wasn't sorry that I was out fooling around. I wasn't even sorry that I inconvenienced my wife in the middle of the night. I mouthed those words because I thought that's what I was expected to say. You see, I didn't feel like I had done anything wrong. I just had a little bit too much to drink, that's all. I was in the wrong place at the wrong time.

I felt a lot more sorry, however, after I learned how much this DUI cost me in attorney fees, fines, and increased insurance rates. I had to pay over $5,000 for this silly little mistake. I also had to take a long and boring DUI class that ate up one weekend: 6 to 9 p.m. on a Friday night, and 8 a.m. to 5 p.m. on Saturday and Sunday.

I was miserable losing an entire weekend, but I lucked out when I happened to sit next to a really attractive woman. I'll call her Joanie. Obviously, everyone was in the class for the same reason. Amazingly enough, we were all in the wrong place at the wrong time when we were arrested for our DUIs. During breaks, several of us gathered in a circle and told our DUI stories. Many of them were of the *Can you top this?* variety.

By the end of the weekend, Joanie and I had shared a lot of laughs and a couple of lunches. I noticed the silver wedding ring on her finger, and she must have seen the band on mine, but she was sending all the right signals by playing with her hair and smiling at me suggestively. I asked her, "Do you want to get together for a drink next week?"

"Sure," she said.

"What about your husband?"

"We're having all kinds of trouble, and I don't care. You're married, too, right?" she inquired.

"My wife doesn't mind at all. We have an open relationship, so it's okay with her if I see other women."

We got together the following week on a Wednesday and met at a Mexican restaurant near my office for Happy Hour. I ended up seeing Joanie for a long time, and she became one of my regular "friends" who I would see whenever I wanted.

This sort of thing happened throughout my marriage to Donna, but she was having her own fun by hooking up with men on a regular basis. I would encourage her to have a couple of guys on the side who she could see whenever she wanted to, in addition to visiting our favorite pick-up bars to see who she could land for the night.

We never thought what we were doing was cheating or even wrong. That was the arrangement we had agreed to, but she had my back when it counted. One Thursday, we were driving home after meeting with a single man in response to an ad we placed on Adult FriendFinder, billed as the largest social network for singles and swingers looking for fun with no strings attached. After a night of heavy drinking, I was really, really drunk. I must have swerved or something because a cop pulled us over on Highway 400 just before the Windward Parkway exit.

His first question was, "Have you been drinking?"

Before I could come up with some sort of an answer, Donna leaned toward the driver's window. "Oh, no, officer. I guess I was a little too frisky with my husband. We have kids at home, so you know how that can be when you have a little alone time. We're really, really sorry."

I dodged another bullet when I ran our 1999 Volvo S80 into

a ditch after another bender. I had done some serious drinking at a new upscale club in Dunwoody and was driving home when I ran a stop sign, turned left, and skidded off the road in a rainstorm and slid down an embankment. The fog I was in cleared quickly: I knew I had to get out of there before the police arrived.

Fortunately for me, I was in our neighborhood, so I walked around a mile to our home in the rain and told Donna what happened. She called a towing company and made arrangements to meet a wrecker there. By the time she arrived, the Alpharetta police were already on the scene.

Donna identified herself as my wife and said I had been driving when the mishap occurred.

"Is your husband okay?" the officer asked.

"Yes, he's fine, but he's not feeling too well. I saw him crawl into bed."

"Was he drinking?"

"No, he wasn't drinking."

I got lucky when the police decided not to investigate further, but it was another expensive lesson: the Volvo suffered $5,000 in damages, which raised my rates considerably.

I don't think fifteen minutes could save me 15 percent or more on my car insurance with Geico after that happened.

10

THE PERFECT SON

Chris

I know this sounds hard to believe after hearing Dad share some of his drinking stories, but my father didn't keep much, if any, liquor in the house.

His refrigerator was not stocked with beer, and he certainly didn't have a wine cellar or more than a bottle or two of wine in the house for special occasions. I think you can tell by now that Dad was a hard liquor fan in general and a vodka man in particular.

I certainly knew that he liked to drink, but it was something I didn't see him do very often. I picked up through osmosis his idea that when you drank alcohol, you should drink *with* someone . . . it was a social activity. Sitting on the couch at home, all alone and sipping on longnecks while watching the Falcons on Sunday afternoon, was not his scene.

I wasn't attracted to drinking at all in high school. In fact, everybody knew me as the kid who didn't say yes to that stuff. By my junior year, however, I was one of the last of the Mohicans. It seemed like all my peers had tried drinking at parties. Many were regulars at Saturday night bashes that I would go to as well, but I didn't care to partake in the festivities.

During spring break of my junior year, I was invited to a beach house on Navarre Beach in Florida that belonged to the parents of a girl I was dating at the time. Her parents and a few kids were there, and the peer pressure from all of them to throw down was especially strong. At the same time, my resistance against drinking was starting to crumble. I guess all the years of harassment and criticism added up.

This time around, I considered stepping over the boundary line I had set for myself. If I had a beer, maybe they'd stop thinking I was perfect, and the last thing a kid wants to be known as at school is a goody two-shoes.

"Sure, I'll try one," I heard myself say. And that's when I raised a can of Natural Light to my lips. I blanched from the sour taste of fermented hops and didn't like it. I also wondered why everybody made a big deal about drinking because even though I had a beer that night, I wasn't going to drink to get drunk like many of my peers did. That was one line I *wasn't* going to cross.

When I got back from Navarre Beach, though, stories about my "beer drinking episode" had beat me back to campus. Like the "telephone game" where one story gets passed along from one person to the next and mangled along the way, things got exaggerated. Word definitely got around school that *Chris was drinking* and *Ooh, watch out now.*

I went with the flow and decided to keep it on the down low. Drinking was not something I was going to do very often. I probably drank a few more times before I graduated from high school, but I never had the desire to get blitzed like some of my classmates.

There was another issue in play, and that was how my parents continued to make me out to be this perfect kid when I really wasn't all that flawless. Sure, compared to my older brother, I probably looked like an angel, but I was definitely far from that heavenly standard. I just didn't get caught like he did.

There were times when I said I was spending the night at Daniel Bettis' house when it was an excuse to stay out with friends until 3 a.m. It's not like we did anything crazy or got into major trouble, but we were dumb high schoolers wanting to stay out late with friends.

Other times, I knew my mom slept like a log, so I'd sneak out of the house late at night to go see my girlfriend at the time. Sneaking out wasn't very difficult, but sneaking back in was an art. I crafted a technique where I would turn off the headlights on my car and put it in neutral right before I hit the driveway. Then I proceeded to coast my car to my normal parking spot by the basketball goal like a stealth bomber.

While all this stuff was happening on the social front, it was actually a relief not to be perfect in the classroom either. During my junior year, I was handed my only blemish on my report card—a B+ in Physics. Science was never my strong suit anyway, which meant I had to do extra studying to make sure I learned the course material. In this particular Physics class, I scored an 89.4 percent when 90 percent merited an A. I know, I couldn't believe the teacher gave me a B either. Whatever. So I wasn't going to graduate as the class valedictorian. That was never a goal of mine anyway.

But I always performed at an A level on the football field and basketball court through my high school years at Roswell High. Beginning as a sophomore, coaches were telling me that if I kept working hard, I would be good enough to play one of those sports at the college level. They had a stack of college recruiting letters piling up quickly to prove it.

If I had my pick, I wanted to play college football. To be playing in a stadium filled with 80,000 people and millions more looking in on TV seemed like the most awesome thing ever.

But those were my daydreams. I had to deal with the reality around me, which is why I was thankful that I found out there was something in life far more important than sports and academics.

During my high school years, a friend of Mom's named Dennis Blackstone invited Mom to a small church in Roswell named Willeo Baptist Church.

We knew Dennis, who was super involved in the community. He coached my brother and me in football when we were younger, so we knew him well. He had a passion for working out and wanted to help change young people's lives, not just physically, but spiritually as well.

Dennis would invite some of his core players to come to his backyard, where he had built a dingy shed and filled the lean-to with rusty weights. He'd crank up the boom box and blast music from Journey, Garth Brooks, and others to pump us up. During the summer, the little tin shed would heat up to well over 100 degrees. You'd hear the iron weights clanking together as we would lift to get stronger each day.

Before each work out, Dennis would invite us into the house, where he would read and explain Scripture from the Bible. Dennis made Bible stories interesting, and often times, he would talk about how Satan likes to play patty cake with you so that he can draw you away from God without you even thinking twice about it. He knew the temptations that we high schoolers were going through at the time.

Dennis never pushed his church on us, but occasionally he'd

invite Mom to join him at Willeo Baptist. Mom had been a lifelong Catholic, so she was used to taking us to Mass on Sunday, even though Mike and I were adamant about *not* going.

One time, though, Mom said yes to Dennis' invitation. I think she had reached a point in her life where she felt like she wasn't getting anything from attending Mass. Maybe it was all the standing and kneeling, or the constant repetition of the worship experience. I think she needed a change.

I felt the same way, especially after I started attending high school—a time when many teens start to think about who they are and what they believe. I was certainly tired of the rituals that comprised Catholicism and how Mass was the same boring forty minutes each week.

So when Mom told me that Dennis had invited us to Willeo Baptist and that she wanted me to check it out with her, I said sure. I could tell this meant a lot to Mom, and I always wanted to please her.

Coming from the Catholic Church, I didn't know what to expect. Driving up, I saw this old tiny white church that looked like it had been built in the early 1900s. Out front stood a beat-up sign that said Willeo Baptist Church. Cars lined the small parking lot as people started to walk into the chapel. Inside, worn wooden pews lined the rows. At the front was a podium for the pastor. Behind the podium were benches where the choir would stand. As we walked in, everyone seemed genuinely friendly. They greeted us sincerely by saying, "Welcome. We're glad you're here today."

Half the congregation was in the choir so it felt like Mom and I were the only people in the pews. I haven't forgotten how the choir sang old gospel hymns at the top of their lungs. Pastor Ricky was the preacher back then, and when he approached the podium, all business, I remember thinking to myself, *This isn't anything like the Catholic Church. In fact, this isn't half bad.*

I knew who Jesus Christ was and what He did for me, but up to that point, I just knew Him as the guy you talked about when you went to church or noticed the statue of Him hanging on the cross during Mass. That would change the first time I heard Pastor Ricky preach.

When the pastor started talking about the importance of having a "relationship" with Jesus Christ, I had never heard that in my entire life. A relationship . . . with God? Now, I was really confused. But for some reason I wanted to know more, so Mom and me kept coming back. Mike even joined us a few times.

I loved the times when I would sit in the pew and listen to Pastor Ricky, in his Southern twang, explain the gospel and how I could have eternal life with Jesus Christ if only I would believe and surrender all to Him.

One Sunday, he walked us through the "Roman Road," quoting from the Book of Romans that we have "all sinned and fallen short of the glory of God" (Romans 3:23), and the problem we all face is that the "wages of sin is death" (Romans 6:23). But the second part of that verse, he pointed out, says that the "free gift of God is eternal life through Jesus Christ." Pastor Ricky went on to explain that eternal life was more than just being "good enough" to get to heaven. Eternal life was about having a personal relationship with God's son, Jesus Christ (John 17:2).

The preacher then quoted Romans 10:9, saying, "If you will confess with your mouth that Jesus Christ is Lord, and shall believe in your heart that God has raised him from the dead, you shall be saved."

I felt God tugging at my heart like never before, but I held back a bit because I still wasn't ready to make that commitment. I wanted to hear more. I *needed* to hear more. Each week, Mom and I would listen to the pastor's teaching and then have the greatest discussions in the car afterward.

One time, she told me that she wanted to get baptized.

"I've gone to church for most of my life, but I never really understood why I was going and who it was for," she said. "It was like I was going to church to earn favor with God instead of going because I loved God. I think getting baptized is my way of going public with my faith in Jesus Christ. I'm ready to take that next step of faith."

Mom asked my great-grandfather to get baptized with her, and he readily agreed. Their baptism took place at Willeo in a small baptismal pool tucked behind the choir benches. What a special moment seeing them come up out of that water. Their public display of faith inspired me to continue *my* search for faith. I admired Mom for taking that step.

I also noticed some slight changes in my mother. She was a huge warrior—someone who fought for her place in life—but she was always a bit of a worrier. That part of her started to melt away. It was cool to see her let go of things she couldn't control, like worrying about what other people thought of her and our family, especially since people would give us snooty stares and talk bad about us behind our backs after catching wind of some of Mike's downfalls.

I noticed how Mom never gave up on Mike, even though he'd beat her down emotionally and cause chaos around the house. She continued to love him in spite of everything, but that didn't make any sense to me at the time. How can you love someone who treats you like garbage? Yet when my heart was filled with bitterness and hatred, Mom's was filled with unconditional love. That kind of love isn't a part of our human nature. It was inspiring and made me take notice.

As for my spiritual walk, things built to a head as I was start-ing my senior year in August 2001. I had several colleges inter-ested in having me play football for them, but I needed to keep my game at a high level throughout my last season of high school football.

The pressure to perform on the field and in the classroom was weighing heavily on my shoulders. Would I measure up? Would I make something of myself? In many ways, I felt like I was the product of a broken home, yet my family was counting on me to become somebody.

Then one steamy summer afternoon, where the heat was so bad it felt like a hot hair dryer blowing in your face, I had a ter-rible practice during preseason training camp—you know, one of those practices that just eats at you constantly. What made it worse was that I couldn't get this worrisome stuff out of my mind.

Still sweating after my shower, I headed toward the parking lot, beating myself up over everything going on. I got behind the wheel of my car—a beat-up silver 1989 Volvo 240 DL with 250,000 miles on the odometer. Even though home was five min-utes away, I took a detour and drove around in circles for the next hour. I needed to think.

Lost in deep thoughts, I knew I had to pull over. I stopped the car as warm tears rolled down my cheeks. I cried out to God, "I can't do this anymore!" I was trying to hold everything together—the "perfect" athlete who did everything the coaches asked him, the "perfect" kid who never got in trouble in the classroom, the "perfect son" who always made the family proud—but inside I was falling apart.

I didn't feel fulfilled. It felt like something was missing, like I had a huge void in my life that athletics, academics, and accolades couldn't satisfy. I didn't feel like I was going anywhere in life, even though I had coaches and teachers bragging on my abilities. My purpose in life hung in the balance of what I could do. I was tired of trying to carry it alone.

I bowed my head in desperation as I had nowhere else to turn. This was gut check time. This was time to put my pride aside and heed the call that God had wanted me to answer for so long.

It's time, Chris. Place your burdens on Me.

God was calling me to something greater, and I just had to put my trust in Him. And that's what I did when I bowed my head and prayed, "Lord, I don't want to do this by myself anymore. I believe You have a plan for my life. I want to trust in You."

When I placed my faith in Christ, I felt this tremendous weight fall off my shoulders. It's not like I saw a bright light or heard the thundering voice of God, but what happened that day was an honest cry and a surrender to a heavenly Father who had been pursuing me since the beginning of time and still pursues me passionately today. I had been beat up and broken from the world around me, and even though it looked as though I had everything, I realized right then that nothing else made sense in my life except for this—having a personal relationship with Jesus Christ.

That night, I told Mom what had happened. She was so happy for me, and we sat and talked for the longest time about the things that matter most in life, like following God's will and the path He has set out for us.

Let's not get twisted here: my life didn't change overnight. It's not like everything was magically fixed. But what I can tell you is that I didn't feel like I was going through life alone anymore. I didn't feel like I had to put on a façade and act like everything was "perfect." I understood what people were talking about when they said that knowing Jesus was like experiencing freedom. Now, I had a purpose—something bigger than myself.

Change is a process that takes time. I was changing from the inside out. Little did I know that God was about to put some amazing people in my life to help spur my faith in ways I didn't think were possible.

But for now, I had just taken the first step of a long journey. I was excited to see where the Lord was going to take me.

It turned out to be some really neat places.

11

ARRIVING AT A CROSSROADS

Chris

Right around the time I accepted Christ into my life, Coach Mac called me into his office.

Coach Mac was Coach Tim McFarlin, and he'd been coaching football at Roswell High for nearly twenty-five years, so he certainly knew how to evaluate talent and what it took to play at the next level.

Coach Mac, the type of coach who looked after his players, had always been in my corner. The topic that day was what to make of the scholarship offers I was receiving from a number of schools. Big-time football programs like Auburn, Michigan State, North Carolina, and Northwestern were dangling full-ride scholarships—tuition, books, room and board—in front of me. These schools wanted me to play football on Saturday afternoons for them, and it wasn't going to be an easy choice.

"Chris, you're getting a lot of offers, but let's talk about this for a second," Coach Mac said.

"Sure, Coach." I certainly respected his opinion since I knew he only wanted the best for me.

"I think you're a phenomenal player. You were a PrepStar All-American with a ton of interceptions and pass catches last year, and I know you're going to be awesome this season. But if you play for a Division 1-AA school like Appalachian State next year, you'll be a big fish in a little pond. If you go to somewhere like Georgia Tech or some other Division 1 school, you'll be swimming in a much larger pond with much bigger fish than you. You probably won't play very much, which would be a shame. This will be your choice, but I want to lay it out there so that you know your options."

Mike

Tim was much more direct with me. "Look, I have to be honest with you," he said. "Chris might be able to play at a lower-level ACC or SEC school like Wake Forest or Ole Miss, but there's no way he could ever play for a Top 25 team. I just don't think he's big enough or fast enough."

The ACC was the Atlantic Coast Conference with powerhouse teams like Florida State University, Virginia Tech, and Miami. There was even an ACC school a short drive from Alpharetta—Georgia Tech in downtown Atlanta. As for the Southeastern Conference, many football experts regarded the SEC as much more physical and having the best college football teams in the country—teams like the University of Alabama, Louisiana State University, and the University of Florida.

I appreciated his candor, but after watching how well Chris performed in three seasons of high school football, I knew he was capable of rising to the highest levels of college ball. He was just one of those special athletes blessed with tremendous hand-eye coordination, an uncanny ability to see the entire field, and the heart of a lion. It was his passion for the game, work ethic, and unstoppable determination that made Chris an exceptional player.

Chris

At six feet in height, I was a good size for a defensive back or safety position, and I always thought I had good speed. After all, few could beat me when we ran sprints at the end of a long, difficult practice. For some reason, I was always the underdog because some coaches thought I was just an overachieving white guy. Their feeling was that at some point, my overachieving would reach its logical end.

I ran into that mindset when I attended a wide receiver/tight end/quarterback passing camp in Troy, Alabama, during the summer before my senior year. Called the Bowden Camp, the three-day mini-camp was headed by Bobby Bowden, legendary coach of the Florida State Seminoles, and his son, Jeff Bowden, FSU's offensive coordinator.

The Bowden Camp was a place where high school athletes could build skills while getting looked at for a possible scholarship with Florida State. With over two hundred rising juniors and seniors in the camp, I knew it would take a lot to impress the Florida State coaches and stand out from the crowd.

On the first day, I heard Jeff Bowden announce, "Gentlemen, I want the wide receivers over there, tight ends over there, and quarterbacks over here. Get to your spots on the hop."

I trotted over to the portion of the field where the wide receivers were gathering. "Line up, everyone," Jeff Bowden said. He took his time inspecting the wide receivers, looking each of us up and down until he stopped in front of me.

"Son, the tight ends are over there," he said in a raspy baritone voice. "You might want to go to the other group."

"No, sir, I'm a wide receiver," I said confidently. This wasn't the first time this happened. I knew I lacked the bulk to be a tight end, who has major blocking responsibilities in any offense.

"Are you sure?" Coach Bowden repeated.

I didn't want to sound disrespectful, but I knew I'd never get anywhere as a tight end. My glue-like hands and ability to catch just about any football thrown my way were the skills that had carried me this far.

"Coach, I really do think I'm a wide receiver."

Coach Jeff Bowden shrugged his shoulders and kept moving on.

Throughout the three days of camp, I made catches right and left, not dropping one ball thrown my way. When camp was over, I won the award for "Best Wide Receiver" against competition that included some of the best pass catchers in the states of Georgia and Alabama.

As I was walking off the field following the final session, Coach Jeff Bowden pulled me over to the sidelines. "Young man, I want to apologize. You were right—you are a wide receiver—and a damn good one at that!"

Coaches were always underestimating how good I was by how I looked on the field. This was not the last time coaches would doubt my abilities.

Mike

Besides getting on the radar of Florida State, we knew that Chris was getting a serious look by Georgia Tech, who first noticed him as a freshman. The Georgia Tech coaches were combing through film of Joe Don Jordan, a senior standout at Roswell, but they kept seeing great catches by Chris at the wide receiver position and well-defended passes as a safety. What really made the GT coaches take notice, though, was a jaw-dropping 65-yard punt return for a touchdown against Pope High School that propelled Roswell into the state playoffs in the last game of the season.

A Georgia Tech coach called Coach Mac and asked about the

kid making all those great plays.

"That's Chris Reis," Coach said.

"So is he going to be a senior next fall?"

"No, he'll be a sophomore. He's a freshman this year."

There was a long silence on the other end of the phone. I'm sure that the Tech coach was thinking, *How good is this Reis kid going to be when he's a senior?*

So we knew that Georgia Tech was tracking Chris throughout his high school career, and they were the first to send him a letter of interest. As more schools took notice, Stephanie asked me to help Chris manage the recruiting process. All this was too much for her, and she knew that I would protect Chris.

I was in seventh heaven! Every week Stephanie would hand me a bag of full of letters from colleges and universities across the country to sort through to gauge their level of interest. I kept a big cardboard box in the closet of my home office and dropped in letters from over forty schools, including top-drawer teams like Notre Dame, Michigan, and Tennessee. The interest was out there for sure. They could all see how good he was on film.

Chris

The recruiting process was interesting. I recall a Northwestern coach dropping by Roswell High, which wasn't uncommon for college coaches to do. The first thing he said was, "You're a lot bigger than we thought you'd be. Let's talk a little bit."

The coach began selling me on Northwestern, a Big 10 school in Evanston, Illinois, that was strong on academics. The football program was on the upswing after lots of horrible seasons in the '70s and '80s. I listened, didn't ask too many questions, but all I was thinking was that Illinois might be too far away from home.

The school I wanted to go to was just a twenty-five minute

drive away—Georgia Tech. I knew Tech was a great school with strong academics and had a great football program. I had gone to their summer camp—a good place for them to get a look at you while you get a look at them—and performed really well.

Before the start of my senior year, Georgia Tech head coach George O'Leary invited me to his office. Everyone in the state of Georgia knew who Coach O'Leary was: he had taken over a team going nowhere in 1994 and led the Yellow Jackets to five bowl games in seven seasons.

Mom and Dad accompanied me for the big moment. Coach started by saying he and the staff had been keeping an eye on me for a long time and felt like I would be a great fit for the program. "You have leadership skills," he said with a slight smile. "I think you could be a captain some day, and I also see you getting playing time early on."

I took a deep breath. Dad beamed, and Mom looked like all the cares in the world had been taken from her shoulders. I know the cost of paying for college had weighed heavily on them, but now everything would be paid for. We also knew that if I stayed in Atlanta, my parents could easily attend all my home games and drive to many of my away games.

Coach O'Leary turned more serious. "Chris, I understand that you are looking at other schools, and I encourage you to do that. But I want you to keep one thing in mind when you visit these schools and it's this: Take a look at the players on the team. Make sure they are the kind of players you want to be associated with. And if they are not like you, and if they don't have the same values as you, and if they don't want to go to class—in other words, if they don't want to do all the things we would want you to do at Georgia Tech—then stay away from them. That is all the advice I'm going to give you."

That was good counsel, but my mind was pretty well made up. I knew, however, I wanted to talk to my parents before I said yes to Georgia Tech. And I also knew I needed to pray about making this huge life-changing decision first.

Remember, all this recruiting stuff was swirling around when I made a decision to become a Christian. I knew my choice of what school to go to was extremely important to my future, but Mom and Dad both said, "It's your decision. Whatever you want to do." They were great in how they did *not* pressure me to go to Georgia Tech or any other college. I could tell, though, that they secretly hoped I would pick Tech at the end of the day.

I had never prayed about a big decision before. Remember, all this "personal relationship with Jesus Christ" stuff was new to me. But I knew the Lord cared about where I went to school as well as every little detail in my life. All the prayers I had known were formal—the "Our Father," the "Hail Mary." I just decided to speak to God as I would to a friend.

In the quiet of my bedroom, I got on my knees. "Dear Heavenly Father . . ." I began.

Wait. That was too formal.

"Lord, please send me to a school where I can play a lot. Please. And please send me to the school where You want me to go. You know what's best for me. I pray this in Your name, amen."

There were no lightning bolts or script mysteriously written on my bedroom walls. In fact, I got no direct answer at all. But over the next week or so, as I repeated that simple prayer, I had this good feeling about Georgia Tech. Going there checked off many boxes: close to home, a team that wanted me, great academics, a highly ranked program, and a good chance to go to a bowl game every season. Georgia Tech had been recruiting me the longest.

I discussed the pros and cons with my parents one last time, and then I made up my mind: I was going to become a Yellow Jacket. Mom and Dad were ecstatic.

I called Coach O'Leary and got right to the point. With my hands shaking, butterflies in my stomach, and a smile on my face, I said, "Coach, I've decided to come to Georgia Tech." We both knew my commitment was verbal and non-binding since I could not sign a formal letter of intent until February of my senior year, but I took it as seriously as if I was signing a formal agreement.

"Welcome to the Georgia Tech family," Coach replied. "We're really excited to have you and can't wait for you to join us here next year."

That was the extent of our conversation, but then again, Coach O'Leary seemed like a man of few words.

Mike

Things were also building to a head in my life in 2001, which turned out to be a crossroads year for me as well. But where Chris was fueled with optimism and a bright future, I was heading in the opposite direction—toward despair and uncertainty.

It all began when I got sideways with my boss at Pepsi—I'll call him John—in early 2001 after a breakfast meeting at the Monte Carlo hotel in Las Vegas for my annual performance review. I had always known that we were like oil and water on a personal level. John was a straight arrow and a former Army Ranger who didn't drink, and I don't think he appreciated how I had formed close relationships with my customers that included a lot of expensive dinners, golf outings, ski trips, and sporting events—not to mention all the drinking and late-night entertainment.

John did appreciate, though, the results my team produced after I was promoted to director of the Southeast Region for the Fountain Beverage Division just a year earlier—No. 1 in the country in operating profits. At this point in my Pepsi career, I was addicted to my job, working day and night, weekends and holidays.

I reasoned that all the long hours were all for my family, but it was really about me and my need for *more*—more alcohol, more woman, more sex, more excitement, more money, more material things, more control over the people I loved . . . the list was growing. My accomplishments at work fueled my ego and led me to believe I was entitled to another promotion.

After all, it was hard for the powers-to-be at Pepsi to argue with my success even if my expense reports were sprinkled with credit card receipts from strip clubs and upscale bars with time stamps after midnight. Imagine my surprise, though, when John delivered a less-than-stellar performance review. He rattled off a whole list of things I needed to work on, but in my twisted mind, the underlying message was that he felt threatened by me and was showing me who was boss.

He knew my ego and drinking were out of control. He had also heard scuttlebutt throughout the company that I thought he was incompetent. I didn't see it at the time, but John wanted me to change my attitude, be respectful of his position, and party less.

That was a tall order.

Instead of nodding my head and saying I would make improvements, I challenged him. "You've got to be kidding with this @#$%. I'm smarter than you, I'm better than you, and I should have your job. Look, I want a promotion. If you're not going to promote me, then I want a package."

I want a package is corporate speak for a severance package. *Buy me out.* Maybe I should have thought things out before uttering my "pay me more" outburst, but sometimes my lips got ahead of my brain. This was one of those occasions when my mouth was writing a check that my ass couldn't cover. After I cooled down, John acted as if he understood my frustration. "Let me see what I can do to help you," he said.

A few weeks later, John called me from his office in Purchase, New York, and said he was coming down to Atlanta. Nothing unusual with that as he frequently visited the Peach State. "Meet me at the Marriot for breakfast," he said. His tone was friendly, and I looked forward to the appointment because I was armed with reports filled with impressive sales and profit numbers for my region. *Sometimes you have to shake the tree to get some fruit to fall,* I thought in anticipation of another promotion.

We sat down at a small table for two, and he got right down to business after the waitress poured our coffee. "We're going to let you go," he said. "And we have a package for you."

I was shocked. Totally blown away. "You have to be @#$%-ing kidding me," I said. "After thirteen @#$%-ing years?"

He didn't blink an eye. "And here's the severance agreement that's been prepared for your signature."

"I'm not signing that @#$%-ing thing. You know that this is not going to stop here!"

I stormed out of the restaurant. When I got back to my office and started cleaning out my desk, my staff couldn't believe what had happened. My assistants were crying, and my sales managers were hurling expletives about this injustice. After all, I was a great manager. I was a great boss.

True to my word, I hired a lawyer who negotiated a little bit more money for me. The severance package gave me a six-to-eight month cushion, but my whole identity was wrapped up in my work. Being fired helped me realize that I was my job and my job was me. Without my position at Pepsi, I felt worthless, lost, and severely depressed. I had no motivation to look for another job until I absolutely had to.

After a quiet hot summer, the only thing I had to look forward to was the start of Chris' senior year of football and cheering him on at Friday night football games. Without any hobbies to fall back on or much else to do, I hung around my home office all day long. Since this was 2001, we had just joined the online revolution and were hooked up to the Internet. Now that I had some time on my hands, I couldn't help but notice that there were a lot of porn sites out there waiting for me to discover. And most let you look for free.

This is when I became addicted to Internet porn. Who should be surprised? I wasn't. It was all right there, a few clicks away, available any time of the day or night. I was mesmerized by the pixelized pictures of naked women in unbelievable poses. I was so spellbound by the hot *Penthouse Forum* stories and others just like them that I could read online for hours. Clicking through these pages helped me take my mind off my troubles and pass the time.

I had to show Donna my discoveries, of course, which opened up a big playground for us. Sure, you couldn't touch any flesh, but those images were imprinted onto my brain and could be called up at any time.

Then on the morning of September 11, 2001, I was readying myself for my first interview since I had lost my job. Donna was dressing to go work out at a nearby health club.

I was adjusting my tie as I walked down the stairs into the family room. NBC's *The Today Show* was on the TV. I glanced at the image on the screen . . . and recognized the pair of skyscrapers that dominated the New York City skyline. That was the World Trade Center in lower Manhattan. But why was one of them burning like a towering inferno?

And then I witnessed the chilling sight of a passenger jet flying straight into the South Tower. Obviously, I did not go to my interview that day. The horrific sight of the Twin Towers tumbling down into a gigantic slag heap also cratered the American economy as business came to a standstill. In the aftermath of 9/11, many companies imposed a hiring freeze.

There weren't many jobs out there—especially high-paying, six-figure ones like the position I had left behind at Pepsi. I was bound and determined, though, to keep up appearances and keep my family in our 5,000-square-foot house. We had upgraded to a five-bedroom, five-bath, three-level red brick home on a leafy cul-de-sac in Alpharetta as my salary rose considerably over the years—but the waterline of debt remained at chin level. We paid $325,000 for our home in 1997 and lived five miles or fifteen minutes from the boys' place in Roswell.

At the time, I knew I had purchased too much house for my salary, which was in the $60,000 range at the time. But I wanted Mike and Chris to have a nice place to stay, a home where they didn't have to share a room with Jack and Katy. I thought everything I did was for my family, for a better lifestyle. That was my justification to buy a bit more house than I really should have. At the same time, though, I saw myself coming into some big income years with hefty pay raises and year-end bonuses. Turns out I was right: I was making more than $200,000 a year in salary and bonuses before I was fired by Pepsi.

It's amazing how you get accustomed to a lifestyle that only money can buy. The more money I made, the more I spent, always living from paycheck to paycheck. When I lost my job, I did the smart thing (sarcasm alert!) and refinanced my mortgage into an interest-only loan. This cut my monthly payments by 40 percent or so, but it also meant I wasn't paying down any of the loan principal. In other words, I wasn't building up any equity, which was around $135,000 since my home had risen in value to $425,000 in just a few years. Remember, these were the go-go "tech bubble" years in the late '90s and early '00s when home prices were exploding.

Then I got even smarter. I took out a second mortgage for $75,000, figuring I could use this money to tide us over until I landed a good job. I *knew* it was a matter of time until a Fortune 500 corporation swooped in and hired me for their team. Remember, I had a great résumé to go along with my killer smile and winning personality. Once I got back on my feet, I'd pay that second home loan back in no time.

Five, six months passed, but I couldn't find a job to save my life. I connected with a former colleague that I'll call Keith, who had also been terminated by Pepsi a few years earlier during a corporate housecleaning. Keith heard I was looking for a job. He had started a restaurant marketing and merchandising firm with a former Hardee's franchisee, and they needed someone to expand their business into the Southeast.

The 50 percent commission rate sounded promising, so I said I'd do it. I gave myself an impressive vice president title, got some business cards printed up, and hit the phones, calling my former customers and drinking buddies. I made a few deals here and there, enough to make a little bit of money but not enough to support my lifestyle.

I needed another infusion of cash since I burned through nearly seventy-five grand in six months. I figured another $75,000 dollars should do it, but refinancing my second mortgage to get more equity out of the house proved a little more difficult. Whereas the qualifications to qualify for a home loan before amounted to being able to fog a mirror, now the bank wanted salary verification.

I didn't have a salary—just a few sales commissions on the side. Since I didn't have a job—or much prospects—I had to get creative like I did back in the day with Johnson Builders.

I went back to Keith, my old Pepsi buddy. "Look, would you mind verifying that I make $150,000 in salary for my loan app?" I asked.

My colleague didn't bat an eye. "Sure, no problem." I didn't see anything wrong with doing that. Neither did he. Just like my dad, I thought the ends justified the means.

And that's how I got another $75,000. But now I had to make payments on those mortgage loans—plus all the other bills landing in my mailbox. It seemed like everyone had their hand out, and I was at risk of falling behind. Then I noticed these small blank checks in my Visa and MasterCard credit card statements. My combined line of available credit was over $200,000 at the time, so all I had to was fill in a number, usually $3,000 at a time, and deposit it into my checking account. Each time I wrote a check, the amount would be added to my credit card balance. Easy—like money growing on trees!

I used one of those blank checks every few weeks to pay the first and second mortgage, pay for all the household expenses, and even to make payments on the credit card I was borrowing the money from to write the checks. And this continued for three-and-a-half years.

Chris

My dad still acted like he had a lot of money. I was just a teen kid at the time, but even I could see that material things and appearances meant everything to him. He always made us take off our shoes when we came into the house. He'd get furious if we got one speck of dirt on the carpet. We had to treat the furniture like another member of the family, and we also had to keep the kitchen spic-and-span. He was compulsive about anything having to do with his possessions. It felt like I was living in a glass house.

He and his family certainly lived in a nicer place than we did with Mom. Our home was built in the late 1960s, had three bedrooms and two baths with 1,400 square feet, and was real dated. Actually, our place was falling apart. There were holes in the wall everywhere from my bother and me fighting, cabinet doors were falling off the hinges in the kitchen, and some drawers would stick, making it difficult to get a kitchen utensil.

On top of that, we didn't have money to fix anything. Mom did the best she could, but she was embarrassed whenever Mike and I had any friends over or when parents picked up their kids. She didn't want them seeing how worn-out our house was.

Mike

That's another reason why I bought the big house in Alpharetta. I wanted Mike and Chris to have their friends over to our place so they wouldn't have to be embarrassed. There was plenty of room to have their friends over to spend the night.

Again, I thought I was doing all this for my family, when the reality was I was doing all this for me—my ego—to show everyone that I could provide for my family. I never missed a child support payment to Stephanie, now at $1,050 a month, either. That's what a *real* man does . . . right?

Chris

I was kind of wondering how Dad could afford everything. I mean, he didn't really have a job. He was still going to all my games, and he even accompanied me on recruiting trips, which he paid for. Plus, he continued to take the family out to big expensive dinners whenever Mike and I stayed for a weekend. I didn't know how he was paying for everything because even I could tell that he wasn't working much.

Mike

Chris is right—I wasn't working much, if at all. I made the choice to just let everything go day after day and ignore the reality of my circumstances. I don't mean that I hung around the house all day unshaven and in my pajamas, but I took my time reading the *Atlanta Journal-Constitution* with my morning coffee, took my time checking to see if I had any interesting emails, took my time flipping through the regular mail, and took my time talking to old friends on the phone. Most days, I would pretend that I was looking for a job when I was really just looking at porn until I could get out of the house for some real fun.

Before I knew it, it was four o'clock in the afternoon and time to get ready for another night out. Donna would usually put on a tight-fitting sexy black dress while I would change into some trendy attire. Then we would hit a couple of our favorite bars for Happy Hour drink specials and free hors d'oeuvres. Jack and Katy, young teenagers at the time, fended for themselves at least three or four nights a week.

I was like Captain Smith of the *Titanic* the day before the massive ship hit an iceberg. I didn't have a worry in the world, even though I was speeding faster and faster into debt. As far as I was concerned, there was no need to slow down.

You may be wondering, *Mike, didn't anyone teach you the basics about finances?*

Where would I have learned that? I was great at helping my

customers make money from a business standpoint, but I certainly didn't learn anything about managing my personal finances from them or from my dad. I really thought that everything was okay since I was still taking care of my family. I didn't miss a ball game, didn't miss a school event. I was a good dad. But the debt kept getting bigger and bigger—kind of like the iceberg looming larger and larger from the crow's nest.

Meanwhile, I was too busy having a good time enjoying the open bar in the *Titanic*'s wood-paneled lounge.

Chris

My senior year of football was a pleasure cruise. I had a solid season at Roswell High and received my fair share of honors:

- first team 5A All-State selection by an *Atlanta Journal-Constitution* panel
- rated the No. 22 safety prospect in the nation by *Students Sports* magazine
- named to the All-South third team with career totals of 226 tackles and ten interceptions.

Best of all, I was a team captain who started a school-record 44 consecutive games at Roswell High from my freshman to senior years.

During the state playoffs in the first week of December 2001, I heard some shocking news when I got home from basketball practice one night: Coach O'Leary had accepted the head coaching job at Notre Dame.

"Notre Dame is the only job I would ever leave Georgia Tech for," Coach told the media. "It's the pinnacle of all coaching jobs."

Feeling jilted, I was suddenly very nervous about my future. The fact that Coach O'Leary and his staff knew me and had recruited me a long time counted a great deal when I made my verbal commitment to come to Georgia Tech. I had staked my athletic future on Coach being there.

Then I got a call from a reporter in South Bend, Indiana, asking if I was going to "decommit" from Tech and follow Coach O'Leary to Notre Dame. The reporter's question—a valid one—crystallized my vision. I knew what I had to do.

"I don't care who Georgia Tech brings in, I'm going to Tech," I said. "My commitment is my commitment. My word is my word."

I'm glad I followed my gut because five days after Coach O'Leary accepted the Notre Dame job, he suddenly resigned after he admitted that he lied about his academic and athletic background on his résumé. Coach claimed to have a master's degree in physical education and to have played college football for three years, but a background check revealed that wasn't true.

What a mess that would have been if I said I was following Coach O'Leary to Notre Dame! Within a few weeks, Georgia Tech announced that Chan Gailey, the offensive coordinator with the Miami Dolphins, would become the new Georgia Tech head coach once the NFL season was over.

Mike

Coach Gailey had an impressive résumé. He had been the head coach of the Dallas Cowboys in 1998 and 1999, taking the Cowboys to the playoffs both times. Since America's Team lost both times in the first round, team owner and general manager Jerry Jones—a man of limited patience—fired him for the indiscretion.

So it was with a great deal of excitement that Chris, his mom, and me were the first family that Coach Gailey met with after accepting the new head coach position. He wanted to make sure that Chris was still committed to Georgia Tech.

In his homespun way, Coach Gailey said, "It's been a whirl-wind, the last coupla weeks, but I'm really excited to be here at Georgia Tech, and I jus' think this is gonna be a great place. I jus' want to make sure that you're still committed to being here."

Chris didn't miss a beat. "Coach, I'm here, I'm excited, I said I was already committed, and I'm here to play."

Coach Gailey beamed. "That's fantastic to hear. I'm very happy you're gonna be part of this program."

Chris

One of the great things about saying yes to Coach Gailey was learning he was a Christian. I would come to find out that this was unusual in the coaching world, but because Coach was a believer, he made several key decisions about how he ran the team that would greatly impact my life *and* help start my father down a path toward recovery from certain addictions.

Addictions that were mercilessly tormenting his life.

12

College Game Day

Chris

I enrolled at Georgia Tech a few weeks after high school graduation because the school had a special program for incoming freshmen—athletes and non-athletes—to help acclimate us to the rigor-
ous academic demands placed on students. Georgia Tech coveted
a proud reputation as being a tough, tough school, and I quickly
learned that college classwork demanded my full attention.

I came into training camp as a safety, but it became evident
early on that I was at the bottom of the depth chart—third string.
That was fine with me. Nowhere to go but up—and another
chance to prove myself.

I was shuttled onto the "look squad," which is a nice way of
saying the scout team, with the other freshmen and walk-ons.
Early in training camp, I was playing on the punt return team for
the look squad. My position was "jammer"—someone who usually blocks the "gunner" whose job is to sprint down the field and
tackle the returner. This time, however, I crept down the line of
scrimmage to rush the punter and try to block the punt.

The "personal protector"—the guy who lines up right behind
the long snapper and has the job of blocking anyone who gets
into the backfield—came out to stop me. We're talking about a

fullback-type player, a big guy, but I dropped my shoulder and knocked him on his butt even though he weighed sixty pounds more than me. Then I ran over him like road kill and came within inches of blocking the punt.

I heard a lot of "oohs" from the players and "atta-boys" from the coaches, especially since I was a freshman and the guy I flattened was a senior. That hit was a turning point for me in training camp. Even though the older guys didn't like me because they thought I was trying to show them up, I earned their respect.

I also impressed our defensive coordinator, Jon Tenuta, an old school, tough-minded coach who loved giving out nicknames. Most of them had no rhyme or reason, but if he gave you a nickname, that meant he liked you. He called Reuben Houston, one of our cornerbacks, "Hurricane" because there was a boxer in the 1960s named Rubin "Hurricane" Carter who was falsely accused of murder and celebrated in a Bob Dylan song known as "Hurricane." Another player was called "Ickey" by Coach Tenuta after Elbert "Ickey" Woods, a Cincinnati Bengals running back from the late 1980s who was best known for his lumbering "Ickey Shuffle" end zone dance after making a touchdown.

At the end of training camp, Coach Tenuta was suitably impressed to give me a pet name: "Torpedo." He never told me how or why he came up with that moniker, but I figure it's because I always attacked the ball and flew around at full speed trying to blow up plays. Coach Tenuta was a gruff guy, but when he said, "Torpedo, get your ass over here," I knew he was using a term of endearment.

Mike

I laughed when I heard that Chris' nickname was "Torpedo" because that fit him perfectly. A torpedo is a self-propelled weapon with an explosive warhead designed to detonate on contact with its target. A torpedo either hits its mark and blows everything up . . . or it misses. There's no in-between, but Chris hit his target much more often than he missed.

Chris

The Torpedo played in every game of his freshman year—but only on special teams. I never saw a down on defense. I didn't blow anyone's mind with my play, but I was a solid contributor. I was trying to fit in where I could and find my way in college football.

I also wanted to get in with the right crowd on the Georgia Tech campus. I knew it was important for me to get plugged into some type of Christian ministry that would act as a counterweight against the heavy peer pressure to party and be part of the hook-up scene.

Then something happened that would change my life. It began when Coach Gailey appointed a chaplain for the team, a charismatic fellow named Derrick Moore who had played several seasons in the NFL, mainly with the Detroit Lions. Derrick, a former running back, knew football and the warrior mentality.

When Coach introduced Derrick to the team, there was something about his demeanor that commanded respect. Six feet tall and sporting a shaved head, Derrick was an imposing African-American in his mid-thirties who looked like he could still suit up and knock over a few players if given half a chance. The players listened to him announce that he was starting a Fellowship of Christian Athletes (FCA) group on the Tech campus. This Christian outreach program had died out during the Coach O'Leary era.

"Our first meeting will be next Wednesday night in the AA

cafeteria," Derrick said, referring to the Athletic Association dining hall. "You're all invited. We start at 7:30."

I made sure I was there that evening, but I was disappointed
when only five people showed up in the dark and dingy cafeteria.
Even worse, I was the only football player from the Tech team—
the rest were athletes from other sports.

Even though the turnout was small and the AA dining hall
wasn't an ideal meeting place, Derrick turned out to be an emotional speaker who was passionate about God. He spoke from his
heart like there were five hundred in the room, not five.

I kept coming back every Wednesday night because I could
really relate to him. Derrick has one of those infectious attitudes
that you just want to be around. God had given Derrick the gift
of public speaking, but he also proved to be a great listener, too.
We connected right away and developed an amazing relationship
that greatly impacted my life.

I told several teammates that they really had to come hear
Derrick talk, which helped our numbers grow. Sometime during my freshman football season, Derrick approached me with a
proposition. "Chris, I want you to be my FCA president here at
Georgia Tech."

Me? I was a lowly, pink-cheeked freshman. A special teams
guy barely getting any playing time. My other concern was that
I was a young Christian, having just marked my first "spiritual
birthday."

Furthermore, becoming the FCA president would put me on
a pedestal for everyone to see—like if I had *Christian* tattooed on
my forehead. To say you're a believer is one thing, but to actually
be a leader was a totally different thing altogether. I knew there
would be people waiting for me to fall.

"I don't know," I told Derrick. "This seems like too much

responsibility for me."

Derrick could sense my hesitancy. "Tell you what," he said in a calming tone. "You go home and pray about it. Then come back next week and tell me your answer."

I followed his advice and prayed about what to do. I didn't receive a text from the Lord or see a burning bush on the way to school, but I did feel like God, in the stillness of my heart, was saying, *Just trust me and take a step out.*

Trusting God is definitely what I did. The next week, I gave Derrick the verdict: "Sure, I'll be the FCA president." I carried that responsibility for the next four years.

With Derrick coming alongside me, my faith grew by leaps and bounds. This leadership role was a big deal for me. I was responsible for organizing the Wednesday night meetings, introducing the speaker (usually Derrick), and even leading the singing of a few worship songs.

In other words, I couldn't be bashful standing up in front of people. I couldn't act like a Christian on Wednesdays and live however I wanted the rest of the week. The fact that I was in a visible role as the FCA president put a target on my back. Even though I didn't outwardly preach to my teammates, I could tell that not everyone liked what I stood for.

This was also the time I really started praying for my dad to come to know Christ. As I grew in my faith, I could tell that our lives were going in two completely different directions, and our relationship was surface level and superficial.

I knew little about his drinking exploits and nothing about his extracurricular sexual activity, but I understood that no matter where we were in life, we were all sinners at the foot of the cross and needed Jesus in our lives. Maybe Dad would listen if I ever had the chance to share the gospel with him. Maybe he'd understand his need to accept Christ into his heart and stop trying to fill his life with meaningless garbage.

Mike

Even though there was turmoil everywhere I turned, I wasn't about to turn in the direction of God. Why would I? He wasn't even on my radar. Besides, after all the horrible things I'd done and the way I'd lived my life, I could never be good enough for God to want to help me.

Throughout Chris' freshman year, I was still without a job even though I tried my hand at a few other things, like doing sales for Peter Anthony Designs, a restaurant furniture manufacturer based in Windsor, Ontario. As a supplier of restaurant seating and décor packages, this Canadian firm wanted to hire me as an independent contractor, paid solely on commission, but I was a good negotiator . . . always getting what I wanted.

"I can't do this job unless you're going to pay me," I said to the hiring manager back in Canada. I'll call him Kevin.

"Well, we're not set up to do that," Kevin replied. "We're expanding our market into the States and building a sales force, but the budget isn't there yet."

"You won't find anyone else with my experience and contacts from my days at Pepsi," I boasted. "You're going to have to pay me a salary, or I'll just move on to the next opportunity." I liked bluffing.

"How much do you need?"

"Three thousand every two weeks. If you can do that for four months, I'll easily sell enough to offset my salary. It's a great investment for Peter Anthony."

Just as Kevin promised, the $3,000 checks arrived every two weeks like clockwork, but I sold only one furniture package the entire time—to an Arby's franchisee friend of mine in Idaho. When pressed on why I wasn't selling more, I replied, "The economy is still sluggish after 9/11, and the U.S. is a tough market to break into. This is a process, so I counsel patience." My comments were accurate, but I was running out of time.

The décor packages proved too pricey for most restaurant operators. I hated this job with a passion, but those Canadian checks helped me stay afloat. Even though I no longer had to pay child support for Mike or Chris since they had turned eighteen, I still had two adolescents at home—Jack and Katy—so we were in the midst of the expensive teen years. That, coupled with the expense of my addictive lifestyle, was causing my debt to spiral out of control.

It was during these turbulent times that Jack was really struggling in middle school with his behavior and grades. Totally out of the blue, he began asking me a lot of questions about church and faith. At the time, I thought his inquisitiveness about spiritual matters was fueled by a desire to figure out who he was.

The questions were significant enough for me to call Chris and ask him if he could talk to Jack and explain a few things about God and the Bible since I had no idea what to say to Jack. I knew religion had become a lot more important to Chris since he started attending Willeo Baptist with his mother.

Chris

When Dad called, I was excited to hear him asking questions about God—on behalf of Jack, of course. I thought to myself, *This is my chance to share Christ with my dad indirectly. God, thank you for giving me this opportunity. I won't let You down.*

Talk about pressure. Playing in front of 50,000 fans screaming at the top of their lungs was nothing compared to the magnitude of what hung in the balance.

"You know, Dad, Jesus died on a cross so that we can have freedom in Him and we can have a great life—a life free of sins," I said.

"Yeah, that's all well and good, but how am I going to explain that to Jack? He's asking me all these questions, and I don't know what to say."

"You can tell Jack to open a Bible and start reading in Matthew. Tell him to read all the way through Matthew, which explains what a great God we have and how He sent his Son to a dark world to die as a sacrifice for our sins. Then He rose from the dead to prove who He said He was. Jesus is both man and God and wants us to have a personal relationship with Him."

"That sounds great," my dad said, but I could tell that he was brushing everything aside. "Can't you call Jack and explain everything to him?"

I sighed. I didn't know what I was expecting, but nothing was getting through to my father. It was apparent that he had a huge hole—a Grand Canyon-sized hole—in his heart. Why wasn't he asking the same questions about what really matters in life like Jack was doing?

After hanging up the phone in disappointment, I called Mom. I was in tears as I hung my head. "Mom, I tried my best to tell him about Christ, but he didn't respond at all. God gave me my chance, and I blew it."

I was crushed, but I also knew that I could not preach to my dad. Confronting him wasn't going to work because I knew my father would tell me what I wanted to hear. If I had said, "Hey, Dad, will you come to know Christ?" he would have said, "Sure." That's because he would do or say almost anything to make me happy, but I'd know he wasn't being authentic.

For true belief to happen, as well as repentance, God would have to make that happen—not me. Hopefully, I helped plant a seed for God to grow.

I began getting on my knees nearly every night, praying for Dad to come to know Christ. I tried to live in a way that he would notice and say to himself, *There is something different about Chris. He could be high and mighty since he's a big-time football player, but instead he's a humble servant who's helping others. There is something more to him than what I have.*

Mike

I actually thought the FCA was a social club, something good to put on his résumé. He'd be able to say that he played on the GT football team and was president of FCA . . . and that would impress people. To me, it was always about impressing others.

Chris

Being the FCA president pushed me out of my comfort zone. When I started the Wednesday night meetings, I would open in prayer, give announcements, play a fun game to break the ice, and sometimes lead worship by playing the guitar and singing. It was scary the first few times, but I got used to it.

Experiencing these growing pains helped me open up to God and trust that He'd provide. I always breathed a sigh of relief, though, when I turned the podium over to Derrick for the message of the evening.

I got a lot more ministry experience when Derrick asked me to be a huddle leader for a group of high school students at a place called Black Mountain FCA in North Carolina during the summer after my freshman year. Even though I had grown in my faith in recent months, I still doubted what God could do through me.

"Are you sure I'd be a good huddle leader?" I asked Derrick. "I don't know enough about the Bible." I was scared that I wouldn't know what to say to these high schoolers.

Once again, Derrick said, "Just trust God. He'll give you everything you need. You can do it."

Little did I know, but that FCA camp was a crucial point in my walk with Christ. It was amazing to see the other huddle leaders—college athletes from all across the country—on fire and passionate about God. I had never experienced that in my life. I wanted to have faith like they did, talk like they did, pray like they did, and live like they did. This is when I really knew Christianity wasn't a religion but a true relationship with the Lord of the Universe.

I don't know if I really taught those kids anything, but that wasn't the point. God was working in me in a mighty way. When Derrick asked if I would share my testimony before the entire camp, I gulped once again, but I said yes.

I was super nervous standing up in front of five hundred kids—much more nervous than playing football before 50,000 fans back in Atlanta. I shared the struggles of growing up with my older brother, how I learned about Christ at Willeo Baptist, asked Him into my life while driving my car, and how my dad wasn't a Christian but that was what I was living for now. I told the high school kids that my great hope in sharing my testimony was that God could possibly use one of them to help my dad come to know Christ.

I didn't have notes that day, but it felt like it was the Holy Spirit speaking through me. I talked about what it means to be a real man. "A real man is not somebody who goes around cussing, goes around looking at pornography, and doing all those things. A real man steps up and accepts Jesus Christ as his Lord and Savior and steps out in his faith," I said. Afterwards, I was humbled when adults and kids came by and said, "Man, your testimony was powerful. Thanks for sharing it."

When I returned for my second year on the Georgia Tech campus, I lived with three Christian guys this time around. I can't say enough about my roommates—Brad Brezina, Nathan Burton, and Gavin Tarquinio—because iron really does sharpen iron. We lived in an apartment-style student housing with two bedrooms and a bathroom on one side, a kitchen and living room in the middle, and two bedrooms and a bathroom on the other side. My roommates and I would get together once a week for a Bible study in the main living room, where we would encourage and hold each other accountable. That means asking each other tough questions like:

- Are you finding time to read the Bible each day and get in the Word—even if it's only for a few minutes?
- What's happening in your life? How can we help?
- Are you living your life each day to glorify the Lord? Are your actions pointing to the cross or yourself?
- Are there any areas you're struggling with or temptations?

By no means were we perfect, and that's the reason we knew that we needed each other to help us in our daily walk. This wasn't "cheesy" Christian stuff. The four of us went through a lot of tough times, and we had life-changing seasons during the three years we were together, baring our souls and growing incredibly close to each other. We moved in together as kids but left as real men.

For my sophomore season, I moved up to No. 2 on the depth chart as a safety, but we had two people in the defensive backfield who would go on to the NFL: James Butler and Dawan Landry. Believe me, they weren't chumps, and their presence meant I wouldn't get much playing time at free safety or strong safety.

Coach Tenuta, our defensive coordinator, knew I was a weapon and wanted to get me on the field to make some plays. Because of the skilled athletes in front of me, he created a spot for me whenever the opposing team was in second- or third-and-long situations and thinking pass. I became part of a "dime package" where the defense plays with six defensive backs (instead of four), replacing two slower linebackers.

As a dime back, I was kind of a rover. This position utilized my tenacity and hard-nosed play as I would either blitz off the edge or drop back into coverage. I loved getting in the game—especially when it was an important third-down situation—and receiving the signal to blitz. I'll never forget getting my first career sack on Jason Campbell, the star quarterback for Auburn who went on to play for the Washington Redskins and is now with the Chicago Bears.

Mike

Auburn was Georgia Tech's first home game of Chris' sophomore season, and the Tigers were coming in as the No. 17 team in the country. Nobody gave Tech a chance. Chris was still on all the special teams, and I watched him line up five yards behind the snapper as the personal protector on the punt team. I always kept my eyes locked on Chris, not on the football.

Chris

We were ahead 3-0 in the second quarter with a fourth and 1 on Auburn's 41-yard line—too far to attempt a field goal.

"Punt team!"

I joined my teammates and jogged onto the field. In the huddle, our punter Hal Higgins called for a fake punt—with the ball being hiked to me instead of him!

My heart pounded. I knew this could be a key play in the game. I also knew that all I had to get was a little more than a yard. Sure enough, we caught the Auburn defense by surprise. I caught the snap, buried my head, and charged through a gap on the right side of the formation, plowing my way for a three-yard gain.

First down, Georgia Tech!

We drove the ball for a touchdown to give us a 10-0 lead that eventually earned us a 17-3 victory over the Tigers.

Mike

This was our first win over Auburn since 1978, and I loved watching the student body charge the field and tear down the goalposts after the game.

I didn't love every moment that Chris played, however. Many times, I held my breath until I made sure that my son was okay after he was knocked to the ground. During Chris' sophomore year, the Yellow Jackets played Florida State University in Tallahassee, Florida. When Tech was kicking off, I kept my eyes on No. 18 as he sprinted down the field. On this kickoff coverage play, he was blindsided by the nastiest hit I'd ever seen him take. Florida State's Ernie Sims, who's a linebacker with the Indianapolis Colts today, blasted him like there was no tomorrow. Chris never saw the bone-rattling collision coming.

We were all frightened to death. By "we," I mean Stephanie, Mike, and me as we sat together in the parents' section. (Donna viewed this horrible hit on TV back in Alpharetta since she stayed behind to care for Jack and Katy.) Our hearts were in our throats when we witnessed the wallop that leveled Chris and laid him out near the 30-yard line. Then to compound our concern, he didn't get up. Teammates gathered around him, and a pair of Georgia Tech trainers came running from the bench. After tending to him for a couple of minutes, a white cart marked EMS zoomed across the field, and that's when I feared this could be really serious.

Through my binoculars, though, I could see Chris moving his arms and legs, so that was good news. When he was carted off the field, he flashed the crowd a thumb's up upon receiving polite applause from the previously hostile crowd.

The three of us immediately left our seats and went underneath Doak Campbell Stadium, where we found the team doctor looking him over. It looked like someone had taken a baseball bat and beaten him up. He was black and blue and bleeding from his nose. Then they told us that Chris had stopped breathing out on the field—

Chris

Let's not make too big a deal about this. I stopped breathing for a very, very short time . . .

Mike

Oh, like it matters? You stopped *breathing*! The team flew him back to Atlanta on a chartered flight for a CAT scan at Crawford Long Hospital near the Georgia Tech campus. Everything checked out fine, but that was a scary moment for us.

Chris

I'll tell you what that hit taught me: keep your head on a swivel. I recovered quickly and missed only one game. But that hit didn't scare me or slow me down at all. I was the Torpedo, right? I think my best effort came in the post-season Humanitarian Bowl. I got significant playing time and was all over the field: eight tackles (including two tackles for a loss), one sack, a forced fumble, and a pass breakup.

When my junior year came around, we still had James Butler and Dawan Landry creating havoc in the defensive backfield, but the coaches really wanted me on the field for every defensive play. We had a lot of linebackers graduate, so we were young in that position. This time around, Coach Gailey approached me with a question: "What would you think if we moved you to linebacker?"

I was game. I loved smacking running backs, and coaches knew I wasn't afraid to get my hands dirty. At the time I was listed in the program as six feet, one inch—even though I was really a hair over six feet—and 205 pounds, a tad small and a bit light for a major college team where linebackers were usually a couple of inches taller and weighed 215 to 230 pounds.

But Coach Tenuta, our defensive coordinator, loved playing an aggressive, blitz-happy defense. To get around my size, Coach put me at strong side linebacker, which meant I would line up across from the tight end—the strong side of our opponent's offense. Moving me closer to the line of scrimmage allowed me to use my quickness to evade blockers and also shortened the distance from me to the point of contact, giving me a chance to hold my ground even though most blockers outweighed me by sixty, seventy, or even one hundred more pounds. Coach said he wanted to use my speed and agility, so he would have me blitz probably 90 percent of the time I was on the field.

I knew I'd help my cause if I were a little bit heavier, so I bulked up to 218 pounds by eating a lot of protein bars and downing shakes brimming with creatine, a muscle-building compound—and totally legal, I might add. I didn't want to gain a few pounds just to have a few more pounds on my frame. I wanted to gain good, lean muscle so I could take hits because I was in the box, getting blocked by huge tight ends and muscle-bound fullbacks a lot of times.

Mike

When I found out Chris was moving to strong side linebacker, I was very concerned. He was not linebacker size. I remember talking to Dave Wilson, the special teams coach, and he said to me, "Chris has a unique ability to escape blocks. He's too slippery. He will turn his shoulders and give his back to the guy blocking him. Then he slides off any block and can make a play."

I started watching Chris during games, and Coach Wilson was right. Chris was really good at avoiding blocks because of his elusiveness and speed. That's what made him so good at blitzing the quarterback.

Chris

I started at linebacker and played a lot more downs my junior year. I was fourth on the team in tackles and was fifth in the ACC in sacks with eight. These exploits earned me All-Atlantic Coast Conference honorable mention honors for a team that finished 7-5 with a Champs Sports Bowl victory over Syracuse in Orlando, Florida.

I had a highlight film experience in the Champs Sports Bowl. On the second play from scrimmage, I was in my strong side linebacker position opposite the tight end. I saw the quarterback, Perry Patterson, drop back as the outside wide receiver ran toward me and then broke to his right—a little hook route. I saw Patterson following him with his eyes and hung off the route, trying to bait him into throwing the ball. In a split second—at just the right moment—I jumped the route as the quarterback released the ball. I grabbed the pass out of the air and saw nothing but twenty yards of green turf in front of me. Just like that, I had a pick-six that gave us a 7-0 lead, which set the tone for a 51-14 blowout of Syracuse.

Mike

You should have seen Donna, Stephanie, and myself cheering on Chris as he took it to the house. There's nothing like the excitement of college football, which is more varied and some say more interesting than the pro game.

The college years were fantastic for me; I loved every Game-Day because I got to cheer Chris on with 55,000 other Tech fans at Bobby Dodd Stadium. But there was an ancillary reason I looked forward to home games—it was time to tailgate! The Georgia Tech players' parents worked together and reserved a small parking lot a short walk from Tech's stadium for our exclusive pre-game parties. Donna and I would set up our big tent with a barbecue and coolers of beer, mixers, ice and several bottles of vodka.

We always arrived early for the simple reason that the sooner we got there, the sooner we could start drinking. Stephanie and her parents often dropped by to be social, and we became friendly with the other football parents. We were like our own fraternity.

What did Donna and I drink? Vodka with diet Sprite or diet

Mountain Dew and occasionally a Bloody Mary mix if we started early enough in the day. Donna was an awesome drinking buddy before a football game.

I had another drinking pal who I called the Colonel. He was the biggest diehard Tech fan you'd ever come across even though he didn't have a son playing on the team. Whenever we traveled to away games, we'd find him in the visitor's parking lot tailgating in his big luxury RV.

"Come on, over," the Colonel would wave upon our arrival. "You know where the bar is. I'm cooking ribs today."

I never saw so much liquor in one place, but as far as I was concerned, this was free booze. The Colonel liked Donna and me because we could match him drink for drink. His wife was a lot of fun and just as crazy as we were.

You have to have a strategy when you tailgate before a college football game, and mine was this: I had to drink as much as possible *before* the game because I couldn't bring liquor inside the stadium. Most college stadiums don't sell alcohol either, but even if they did, I wasn't about to pay eight bucks for a watery beer in a paper cup.

Let me tell you, once I was in my seat, I was locked and loaded for football. I yelled at the referees and gave them a hard time after every horrible call against Tech, but everyone around me did the same thing. I was conscious, however, of not saying bad things about the other Tech players whenever someone threw an interception or fumbled the ball.

Like Chris, they were someone's son trying to do their best, and they weren't professionals.

Chris

I heard stories from Mom about Dad being loud during the games. "Dad was cussing at the refs when they made a pretty bad call," Mom would tell me. I wasn't that surprised. I knew my dad could get heated at times.

After the games, my family—like a lot of families—would wait outside the locker room to greet me when I came out. When I gave Dad a hug, he'd give me a kiss on the cheek and I could often smell the liquor on his breath.

Mike

I may have been wasted most of the times, but I remember every play like it happened yesterday.

Chris

I know how much playing football at Georgia Tech meant to my father and my mother. When my senior year rolled around, I wanted to finish strong. James Butler had graduated and was drafted by the NFL, so we needed someone to take his spot at strong safety. Coach Tenuta wanted me to fill that role, which was fine with me. I had an eye to the future, and I knew I didn't have the size to play linebacker in the NFL. I did feel that I had the speed and talent to compete at the free safety position, though.

Did I really think I had a chance to play professional football?

Let's just say it was a pipe dream. It wasn't like I was an All-American getting a lot of ink or someone who was on the radar of Mel Kiper, Jr. and Todd McShay, the ESPN draftniks who pro-vide in-depth coverage on the nation's potential draft picks.

Before my senior season, Dad asked me what I was thinking about in regards to playing in the NFL. "Are you thinking it's a possibility?" he asked.

"Dad, I'm not even thinking about the NFL right now. I just want to focus on my senior year and think about that after the season is over."

Midway through my senior year, a couple of low-level player agents on fishing expeditions contacted me. I asked Dad to talk to them. I didn't want to be distracted.

Mike

I spoke with the two agents, and it was rather exciting to hear them say nice things about my son's ability to "play at the next level." I wondered if Chris had what it took to play in the NFL, so I went to Coach Gailey. I figured he'd be a good source since he'd been the Dallas Cowboys head coach and had a lot of experience in the pros.

"Coach, what do you think about Chris' chances to play in the NFL?"

The Tech head coach hemmed and hawed for a moment. "Well, it'll be interesting. We'll have to see what happens."

Not exactly the ringing endorsement I was looking for. I doubted Chris could play in the NFL, but I could tell that in his heart of hearts, that was something he wanted to at least *try* to do. He'd always been underestimated his entire life, even by me at times, but if anyone could do it, that would be my son.

Chris

During training camp before my senior year, a team meeting started with the coaches handing out slips of paper.

"You're voting for your team captains," one of the coaches said. "You can write down four names."

I was voted as one of the four captains, but receiving that honor didn't come as a surprise to me because I had taken a leadership role during spring practice and the off-season workouts. The times when you go through tremendous pain and hardship, like off-season workouts, is when you bond with your teammates the most. The way I motivated and pushed my teammates was the same way I lived out my faith, not with rah-rah spirit but through example. If the guys didn't see me working hard, how could I expect them to follow suit?

I arrived early for workouts and practice every single day. I was No. 1 in every drill I finished. I would demolish everybody. Being the best was not just something I strived for but a lifestyle I lived. I was leagues ahead of my teammates in terms of conditioning, but that's because I wanted it more than anyone else.

Mike

Standing next to other team parents, I watched Chris end practice with a series of sprints. In Georgia, at that time of year, it was 100 degrees out there. They'd run from sideline to sideline, and guys were just trying to survive. Half-gassers they call them. Chris would hit the finish line first before everyone else.

Chris

My goal was to be first every time. That's how I led my teammates. That's how I earned their respect. If you don't play well and perform well and do things to be the best, a lot of times you're not going to be a leader. That's just how it is.

I wanted to project the same kind of attitude off the field, which is why I took my leadership role as the FCA president just as seriously. I was in my fourth year of leading the weekly meetings, leading worship songs, introducing our speaker for the evening, taking prayer requests at the end, and finishing with a time of corporate or group prayer. From just five athletes at the first FCA meeting my freshman year—and me being the only representative from the football team—we were now hosting between forty and fifty Georgia Tech athletes from all sports each week my senior year. That was really awesome and had nothing to do with anything I was doing, but how a great God was using me and moving through Georgia Tech athletics.

Midway through my last college season, Derrick Moore came by to see me one Sunday afternoon.

"I've been doing some thinking, and I'd like to have us do a parents' breakfast and inform them about what's going on with FCA at Georgia Tech," Derrick said with excitement. "We could hold the breakfast on the Sunday morning after the Clemson game."

My heart quickened. I knew Mom would come, but should I invite my dad? The more I gave this thought, the more I figured I had nothing to lose. I had never invited Dad to any Christian event before and didn't even know if he'd want to come. After our last Christian talk—the Jack situation on the phone—I wasn't expecting much. But this was the first time that I had the opportunity to invite him to an event having to do with my faith, and so I had to at least reach out and try.

I sent my father an email:

> Hey, Dad, no pressure, but I want to let you know that we're having an FCA event, a parents' breakfast, to let people know what's going on with the Georgia Tech FCA. I would love it if you could come the morning after our game against Clemson. It'll be held at the Georgia Tech Hotel and Conference Center starting at 9 a.m. If you can't come, it's no big deal.

Mike

I immediately wrote back and said I would love to come. I saw this as another chance to spend time with Chris. I was acutely aware that the window of opportunity was closing now that he was a senior in college. But I had no idea what I was getting myself into.

When Donna and I walked into a conference room at the Georgia Tech Hotel, I saw that several rows of chairs had been set up in front of a riser with a podium and some musical instruments. I got a little nervous because this sure looked like a church service to me. It was Sunday morning, October 30, 2005.

Church held nothing but bad memories for me. On the rare occasions that I did attend church as a child, the experience frightened me to death. The preacher invariably rained fire and brimstone upon the faithful sitting in the pews. I remember feeling judged and condemned by so-called "Christians" and "church people."

You're worthless. You're not worthy of anything. You are certainly not good enough for God's love. You can't overcome your past, especially with everything you've done. You'll never be good enough to get right with God.

All these things were rumbling through my head as I took in the scene. But then several people who didn't know me came over to introduce themselves. They shook my hand and said, "We're really happy that you're here!" They didn't try to get me to sign anything, give them money, or join something.

I started looking around. People were smiling and happy. They looked at peace. I couldn't understand that. What was going on with them? What was it that they had that I didn't have?

Actually, they were more than happy. Happiness is an emotion that can change with the weather. What I saw was joy, and I had never seen pure joy like this in my life.

After we ate a light breakfast consisting of fruit and muffins, we were invited to take a seat in one of the rows. Chris jumped up on the small riser with a guitar in his arms. He started strumming away and leading the singing. I had never seen him play the guitar before. I didn't know he could sing. But here he was, leading the hundred or so people through a series of very inspirational songs. The melodies were so uplifting! Since I didn't know the words to the songs, I was thankful that they were put on a big screen via PowerPoint.

I remember one song that a special guest, former NBA basketball star and Georgia Tech alum Mark Price, sang that morning—"I Can Only Imagine." I had never heard a more beautiful song in my life. The music and the lyrics took my breath away. In fact, I got the chills. It was as if God put His arms around me, hugged me and said, *Mike, I love you, and it's time.*

I was overwhelmed with emotion. I sensed God's presence. It's as if He was speaking directly to me through those worship songs. Something stirred in me, and I realized that the only way I would ever find true peace and joy—to stop the pain and to fill this hole I felt in my heart—was through a relationship with God's son, Jesus Christ. I had to stop my hurtful and destructive behavior.

Chris

I didn't know Dad was experiencing any of this since I was pre-occupied with my responsibilities that morning.

I don't think Dad would have come if he had known Derrick would share the gospel after our buffet breakfast, but Derrick *always* shared the gospel any chance he got. He loved winning souls to the Lord. After I introduced Derrick, I sat down at the end of the aisle next to my mom with Dad and Donna in the middle of the row a few seats down.

Let me tell you something: there are few people who can

bring it like Derrick Moore. The guy is mesmerizing. He has a God-given talent. You can't take your eyes off him. Coach Gailey always had Derrick deliver the pre-game pep talks, and he spoke with that deliberate half-shouting cadence in the black pastor tradition that had a way of penetrating your soul and getting you fired up like there's no tomorrow:

Football is about courage and toughness.

Football is about heart and determination.

Football is about character, about winning at home, about winning on the road . . .

We were ready to break down the doors whenever Derrick fired us up.

At the FCA prayer breakfast, Derrick brought his A game again. After talking about how he carried the rock for the Detroit Lions, Carolina Panthers, and Arizona Cardinals, he described how he discovered his true calling in life: to minister to others and share the Good News of Jesus Christ. "My passion has always been Christ, and the Lord in his sovereign way opened the door for me to come to Georgia Tech. I was available, and I merely heeded the call."

Then this broad-shouldered man brandished the obituary section of a newspaper to make this point: "If you don't make the sports column, you'll make the obituary page one day. You are here this morning because God called you to be here. Life is precious and is like a running game clock. You live your life, but you don't know how much time you have left. What is to become of your life when that clock reaches zero?" he asked.

"God, in His grace, has given us a way to be reconciled with Him," Derrick continued. "All He's asking you to do, today, is to turn away from your sin and follow Jesus as Lord. He is the answer. He is the beginning and the end. He is our great hope.

Admit that you're a sinner. Realize that the penalty of sin is eternal death. Acknowledge that there is nothing you can do to save yourself. Repent of your sin and turn to Jesus Christ alone for salvation."

You could hear the proverbial pin drop. And then I heard a whimper. I glanced to my left and saw my father hunched over, sobbing. I did a double-take. I had never seen my dad cry before, at least not like this.

What I saw excited me, though. Maybe Derrick's gospel message had penetrated his heart. Maybe this was it. I had been praying for this moment for years.

When Derrick finished, that was my cue to finish the breakfast by leading everyone in a worship song that we ended all of our Georgia Tech FCA meetings with—"Your Love Is Deep." After singing several choruses of *Your love is deep, your love is high, your love is long, long, your love is wide*, I took off my guitar and walked over to where Dad and Donna were sitting. Dad looked at me with red-rimmed eyes and said, "I would love to know more about this Jesus thing."

I can't begin to explain how my heart started to dance. Hearing him say that meant everything to me and were the sweetest-sounding words I'd ever heard my dad speak.

Mike

Something blew me away that morning. I wasn't sure what was happening to me, but I knew my life would never be the same. I had never experienced the kind of love that was in that room that morning. I had never found that kind of love in sex. I certainly had never found it through drinking.

What was happening was totally unexpected. You see, I had shown up because Chris asked me to come. I wanted to support him. But singing those songs, seeing those lyrics on the big screen, and then being reminded that my time on earth was getting shorter by the minute hit me like a ton of bricks. In the quiet of my heart, I bowed my head, prayed, and wept.

That's when I asked Jesus to come into my life—a life filled with lies and sex, booze and broads. I was such a sinner unworthy of God's grace and unconditional love.

Upon accepting Christ as my personal Lord and Savior, my relationship with God was restored. For the first time in my life, I accepted responsibility for my bad choices and decisions. How I was living my life was wrong, and I begged God for forgiveness. But now what do I do?

Something just told me that I had just begun a thousand-mile journey with a single step.

13

SECOND-CLASS FAMILY

Chris

I felt God had been preparing me for something big, but I had no idea it would be the moment when my dad accepted Christ. But I was quickly drawn into other conversations that morning, and I didn't get a chance to follow up with Dad before he left the Georgia Tech Hotel and Conference Center.

Mike

I'm not sure what I would have said had I had a chance to pull Chris aside. I was still processing what happened myself.

I remember talking on the phone with him the next day. We had a long conversation—probably an hour or two—because I had questions about what it meant to have a relationship with Christ. There was so much I didn't know.

I asked him questions like:

- How do you know the Bible is true?
- What is the difference between the Old Testament and the New Testament?
- Why does God allow bad things to happen to good people?

Chris said the first thing I needed to do was start reading a

Bible written in contemporary English—not a Bible with a lot of *thees* and *thous.* "Let me take care of that," he said.

Ten days later, Donna and I drove eight hours to Charlottesville, Virginia, to watch Chris play against the University of Virginia. After a disappointing loss, we waited for him to come out of the locker room to give him a hug and spend a few minutes with him before he boarded the team bus for the flight home.

Chris walked out carrying a duffel bag in one hand and clutching a paper bag in the other. "Here, this is yours," he said, handing me the paper bag.

I opened the package and found a paperback book called *God's Game Plan: The Athlete's Bible.*

"That's an FCA Bible," Chris said. "I think you'll like it. There are study notes and questions, too. It's a great way to start reading the Bible."

"Wow, this is so cool," I said with tears forming in my eyes. I gave him another big hug.

When I got home, I opened the *Athlete's Bible* to the New Testament. I liked the easy-to-understand plain language and the notes on each page that provided a good explanation of what the verses meant.

Chris

The Athlete's Bible was geared specifically for student athletes and tied Scripture to sports.

Mike

Which was helpful for me because I was into sports. I enjoyed reading this version of the Bible, but it was still difficult figuring everything out, even in simpler language. The Bible is a big book, and there was a lot to read. I didn't know where to begin.

I found it easier getting into *The Purpose-Driven Life* by Rick Warren, the pastor of a megachurch in Southern California. I heard about this book on one of the morning news shows like *Good Morning America* or *The Today Show*. While traveling to a business meeting on the West Coast, I purchased a copy in an airport bookstore during a layover in Salt Lake City. The back cover said *The Purpose-Driven Life* would help me answer the most basic question that everyone faces in life: *Why am I here?*

In the search for significance, the starting place must be with God and His eternal purposes for each life, wrote Rick Warren. Real meaning and significance comes from understanding and fulfilling God's purposes for putting us on earth.

I dove into *The Purpose-Driven Life* like a thirsty individual who hadn't sipped a glass of water in days. The more I read, the more I realized that I had a lot to learn about God and His plans for me.

Chris

A son teaching and discipling his father was a weird concept for me to grasp, but I have to credit my father for having the humility to ask me questions.

Doubt, however, rolled over me as I realized my dad was expecting me to have all the answers and lead him in this new journey.

Trust Me . . .

I remembered those words as I looked back and saw how far God had brought me. *Just trust Him, Chris*, I reminded myself.

A short time later, I received the nicest email from my father. He wrote, "I want to thank you for being there for me. I realize that I have been filling a hole in my heart solely with material things—things that I know cannot fill me up. I understand that

I need a personal relationship with Jesus Christ to fill that hole. I just want you to know that I now have that personal relationship with Him."

I broke down crying after reading those words that I had prayed to hear for so long.

Mike

These days, people tell me that I had a "road to Damascus" moment, but I wouldn't have known what that meant at the time because I didn't know the story of the Apostle Paul's conversation experience as retold in the Book of Acts. What I was yet to discover was that even though I said yes to God that day, my life would not automatically become better. In many ways, things got worse. I still had to pay for the consequences of my sins, of which there were many.

It turned out that a thousand miles was a long way to walk.

I need to backtrack a bit. About a year *before* the FCA breakfast, I landed my first job in three years when ConAgra Foods hired me as Manager, National Accounts for Lamb Weston, their specialty frozen potato products division. In layman's terms, I sold French fries to national account restaurant chains like Chick-fil-A and Arby's. After not having a full-time job for so long, it felt great to join a $20 billion company that was a major force in U.S. food production. Happy days were here again.

ConAgra Foods was one of North America's largest packaged foods companies. Their products were available everywhere: supermarkets, restaurants, convenience stores—anywhere food was sold or prepared. You're familiar with their brand names: Hebrew National, Healthy Choice, Chef Boyardee, Wesson,

Reddi-Wip, Fleischmann's, La Choy, Peter Pan, and Van Camp's. The complete list is quite extensive.

My job interview was like taking candy from a baby. I flew to Orlando to meet with a guy around my age that I'll call Doug. He knew that I was well qualified from seeing my résumé and speaking to me on the phone a few weeks earlier, so we got to talking about football instead.

Obviously, this gave me a great opening to tell him that my son played for Georgia Tech. Doug was a big ACC fan in general and a Florida State University Seminole fan in particular, so we started swapping stories about games we'd been to and players we'd seen in the past. I knew I had the job by the time I boarded my return flight to Atlanta.

I wasn't offered a really big salary liked my Pepsi heyday, but this was a good $100,000-a-year job where if I performed, I could tack on a $25,000 to $50,000 annual bonus. I soon learned that some of the ConAgra guys I worked with were football fans *and* big drinkers too, so it wasn't long before I was partying like it was 1999 again.

Donna and I were still looking for new frontiers to conquer on the sexual front. The Internet had opened up a world of personal ads like those found in Adult FriendFinder. We'd make an online connection and then go out and meet people and see if things jelled in a foursome kind of way. More often than not, however, they didn't, which soured us on personal ads.

Consequently, Donna started going out on her own more, which I was fine with since we had an "open" relationship anyway. I was content to let her go because when she came home after being with another guy, our sex was unbelievable. Besides, I saw other women over the years when I felt the need to get out on my own to play.

Those were the high moments in our marriage. The low moments were our violent fights when Donna and I would scream and yell at each other. I think it was evident to her that I treated her and Jack and Katy like a second-class family because I always placed Mike and Chris's welfare first. When Chris became a football star at Georgia Tech, I know that's all I talked about.

We also strongly disagreed on how we were raising Jack and Katy. I was the disciplinarian in the home, and I expected our children to make good grades, be respectful, develop a strong work ethic by going to school every day, and help out around the house. When I tried to punish the kids by taking away privileges or grounding them, it would all fall apart. If I happened to go on a business trip for a few days, I'd return home to find they were allowed to go out or miss school, and that's when our fights would resume.

I know I acted like a tyrant at home with all my rules. What I didn't realize was that when you're in the throes of addiction, you try to control your environment as much as you can because the rest of your life is so out of control. But that was me in a nutshell.

I carried around a lot of anger, and it would come out at times. I know Jack and Katy caught the brunt of my horrible outbursts. They also heard the loud, ugly fights between Donna and me whenever we came home after a long night of drinking and carousing because alcohol had one of two effects on me:

1. Alcohol either made me really happy.

2. Or alcohol made me really angry.

Most of the time, it was the latter, which is why alcohol brought the worst out of me when I was around Donna.

I was becoming more miserable with each passing day. I was not happy with my life or my addiction-rattled lifestyle. I knew I was going down the wrong path, but I didn't know how to make a U-turn.

That was my mindset when Chris invited me to the FCA parent's breakfast. There was a lot of pressure on Donna and me. Our marriage was a pressure cooker threatening to blow. A lot of things around us were spiraling out of control.

⁕

Donna was sitting next to me when I was overcome with my need to ask Christ to come into my tattered life at the FCA event on October 30, 2005.

I believed in Him, asked to be pardoned for my sins, and accepted His forgiveness to some degree, but everything was a blur. I didn't fully understand what happened that morning, but I knew the only way I would fill this big hole in my life and find the inner peace I so desperately wanted was to reach out and ask Jesus Christ to come into my life.

Donna and I didn't say anything to each other until we got in the car for the thirty-minute drive back home to Alpharetta. I was the one who spoke first.

"Something happened this morning," I began. "Something changed. Something came over me back there. I really feel like God, in His way, spoke to me. He said it was time for me to come back home and be a part of His family."

I took my eyes off the light freeway traffic—it was a Sunday morning, after all—and looked toward Donna. I remember seeing a puzzled look on her face.

"That's interesting," she said. But that's all she said.

I filled the void with more observations. "I need God in my life. I looked at all those people who were there, and they all had something I wanted. Did you see the peace and joy? They had that because they have Christ."

"That's really nice. That's great," Donna responded. "I hope it makes you happy."

Donna was agreeing with me, but she would often be in accord with what I had to say. I suspected, though, that she thought I was entering another one of my "phases." *This will last a little while, just like all the other things that you try, and then it will be over.*

I knew in my heart that this time around my life would be dramatically different. On the drive home, I was thinking *I have to learn more about Jesus. I have to start figuring this whole thing out. Maybe this is the answer. Maybe this is what I've been looking for.* What I knew was that everything I had tried to make me happy up to that moment hadn't worked.

Reading *The Purpose-Driven Life* shortly thereafter was perfect for me. Rick Warren laid everything out there in a super simple way. One idea that was new to me, though, was his chapter on small groups and the importance of meeting with other believers to read and discuss passages of Scripture. I had never heard about small groups before, and the idea of joining a small group sounded unpleasant to me. I didn't want anyone to know how much I *didn't* know about the Bible. I was embarrassed and feared being judged.

I was also afraid of going to a church because of all the bad experiences I had growing up as a kid. When I expressed to Chris my concerns about stepping inside a church and revealing my story to a bunch of strangers who'd probably raise their eyebrows and decide I wasn't "good enough," my son quickly allayed my fears.

"Dad, there's a really cool church in Alpharetta that I know you'd like. It's called North Point Community Church, and it's a non-denominational church that's exploding in growth. Around

15,000 people go each week to hear Andy Stanley's sermons. He's a phenomenal speaker and teacher. Don't worry—no one's going to try to recruit you. They have rock music and all this other stuff. You'll love it."

Mike

North Point was such a big church in Alpharetta that even I had heard of it. I knew exactly where the church was located. *Okay, it's not too far. I can try it out one Sunday.*

When Chris suggested North Point Community Church, I remember wanting to go the next weekend. I said to Donna, "I'm going to get up on Sunday and go to church. If you would like to go with me, that would be great, but you don't have to."

Once again, she gave me a puzzled look. I might as well have said that I wanted to become an astronaut.

Donna and I liked getting up at the crack of noon on Sundays because we usually drank a lot on Saturday nights and stayed up very, very late . . . sometimes all night. Sundays were for sleeping in and recovering from hangovers. Even though I usually couldn't sleep past 9 a.m., Donna liked to keep snoozing to noontime or even 1 o'clock in the afternoon. The point is, we didn't have to get up for any reason and get the kids to school or go to work.

On this particular Sunday in November, I decided to check out the 11 a.m. service at North Point. I knew this was a casual church, so I put on a pair of blue jeans and a sweater. I let Donna sleep; she was dead to the world anyway.

My first perception that something was different was when I turned right onto North Point Parkway and noticed that traffic was backed up a half mile. I saw traffic cops and people with fluorescent orange vests directing traffic into vast parking lots surrounding the main building of the East auditorium. Seeing so many cars filled with people who *wanted* to go to church was impressive. The other thing that caught my attention was that North Point didn't have a church steeple or even a cross anywhere. The main building looked like a nice two-story professional office building.

Once again, people were nice to me as I stepped inside the main foyer.

Welcome to North Point.

Welcome to North Point.

Welcome to North Point.

I accepted a handshake and a bulletin from one of the greeters and found an empty chair toward the back. No way I was going to sit toward the front of the main sanctuary, which seated several thousand. I wanted to be as unobtrusive as possible.

I took in a deep breath. So far, no one had asked me to sign up for something or join the church. The other thing I noticed was a big stage with state-of-the-art lighting in dramatic purples and blues. I felt like I was sitting down for the start of a Broadway production or a rock concert.

Before I knew it, senior pastor Andy Stanley walked out and welcomed the congregation. Dressed in blue jeans and a long-sleeved shirt that wasn't tucked in, he began by saying that North Point was created for "unchurched" people. He added that their mission was to lead people into a growing relationship with Jesus Christ.

I wrinkled my brow. First of all, he didn't look like any pastor I'd seen before. Was he saying that I didn't have to *do* anything? Or that being part of North Point wasn't based on how good I was? I was contemplating those questions when the worship band started playing a rock 'n' roll version of a Chris Tomlin song, "Indescribable." Once again, I got the same chills that I received when I heard my son singing Christian worship songs at the FCA event a few weeks earlier.

Tears came to my eyes. My soul was stirred by the sweeping melody and powerful words sung by the worship band and the congregation.

Andy delivered a powerful and moving sermon about God's love and grace, but I felt like he was talking directly to me—like a guy sitting in the barstool next to me at my favorite tavern. He was speaking in a language I could understand and relate to. He had taken a big church and made it small and intimate.

It took me forty-minutes to get out of the parking lot. Donna was still in bed but half-awake when I got home in the early afternoon. I came running into the master bedroom like a kid who had found a dollar on the street.

That was the coolest experience. It was incredible. It was like a Broadway show. You really need to come with me some time. It was awesome.

I couldn't stop gushing about North Point. I went back the next Sunday and the next. This started a pattern where I would go to church on Sunday mornings and she would not. I would go to church even if I had drank myself into a stupor at one of Chris' Saturday games or partied into the wee hours. Becoming a Christian hadn't changed that aspect of my life. I still liked the taste of alcohol and what it did for me.

Meanwhile, I tore into the Bible that Chris gave me like a fat kid with a piece of chocolate cake. I started reading from the first page of the Bible with Genesis. I remember calling Chris often to ask him to explain who Abraham was and others whose names I couldn't pronounce, like Abraham's sons: Zimran, Jokshan, Medan, Midian, Ishbak, and Shuah.

I also told Donna about what I was discovering in the Bible because I had to tell *someone*. Oddly enough, the following conversation happened while we were on our way to a downtown Atlanta sex club in hopes of meeting other like-minded couples. Even after accepting Christ, I didn't realize what Donna and I were doing was a sin. After all, we were married and it was consensual.

"Did you know that Abraham is the father of all religions?" I said to Donna as we tooled along Highway 400 in a southerly direction. "That's amazing to me. He had all these sons, and they went on to be kings. It's unbelievable. I can't get enough of this."

Once again, I'm sure that Donna wondered what got into me. At least I hadn't become some religious nut and stopped drinking and having sexual escapades. But no matter what we did sexually or how much I drank during the weekend, she couldn't escape the fact that her husband sure seemed to be reading this Bible a lot and was attending North Point Community Church every Sunday morning.

Beneath the surface of our relationship, though, things were bubbling to the surface that would blow our marriage apart.

Chris

Throughout my college years, Mom and I talked virtually every week. One time, I posed a question that I had never asked her before. "Why did you and Dad get divorced?" I spurted out, not comprehending the weight of the question. I don't know what I was expecting her to say.

Mom got quiet for a second and then took a big sigh. She proceeded to explain how Dad had an affair with Donna and then left us. My stomach dropped when I heard those words, and my heart broke for Mom. Surprisingly though, I wasn't mad at Dad. Forgiveness was the key topic of my Bible study that week, so I could tell God was preparing me for this moment. I began to tear up as I said, "Mom, if Dad hasn't said it to you yet, I just want to say sorry on his behalf." She began to weep.

Mom said she never wanted to tell me, not because she was trying to hide anything but because she wanted me to have a relationship with my father. She knew that if I would have found out about this before I became Christian, I probably would've walked away from my dad and never spoken to him again. She always tried to paint Dad in a good light for me and my brother's sake.

After hanging up the phone, I wiped away fresh tears rolling down my cheeks. I thought about Mom and how difficult it must have been to have to see, be around, and even be cordial with the woman my dad cheated with. But she brushed all of that aside and sacrificed her pride to put my older brother and me first.

Dad had no idea that I knew what had happened between him and Mom. One time, before one of my football games, I put my arms around him and gave him a big hug. My heart whispered, *I forgive you.* For the first time in my life, a layer of Dad's rough exterior flaked off, and I began to see him the way that God had always seen him—fearfully and wonderfully made.

I had a very good senior year at Georgia Tech in 2005, starting every game at strong safety for a team that would go on to another bowl game and finish with our third consecutive 7-5 season. We were ranked as high as No. 15 before falling to No. 24 behind Florida State and Oklahoma. On a personal note, I was Tech's second-leading tackler and a key performer on a defense that ranked in the Top 25 nationally.

Our final game of the regular season was against our greatest rivals—the University of Georgia. Separated by only seventy miles, we had been heated adversaries since 1893, when Georgia Tech beat the Bulldogs 28-6. On the last Saturday in November 2005, Tech and Georgia would be meeting on the gridiron for the

99th time since their rivalry began.

Called the "Clean, Old-Fashioned Hate" game, this intrastate rivalry contest was also our last home game of the season, which made it Senior Day—the time when all Georgia Tech seniors would be honored with a pregame introduction ceremony. Senior players would come onto the field and be joined by their parents, where everyone would stand at midfield. It would be a nice form of recognition as well as a memorable send-off.

During the week leading up to Senior Day, I got a call from Mom. This time, though, I could sense some concern in her voice. "Chris, I don't want to make a big deal about this, but when we go down there onto the field, I would feel uncomfortable if Donna walked out with us. I just want you and your father to be out there with me."

"Why would you feel uncomfortable?" I asked Mom. We both knew why, but I wanted to hear her thoughts.

"If I had a husband, I would never bring him on the field because your dad is your dad. I wouldn't want my husband acting like he is your dad because he's not your father."

"Okay, Mom." I didn't know what to think except that I knew I was put in an awkward position. I had never looked at Donna like she was my mom. I called her Donna because she was my stepmom. I credit her with doing a great job of understanding what her role was. Donna attended nearly all my sporting events growing up, and she was certainly there for all my home games at Georgia Tech and was as supportive as you would expect any stepmom to be. But at this special Senior Day ceremony, I understood why Mom wanted just her and Dad on the field with me.

I wrote Dad an email stating that I just wanted him and Mom to accompany me on Senior Day. I figured that he and Donna might not be happy with my decision, but then again, it was my decision.

He phoned me right away. Dad's always been really good

with his words, which helps when you're in sales. "I'd like you to reconsider," he began in a conciliatory tone. "Donna's been to all your games for sixteen years. She's supported you, she doesn't ask for much, and I know this would mean the world to her."

Dad had a way of trying to guilt my older brother and me into doing certain things, especially when it came to events having to do with the family. But my mind was already made up. My mom had voiced her opinion, which she rarely did unless something was really important to her. She had never said, "Chris, I don't want Donna at your awards banquet" or "I don't want Donna at this game." But for Senior Day, she said, "This is my time with you and your dad, being on the field."

Mike

I wanted to be sensitive to Stephanie and the situation. I wasn't trying to manipulate Chris, but I was trying to tell him why I thought Donna deserved to be there. Had he told me from the beginning, "Mom's just not comfortable with it," then—

Chris

I didn't say that because Mom asked me not to. Mom felt uncomfortable with Donna being there, so I had to be the bad guy. Since Mom had never come out and protested like this before, I knew it was a big deal. So I said, "You know, Dad, I'm just not comfortable with Donna being on the field because it's Mom's time." I wanted to make it seem like it wasn't my mother pushing Donna out of the way. I took the bullet, so to speak.

Mike

I restated how Donna had been there for him over the years, always taking a backseat to everything, and how I thought she deserved to be there, but we went in circles on this. This wasn't a confrontation, and we weren't mad at each other, but we butted heads as we got going around and round . . .

Chris

We kept going in circles because I had made my mind up. I can be stubborn in that way. We ended the conversation with Dad saying, "Okay, that's fine, but if you don't want Donna on the field, you have to tell her yourself."

I could do that.

I wondered how I could best communicate that message. Since we never spoke on the phone—it's not something we did; we had maybe three phone conversations over the years—I decided to send her an email:

> *Dear Donna,*
>
> *I want to thank you for being an awesome step-mom. You've faithfully attended all my events, you've always supported me and Mike, and you've kindly stepped back when my mom was around. I can't begin to explain my appreciation for how you've let my mom step up. However, as you can understand from being a mother, this is my mom's time to shine. But I want you to know how much I appreciate you being there to support me over the years.*

I never received a reply, and Donna never brought it up with me.

Mike

But Donna brought it up to me because she was devastated. In a sense, Senior Day crystallized her position in our marriage—she was Mom No. 2 and would always have that status.

I dreaded Chris' final home game. No. 20 George Tech versus No. 13 Georgia was a night game, so there was plenty of time to tailgate, but Donna and I didn't drink very much because of the importance of the occasion. We gathered with the other senior parents at the Edge Athletic Center before the game, where they played a flashback video of the last four years on a huge flatscreen. I was emotional, but Donna was even more emotional. She couldn't stop crying because she knew that she had not been invited to go on the field.

When it was time to start the Senior Day ceremony, Donna, Jack, and Katy returned to the stands while I went to find Stephanie. While lining up with other families, she motioned to our son Mike to join us for the walk out before the boisterous sellout crowd of 56,412.

From their seats, Donna, Jack, and Katy watched the three of us stride onto the field while Chris entered from the other side and joined up with us as his name was spoken over the loudspeaker. All the time, I was thinking that Donna, Jack, and Katy had to be hurt and very upset because they felt they had been a big part of Chris' life too. I noticed lots of blended families out there—moms and stepmoms and dads and stepdads. I'm sure that development didn't escape Donna's attention.

After our introduction, pictures were taken of the four of us at midfield as we were announced to the home crowd.

When I returned to my seat, there was no mistaking that Donna was devastated. She had been crying and looked as if she had just lost her best friend . . . it was very sad. There was nothing

I could do or say. The damage was done, and her heart was shredded into little pieces.

Senior Day set the tone for what would happen two months later in January 2006, which would be the beginning of the end of our marriage.

14

A Time of Transition

Mike

This may surprise readers, but I never went out on New Year's Eve. I preferred to stay home and do any celebratory drinking under my own roof.

As far as I was concerned, New Year's Eve was Amateur Night. I'm a professional when it comes to drinking, so I'm not going to go out with all those crazy people on New Year's Eve—or St. Patrick's Day or Cinco de Mayo either. Too many idiots in the bars, and way too dangerous to be on the roads.

So Donna and I always stayed home. We never had anyone come over to celebrate with us after the kids got older. It would just be the two of us watching Dick Clark broadcasting from Times Square, cuddling up on the couch and happy we weren't part of that freezing madhouse gathered on the streets of Manhattan.

Early in our marriage, we always tried to have sex as close as possible to midnight, timed with the lowering of the Time Square Ball as it dropped to signal the start of the new year. That was always fun to do, but in recent years that had become too boring.

As we were waiting to usher in 2006 on New Year's Eve, Donna and I were in the kitchen, refilling our empty wine glasses when she said, "We had a lot of fun this year, but it's also been hard and very emotional. Through it all though, you were the best husband a woman could ask for."

For some reason, Donna was in a good mood that night. I'm sure the bottle of Kendall-Jackson we consumed helped that cause as well.

"Thanks sweetheart," I said. "It's hard to believe another year flew by so quickly. I wonder what 2006 will bring?"

It certainly promised to be an interesting year. Chris had one more semester of school at Georgia Tech before graduating, but he was talking about taking a semester off to prepare for the NFL draft. I was growing in my faith at North Point Community Church, but Donna had yet to join me. Jack and Katy continued to present parenting challenges, especially when it came to attending high school.

Fortunately, we had a steady income stream and were on better financial footing since I had joined ConAgra Foods, but I was still struggling to keep my head above water. We lived paycheck to paycheck and managed to get the bills paid and keep the first and second mortgage current each month, but we had accumulated over $150,000 in new debt over the last three years.

Chris

I wondered what 2006 would bring as well. Besides my aspirations about playing in the NFL, I had a serious girlfriend that I was thinking about asking to marry me.

Her name was Michelle Tyree, and I had met her the summer before my junior year at an FCA event known as the Day of Champions. I remember walking into the Georgia Tech Hotel for a student-athlete conference and noticing a really pretty girl sitting behind the registration desk. She had a big smile and long, black hair. *Wow, she's really beautiful,* I thought. *I hope she's a Christian.*

You'd expect that she would be a follower of Christ, considering she was working at an FCA conference, but you can't assume anything these days. She was gorgeous with a bubbly and outgoing personality. Up to that point, the girls I had dated didn't take their faith as seriously as I did, so we never meshed. I had been praying fervently, though, that God would put the right person in my life at the right time—His time.

Derrick Moore, my mentor and the FCA team chaplain, introduced me to the latest addition to the FCA staff. "Michelle's going to be helping us this year, working with the women athletes and leading Bible studies for them." Derrick explained that she had recently graduated from the University of Georgia, where she had been a standout on the women's softball team. Now she was trying her hand at ministry on the Georgia Tech campus.

We shook hands and smiled as I looked into her big brown eyes. The entire conference that night I couldn't take my gaze off of her.

Being new on the FCA staff, she was introduced and gave her testimony in front of all the college student-athletes. I'm not going to lie, but I was a little intimidated. Here was an extremely beautiful woman so strong and convicted about her faith that she had no problem telling a roomful of strangers that she was in love with Jesus. Her composure amazed me and prompted me to ask myself: *Am I strong enough and knowledgeable enough in my faith to lead a woman of God like that?*

I started asking around about Michelle and learned that she had a boyfriend. Talk about deflating news. It was like Lucy pulling the football away just as Charlie Brown was about to kick. *Well, Lord, I guess it wasn't meant to be, but I know I would like to be with a woman like that.*

During the summer, Michelle asked me to help her find an

apartment, which I was glad to do. I enjoyed spending time with this girl, but I also thought it would be a good opportunity to get to know each other better since I was the FCA president and we would be working together. All the time, though, I was thinking how it really sucked that she had a boyfriend back in Athens.

The apartment hunt was comical. We'd find the manager, and he'd look at the two us and invariably say, "You're a cute couple. We have just the right place for you."

"Oh, no, we're not together," I'd say, waving my hands and blushing a little bit. "I'm helping Michelle find an apartment."

We searched over two weekends, which allowed us to spend a significant amount of time together and get to know each other on a friend level. We found her a place that, unfortunately, wasn't in the best part of town. However, that's all Michelle could afford since she had to raise her own support. She was trying to live on a $15,000 annual salary, which was really tough in a major city like Atlanta.

After I helped her move in, we were working together on FCA events all the time. She was also an important part of the planning process for our weekly meetings on Wednesday nights. We talked to each other on the phone nearly every evening, usually about FCA stuff. There were only so many FCA things to talk about, so it wasn't too long before the conversations would move to a more personal level. Our long phone chats allowed our friendship to become deeper and taught us how to communicate on a deeper level.

Some time during my junior season, I heard from another FCA staffer that her boyfriend had broken up with her. The long-distance relationship had fallen apart somehow. She was devastated but didn't tell me because she knew it wouldn't have been appropriate to talk about since I was a student—even though we had grown close to each other.

When I heard she was "available," I raised an eyebrow, but I knew the Georgia Tech FCA staff was not allowed to date students. The no-dating policy made sense. She was staff, and I was still a student. You didn't want anything looking shady, but I knew that I liked her. I didn't know if she liked me, but that was okay. I had time to wait things out.

I hadn't had a girlfriend since my senior year of high school. But in my mind, I was already dating her.

Mike

Here's what I saw. She would sit in the Georgia Tech section during away games and go crazy every time Chris made a great play. For instance, when Chris intercepted a pass for a touchdown at the Champs Bowl in Orlando, she jumped and screamed in a way that was way beyond how a "normal" Tech fan would react.

She always acted like she was interested in who won, but it was apparent to all of us that she came to see Chris play. When the games were over, Michelle would wait—with a couple of her girlfriends, of course—for Chris to come out of the locker room.

We all knew it was a matter of time.

Chris

Michelle and I could sense that as well, but we never said anything to each other. She *was* on staff, so what was there to talk about? My roommates would come up to me and say, "Okay, let's say she wasn't on staff. Would you date her?"

That was a hypothetical question—and I didn't want to play that game. My friends got irritated when I wouldn't answer directly, but I respected what FCA stood for. I didn't want anything to discredit what God was doing on the Georgia Tech campus.

Some may think the no-dating rule was silly, but it was put in place to protect the integrity of FCA. Thus, we acted accordingly and remained good friends.

Since Michelle hadn't raised much support, surviving in Atlanta on $15,000 a year took some real budget-stretching and a lot of faith. One month, she let on to John Rainey, another FCA staff member, and myself that she had over-drafted her checking account to pay the rent. I sympathized for Michelle and wanted to help. I didn't have a lot of money, either—probably $400 in the bank—but I felt led to put $300 in an envelope and bring it with me when we gathered at her place for a Bible study.

There were around a half-dozen student-athletes there as well as John, so I didn't go over to her place alone. I discreetly left behind the envelope filled with cash. The envelope was addressed to her but didn't have my name on it.

While on my way home, she called me, having figured out who would have given her such a gift. She was crying and thanking me for my generosity. "This was an answer to prayer," she said. "You really didn't have to do that."

I didn't tell her that I nearly emptied my bank account, but I think she realized I would give up anything and everything for her, even down to the last penny. From that moment on, I knew she was the one for me. That experience really drew us together, even before we started dating.

At the end of the school year, she believed that God was calling her to move back to Athens and teach softball hitting lessons at All-Sports Training. She knew a couple of friends there who had done quite well giving hitting lessons to high school softball players.

I was sad that she was leaving Tech and moving seventy miles away, but I was happy she was leaving the FCA staff because that meant I could ask her out.

I'll never forget our first "date," if you can call it that. I invited her to meet me at my mom's house, saying we'd hang out and then go grab a bite to eat somewhere.

She knocked on the front door. I answered the door. So did my mom. And so did my brother. Everyone was glad to see her because she already knew my family pretty well since she was one of my best friends and she had hung out with them at the Tech football games. After welcoming her inside and catching up some, I asked where she'd like to go grab a bite to eat.

"Wherever you want to go," she said with that bright smile of hers.

Neither one of us cared where we went to eat; we were ecstatic to finally hang out alone together. I suggested Zaxby's, a fast-casual restaurant like Chick-fil-A, for a quick bite. Trying to be polite and courteous, I said "Hey, Mom, Mike, do want to come with us?" I never imagined that they would say yes since they knew this was our first official "date."

The next thing I knew, the four of us were jumping into the car for the short drive to Zaxby's, whose calling card is wings and fried chicken. Michelle couldn't have cared less, secretly smiling at me about the whole situation as the four of us scrunched into a booth.

We had a great time interacting, and everyone enjoyed themselves. I could tell Michelle loved and appreciated the fact that I was so family-oriented, even though inviting Mom and my brother to come along wasn't planned. After we got home, Michelle and I—alone—watched a movie and chatted for awhile. Later when Michelle departed, my mother, grinning from ear to ear, turned to me and said, "I'm glad you guys are together now."

Funny she said that since I hadn't told Mom how I felt about Michelle, but I guess she could see the look in my eyes. I thought I did a good job of masking my true feelings for her over the past year, but maybe I didn't.

We continued to see each other as much as we could during my senior year, but it wasn't easy since she lived in Athens. Sometimes I'd only see her once a week after home football games, but I had fallen hard for her. All along I knew I was going to ask her to marry me. I was looking for the right moment.

Mike

January 1, 2006, fell on a Sunday, so by the following weekend, Donna and I were itching to get out of the house and have some adult fun. Even though I was hanging on to every word of Andy Stanley's preaching and working my way through the Bible after starting with Genesis, I was still hopelessly addicted to alcohol and sex. Talk about strongholds in my life.

Our frustrations with finding attractive partners on Adult FriendFinder and other online personal ads led Donna and me to visit upscale private "lifestyle" clubs in Atlanta where we could meet all sorts of different people.

These lifestyle clubs were quite different from the low-rent "swingers" parties held monthly at Holiday Inns and Ramada hotels that we attended in the mid-1990s. Our favorite lifestyle club was a place called Trapeze, a private club that advertised itself on their website as "an upscale adult private membership club that caters to adventurous and open-minded couples, as well as to select single males and sexy single females. We offer a little something for everyone." Trapeze was located in an industrial part of west Atlanta.

My thoughts turned back to our last visit to Trapeze. Donna and I dressed like we were going out to a New Year's Eve bash—a fashionable but sexy cocktail dress for her and a trendy all-black suit with a black silk mock turtleneck sweater for me. As we pulled up to a nondescript low-rise building amidst other industrial properties, a valet attendant jumped out the darkness to take my car. We arrived around 9 p.m. after dinner and drinks at Chops, a ritzy restaurant in trendy Buckhead.

I left the key in the ignition and popped open the trunk, where I had stashed two bottles of Ketel One vodka. I grabbed them and started walking toward the front entrance with Donna. Trapeze didn't have a liquor license because of zoning laws. Hence it was BYOB—bring your own booze—which was great by me.

I paid the $100 entry fee at the club entrance and handed both bottles of vodka to the hostess. She immediately slapped two stickers with the number 57 imprinted on them. From then on until my departure, all I would have to do was give my number to the bartenders, and they would make us drinks using my vodka.

The foyer led to a full-service bar and lounge paneled with dark wood and featuring a fifty-foot long bar made of Spanish limestone. The furnishings were upscale and well-appointed. On the other side of the club was a large dance floor surrounded by mirrors with multi-colored lights flashing to the pulsating beat of the loud music. Along one wall, tables with white tablecloths presented a fabulous buffet of gourmet food.

Dozens of couples and a few single men and woman milled about with drinks in their hands. Everyone was nicely dressed, although the women were attired more proactively than you'd normally see at a bar scene. I'm talking waist-high slits in skirts, plunging V-necklines, and enough cleavage to open a Victoria's Secret store.

I quickly made my way to the bar and said, "I'd like one vodka on the rocks and one vodka and cranberry juice from number 57."

Let the party begin.

Donna and I liked to mingle with others, introducing ourselves and making light conversation. There was a certain etiquette to this lifestyle: You never asked for last names, and you never asked for any personal details, like what people did for a living. If someone wasn't interested in connecting for sex, then "No, thank you" meant no and you would politely move on to another couple.

We probably stayed in the bar area for an hour . . . a sense of anticipation building within the both of us. Besides, I usually needed a good hour of liquid courage to work up the nerve to proceed. When Donna and I thought we were ready, we gave each other a sexy smile and nodded our heads. We both knew what would happen next.

We walked around a corner and through a set of double doors that steered us toward the second half of the club. The next doorway led to a dimly lit room lined with lockers and wooden benches. At attendant handed over locker keys and pointed us toward cabinets filled with white towels and bathrobes. A few other couples were getting undressed, but people generally kept to themselves.

Donna and I disrobed and removed every stitch of clothing, which we placed in lockers with our personal belongings. Then we wrapped our bodies in bathrobes.

There was another set of doors that led to various rooms— some communal and some private. Donna and I headed to one of the communal rooms, which was even darker than the locker room. Inside this communal room, there were perhaps twenty couples on the mat floor in various stages of having sex. You can imagine what we did next.

When we were finished "playing," we took a break. There was a nice mahogany mini-bar at one end of the main room, where we sat on a nice leather barstool and had a few drinks to recharge. They was also a large indoor swimming pool where we could sit while sipping our cocktails, but we preferred to stay put and watch others having fun in the communal room. It was a great spectator sport. Some enjoy watching people at airports or malls; Donna and I happened to like watching other people having sex. That was our hobby. We never thought this was wrong, just different.

We stayed until four or five in the morning, and then we went home to bed, where the two of us went at it again while discussing the highlights of the evening. The addiction to sex was always there, and alcohol made it even better.

After I had my conversion experience at the FCA event, I started having guilty feelings about visiting places like Trapeze. Experiencing pangs of guilt was new to me. I didn't think having sex with another woman was wrong if my wife consented. But the Bible made it clear that this was a sin and dishonored God.

As I worked my way through the Apostle Paul's Epistles, the scales were being lifted from my eyes. My vision was still cloudy, but I was getting the picture of what I should be doing—and that was to flee this life of immorality.

On Saturday, January 7, 2006, Donna and I were planning our first trip to Trapeze in several months. Instead of looking forward to a night of drinking and sex, I wasn't feeling right about going out. In fact, I was miserable and deeply depressed that day. I really couldn't pinpoint the cause of my distress, but I was confused by what I was feeling.

Keep in mind that being a Christian was totally new for me.

It had only been two months since I had accepted Christ as my savior. I felt like a stranger in a foreign country. When you ask Jesus to come into your life, your life doesn't suddenly become perfect. You don't stop a lifetime of destructive behavior overnight. I struggled with concepts like trust and forgiveness, and I was hesitant to turn total control of my life over to God.

I was in a very bad mood that morning, knowing what we would be doing later that night. I was on edge and blamed Donna for how I was feeling that day. As for Donna, she had grown tired of our drama and my mood swings over nineteen years of marriage. I could be the most thoughtful loving husband in the world at times, but if I was upset with Donna, I'd withdraw completely and stop speaking to her, or my volcanic temper would erupt.

"What's wrong now?" she asked in a condescending tone. I hated it when she used that tone of voice with me. I was on the verge of a meltdown after she said that.

"I'm not sure." I really didn't know myself.

"We're still going out tonight, aren't we?"

"Yeah, but it's not going to be any fun. I don't even know if I want to go."

Donna tried to change my mood. "Don't worry about it. We always have a good time."

Something snapped within me, and I started screaming at her at the top of my lungs. "I'm just so sick of this #@%&. I'm sick of our lives. I'm sick of everything. I'm especially sick of you and the way you act. You're such a slut. You're such a whore."

When I would yell, it was always very loud and very, very scary, especially to the kids. We had a large open floor plan in the house, and my shouting would echo throughout the house.

Jack, who was seventeen years old at the time and an imposing figure at six feet tall and 220 pounds, heard my outburst and came storming into our master bedroom. He immediately got into my face.

"You @#$%-ing stop talking to Mom like that!"

"Mind your own @#$%-ing business," I retorted.

Jack started shoving me. I was appalled by his blatant disrespect, so I grabbed him, and we started to fight. We wrestled with each other, and then he grabbed one of the Queen Anne chairs in the corner and threw it in my direction.

Tossing a chair was a dramatic but ineffective gesture on his part, so I retaliated with my own weapons of mass destruction—words. "You're such a loser. You can't do anything right."

There was more wrestling, more pushing. Donna got into the middle of the brawl. We never came to blows, but it was all very violent. I realize now that this was eerily reminiscent of scenes that took place between my father and me thirty years earlier.

I had to get out of there. I stormed out of the house, slamming every door I could to make a statement, and drove to a nearby bar. Shockingly, I had something to drink. Then, a second and a third and a fourth vodka on the rocks.

Hours later, I drove back to the house. It was dark. Everyone was gone. I went downstairs and slept on one of the couches in the finished basement.

I heard Donna and Katy come into the house sometime during the night. I figured Jack was staying at some friend's house. Donna and I didn't talk for four days: I would stay in the basement, and she would stay upstairs. Eventually, she came down to the basement and said, "Don't you want to talk about this? We have to figure something out."

"No, it's over. I'm done. I've had it with everything," I mumbled.

She turned around and walked back upstairs. I didn't speak

to her for another week.

"Are we ever going to talk about this?" she asked one time when she came down to the basement.

"I didn't do anything wrong. Jack attacked me," I rationalized. "We were yelling, and he attacked me. You're taking his side?"

"He was trying to protect me."

"I'm not talking about this anymore." I rolled over on the couch, turned my back to her, and covered my head with a blanket.

She went upstairs, and another week slipped by. This went on for another month. In the meantime, I was working for ConAgra Foods behind the closed doors of my home office most days and traveled a bit now and then to get away. I was still going to North Point Community Church on Sundays. Donna was gone most days, working retail for a major department store at Perimeter Mall. I was oblivious to what was going on in the lives of Jack and Katy.

After six weeks of living-separate-lives existence, I decided it was time to get past this. I approached Donna and said I was finally ready to talk.

"Save your breath," she said. "It's over. Our marriage has been horrible forever and ever. I want a divorce."

"What do you mean it's over? A divorce? I'm sorry for what happened. Look, I'm going to church now. I'm changing who I am. Come on, we can work this out."

"No, that's it. We're done."

I started begging. "I know I have issues, but we can work this out. I'm changing and learning about how I can be a better person through God's Word. I'm learning a lot about myself."

"This is just another phase you're going through. I've seen a lot of them over the years. This is another one of your bull@#$% phases."

"We can't throw in the towel now," I pleaded.

"Things have been this way since we met, and I can't stand living like this anymore. You're horrible, and I'm tired of walking on eggshells all the time. You've been abusive to me long enough, so that's it."

Even though we were estranged, we continued to live under the same roof. She stayed as far away from me as she could, and I avoided her as well. We certainly didn't have a marriage.

Talk about some major lifestyle changes. This was the longest I had gone without sex since I was fifteen years old. If there was one thing that stuck with me from reading the Bible, it was that sex was reserved for married couples—but my wife wasn't making pillow time for me because we were legally and physically separated. There was no outlet for me—which is why my drinking escalated. With nothing else to do, drinking helped medicate my pain.

My moral compass was starting to function for the first time in my life, but my drinking got worse because I was hanging out in my favorite bars to pass the time. I would still flirt since I liked the attention and needed to prop up my self-esteem, but I wasn't about to have sex with women I chatted up in bars. I drank right up until closing time.

Being the responsible person that I was—a "professional" drinker right?—I would get in my car and drive to a nearby office building parking lot and sleep it off. Actually, sleep isn't the right word. I would pass out. I was usually too bombed to take the keys out of the ignition, and that could have created a huge problem if a police officer happened to stop by to check up on me. Even if the car is parked and the engine isn't running, it's still considered driving under the influence—a DUI. Unfortunately, I usually wasn't that cognizant to take the keys out of the ignition.

Donna, meanwhile, continued to live her life under that tacit agreement that we had an "open" marriage. She was still hooking up with other men. I'm assuming that's why she would come home at four or five o'clock in the morning after being out on Friday and Saturday nights.

As I continued to read the Bible, I decided to put my newfound knowledge to good use on my marriage. I waited up for her on one occasion as she rolled in at four o'clock in the morning. I wasn't mad. I wasn't raising my voice. I merely stated, "What you're doing is wrong. We're still married. You're sinning. Look, it's right here in the Bible," I said, pointing to Proverbs 5:3-9, a passage of Scripture about adultery.

"Go to hell. I have my life, and you have yours."

The next Saturday night, I decided to take control of the situation so I let the air out of one of her tires so she couldn't go out. She thought she had a flat tire. I offered to drive her to work that Sunday while I got her flat fixed. While we were driving in the car, I said, "You know, I still love you. I'm so sorry about everything. We can still work this out."

"No, we can't. It's too late. Seeing you and Jack go at each other like that made me realize how violent and destructive our relationship has been over the years. I lost myself in our marriage. I need to find out who I am."

"But I'm different now and starting to change from the inside. I'm going to church, I'm reading the Bible, and I'm meeting good Christian people. There are big changes happening in my life. At least go to church with me."

She surprised me when she said yes and joined me for a couple of times at North Point. But Andy Stanley's and God's Word didn't penetrate her heart. Donna didn't believe I could ever change, and she thought I was hiding my life behind the cross.

Chris was the only one I could talk to about this stalemate.

Chris

Dad didn't tell me everything that was going on. He said that he knew divorce was wrong and that he didn't really want to split up with Donna, but he didn't know what to do.

It broke my heart to see Dad going through this, especially with him being a young Christian, but I didn't know what to say to him. I was twenty-two years old, never been married. But what I could offer was some advice that I had learned from my leadership role in FCA.

"Dad, you can't force people to come to know Christ. I didn't force you to come to know Christ. You kind of have to let God handle it. All you can do is be there and try to live out your faith for her—show her the Way."

"Yeah, but I'm going one way and she's going another . . ."

"I get that. Obviously, all you can do is be able to say that you did the best you could to hold this marriage together. The rest is up to God."

Mike

I told Chris, "I'm trying."

When Donna kept telling me, "It's over, it's over, it's over," I was having a hard time hearing that. I was devastated. I wanted to work everything out. I didn't want to be single again. But in my heart, I also knew that I couldn't go back to our old lifestyle of extramarital sex and drinking to get drunk.

I had finally learned right from wrong, and the way I had lived my life for decades was a sin against everything God stands for. I felt tremendously guilty for my destructive behavior over the decades. I felt deep shame for my actions.

I was praying a lot: *God, please soften her heart. Please help her to see I'm becoming the man that You want me to be. That I'm finally becoming the man You always intended me to be.*

Months passed by with no change in her attitude. I made the decision, after half a year, that I could no longer sleep in my house. Hearing her come home in the pre-dawn hours and having a good idea what she had been doing was painful and too hard to deal with.

I found a condo close by, just five minutes away, and put a deposit down. But I didn't sign the lease. I was still holding out hope.

In July, I flew to Pasco, Washington, for a ConAgra meeting. I knew I would have to sign the rental lease to meet a deadline, so I got down on my knees in my hotel room and prayed, *Heavenly Father, please, if something is going to happen to save this marriage, please let that happen now before I sign this lease.*

But nothing happened to stop me. I signed the agreement and faxed it in from the hotel lobby to my new landlord.

A few days later, I was driving to the airport in Pasco, Washington, for the return trip home. While connecting in Salt Lake City, I checked my cell phone to find that my sister, Ellen, had left a message for me to call her. I ringed her immediately.

"Mike, the first thing I want you to know is that everything is okay."

My heart skipped a beat. "What happened?"

"Donna is in the hospital. She had a car accident."

"Oh, my God. Is she all right?"

"She's bruised, but she's okay."

"How did it happen?"

"We don't know a lot of details. Apparently, she was coming home late at night and had a head-on collision with a truck."

I thanked Ellen for the call and returned to the departure gate, my hands shaking from the news.

As soon as I arrived in Atlanta, I hustled to the hospital. When I arrived, Mom was in the room. My mother and Donna were never close, but my wife had no one else to call but my mom. Donna had no real friends. No extended family in Atlanta. She didn't know who else to call.

The story she told me was that she had gone out to a concert with a friend that night and then had stopped at Johnny's Hideaway in Buckhead before heading home. Johnny's is a "must visit" for male business travelers coming to Atlanta because it's a great place to find readily available woman. I'd been going there since my high school days, and we had a saying that's as true today as it was back then: *If you can't get laid at Johnny's, you can't get laid anywhere.*

Donna was bruised all over and looked terrible. She cried and apologized for her behavior and what happened. Over the next few days, I pieced together the entire story. She was driving home on Highway 400, heading north around 3 a.m. She apparently got off on Mansell Road—three exits south of our exit at Windward Parkway.

What she was doing there, I'll never know, but somehow she was driving on the wrong side of the road and ran head-on into a delivery truck that must have been stopped at a traffic light. Her 2004 Jeep Wrangler SUV was totaled in the accident.

She was rushed to the hospital, patched up, and given a blood test. She was well over the legal limit, but I was never told the number. She was charged with a DUI.

I was set to move into my condo, but now I had to help her recuperate. She was apologetic about what happened and having me care for her, but I said it was all right.

Half of me was thinking, *Maybe this is an opportunity to reconcile,* but the other half of me was saying, *I don't know if it's God will for us to be together*. I could feel that our lives were going in different directions, however. I was moving toward a life of faith, and she was stuck in the same sex-soaked lifestyle.

I waited on her hand and foot for the next week, thinking that maybe things would work out. But after a while, Donna used the opportunity to tell me the accident was really all my fault. The way I treated her all these years had caused her to drink so much.

It was apparent that her attitude against me was set in concrete. I moved into my condo not too far away. For the first time in my life, I had a moral dilemma. Should I stay married to her—or move on? I had recently started attending a divorce recovery class called Oasis at North Point Community Church. The class was for those who were in the midst of a divorce or separation. One of the first things I learned was that I should pull out all the stops to save the marriage. It's what God wants us to do.

Once again, I called Chris.

"Am I giving up?" I asked. "On the other hand, I know in my heart that there's no way this is going to work."

"Dad, it's more than likely, after all this wears off, that she's going to be the way she's always been. There's nothing you can do about it. Just go with what's in your heart."

The Oasis divorce recovery group was a godsend. I really connected with everyone since we were all going through the same thing. I didn't see any change in Donna the few times we interacted. I knew she was still involved in the casual hook-up scene, doing whatever she wanted.

I felt like my life was finally getting on the right track. I decided that the marriage couldn't be saved, which meant that we needed to get a divorce and move on. Donna didn't disagree with me. We got together and negotiated an agreement that was put into writing by an attorney we mutually knew. The divorce decree was finalized on December 6, 2006, and I was a single man again.

Redemption had started, but I knew I wasn't there yet. There was a reason that the process was called a "walk." You don't start at the finish line.

Even though I had come a long way, I still had a long ways to go.

15

BEATING THE ODDS

Chris

A lot was happening in 2006, and big changes loomed ahead of me. I knew I wanted to marry Michelle, so I asked Mom and Dad to go ring shopping with me. I thought it would be nice to have them be part of that.

A couple of weeks after Valentine's Day, my parents accompanied me to Solomon Brothers in downtown Atlanta. Dad had done some research and thought this well-regarded fine jewelry store would be a good place to buy a diamond ring and engagement band.

We had fun picking out the right diamond and setting. As we were walking out of the building, Dad turned and congratulated me. "I think you're getting a really good diamond. Plus, if it doesn't work out, you can return it and get your money back."

I didn't think I heard right. "What do you mean?"

"You never know how it's going to work out between you and Michelle. You can't say anything lasts forever these days."

I felt a little offended. "Dad, once I marry Michelle, it's forever."

"No, you can't say forever. Things happen. Feelings change."

"No, Dad. I'm never going to leave her. I'm never going to

do those things. This is a forever commitment, so I don't need to think about whether I can get a refund on the ring."

I couldn't blame him for thinking that way after coming from two disastrous marriages. That was all he had ever known. It broke my heart as I realized that he had never seen or been in a "real" relationship—a relationship with a solid foundation. I wasn't mad at Dad, but I explained to him that Michelle and I would be making a lifelong covenant before God that would stand the test of time for better or worse.

I could tell that he was skeptical, but he agreed and we left it at that.

I called Michelle's parents, who lived in Brentwood, Tennessee. I certainly wanted their blessing before I asked their daughter for her hand in marriage.

"We love you," her father said. "We think you'd be great for Michelle."

Meanwhile, I was preparing for the NFL draft. I knew the daunting odds I faced. I had been overlooked all my life when it came to sports, so why would things be any different now?

I wasn't surprised when I wasn't invited to the NFL Combine held every March in Indianapolis, where three hundred players were weighed and measured and participated in various drills under the watchful eyes of hundreds of NFL general managers, coaches, and scouts. I could, however, participate in Georgia Tech's Pro Day, in which graduating seniors can perform similar drills before NFL scouts.

I worked hard in the off-season to increase my weight to 222 pounds and had an amazing Pro Day. I ran 4.4 seconds in the 40-yard dash, bench-pressed 225 pounds twenty-one times, and ran 3.85 seconds in the shuttle drill—the fastest time in the country in that drill.

Shortly after my Pro Day, I drove with Michelle to my uncle's beach house on Fripp Island in South Carolina, where I planned to ask her for her hand in marriage. The week leading up to our trip, however, didn't give me a good feeling that everything would go smoothly. Michelle was teaching a softball-hitting lesson when the ball ricocheted off the bat, smacking her square in the eye. She had to go to the hospital to get stitched up, which left her with a swollen black eye.

Knowing I was going to propose to her the following week, I thought to myself, *Great. Now she's going to be reminded of that horrible black eye every time she looks at our engagement pictures.* But her shiner didn't deter me from trying to make this the most memorable engagement for her.

We arrived at the Fripp Island beach house as the sun was setting in the west. (We stayed in separate bedrooms, of course.) It was a chilly March evening, so we put on sweatshirts and took blankets to the deck overlooking the beautiful beach. All I could think about was my next move. The ring was burning a hole in my pocket, so I took out my guitar and told her I had written a song just for her. She thought that was a sweet gesture as she listened to me play. As the sun started to fade, I sang the last line of the song—"Will you marry me?"

With a shocked expression and a black-and-blue eye, Michelle looked at me as if she wasn't sure if she heard right. She didn't make the connection. I could tell she was thinking, *Did he just say what I thought he said?* So I put the guitar down, got down on one knee, and proposed to her.

She screamed in happiness, crying out, "Yes, of course!" It wasn't long before she was calling all her family and friends with the great news.

We set a date: February 17, 2007. We had to plan our wedding around the NFL off-season. Of course, I had no idea if I'd be playing professional football, but I had to have faith that I would make it.

The NFL draft process is an interesting one. I call the NFL a "paper league," and the reason why it's a paper league is because the scouts have to justify their draft picks to the general manager and everyone else in the organization with factual data that can be put onto paper. While the scouting staff can say this guy is a better pick because he runs a 4.3 in the 40-yard dash while the other prospect is half a step slower at 4.4, they can't measure heart. They can't measure passion, and they can't measure work ethic. All those attributes are subjective, and NFL organizations haven't figured out a good way to measure those yet.

In calling around the league, my agent confirmed what we both figured: I was a long shot to be drafted in one of the seven rounds of the NFL draft. "Time to prepare for Plan B, which is getting you signed as a free agent," he said.

The Atlanta Falcons were the only team showing any interest in me, probably because I was a hometown product. I had been a lifelong Falcons fan growing up in Atlanta, so hearing of their interest was an exciting prospect. But the Falcons gave no indication on whether they would spend a draft choice on me.

Draft day was nerve-wracking. I held out faint hope that I'd be picked in the seventh and last round, but I was passed over. My agent told me that once the NFL draft was over, he had less than an hour to sign me as a free agent because that's when teams fill up their ninety-man training camp roster. He did a great job working the phones with the Falcons organization, lobbying on my behalf. The Falcons said yes to signing me as a free agent, and we quickly wrapped negotiations for the contract. The amount of the signing bonus: $12,000.

A few weeks later, I arrived at the Falcons' training camp for the rookie mini-camp followed by OTAs—organized team activities, which is another way of saying "practice." As I walked into the facility, I don't remember any players welcoming me or offering to show me the ropes. I wasn't looking for a parade or anything, but I soon found out that I was on my own in the locker room. I know what the other players were thinking: *This guy is coming in to take my job, trying to take food off my table. I'm not going to help him.*

That was really eye-opening to me. The NFL, I learned, was cutthroat. Guys were playing for themselves, and they were playing for the money—a completely different atmosphere than college football. Not that it was wrong, but it was a rude awakening.

Throughout training camp, the team parked me on the sidelines. I stood around a lot, tossing a football back and forth in my hands. Would I ever get a chance to play in any drills or scrimmages? Sitting out was super frustrating. I knew I was good enough to play in the NFL, but I wasn't getting a fair shot. When the coaches did throw me a bone, I didn't know what I should be doing on the field because I hadn't taken many reps.

After the third game of the preseason, I got a phone call at my dorm room. One of the scouts in the Pro Personnel department was on the line. "Hey, Chris, we want to talk to you. Can you bring your playbook?"

Bring your playbook is NFL code for *We're cutting you.*

I knew what was going to happen. With a bad feeling in my stomach, I hung my head as I walked upstairs, where the front office scout invited me into his office. "Chris, we're going to let you go," he said without introduction.

I didn't say anything because there was nothing to say. I shook my head and nodded, and just like that, my NFL dream had died. No coaches or players said goodbye or wished me luck in the future. I came into the league alone, and I left alone. All I wanted to do was to go home and start the rest of my life.

I still held out hope that another team would pick me up. I decided to keep living at home with Mom and my older brother Mike and continue to work out to stay in shape. Meanwhile, Michelle had gotten a job with LA Fitness in Atlanta. She moved into my old bedroom while I slept on the couch downstairs so that we could save some money.

Since I was living off my signing bonus, I felt like a nobody with no job, no degree, and no sense of purpose. No team called during the season, so I decided that I should go back to school in January and finish college. I was just four hours short of a degree. Then I'd get married in February and figure out what I would do for the rest of my life.

Something interesting happened at the end of December. My agent called and said the New Orleans Saints were interested in picking me up and allocating me to NFL Europe, which was kind of a farm system for the NFL. At the time, the Saints had some older defensive backs, and I suspect they were on the lookout for some young, inexpensive talent to develop.

NFL Europe was comprised of six teams: five in Germany and one in the Netherlands. Younger, "developmental" players received game experience and coaching—and kept their dreams of playing in the NFL alive. The players the Saints allocated ended up playing for the Cologne Centurions.

I told my agent to tell New Orleans that I was packing my bags. Of course, I talked with Michelle before agreeing to go because I was due in Germany two weeks after the wedding. There was no way I would go play football in Europe for ten weeks without Michelle, so I wanted to make sure we were in this together.

Michelle was game, which shows how adventurous she was. I

was a happy man when we tied the knot on February 17, 2007, at Roswell Presbyterian Church. We spent our wedding night at the Buckhead Ritz-Carlton, and the next morning we flew to an all-inclusive beachfront resort in Ocho Rios, Jamaica, known as Couples.

Our ten days in Jamaica were magical, but I was still working out all the time. The little gym at the Couples resort had a few weights and dumbbells, so I got my share of strange looks from other vacationers as I did my power cleans and hang snatches, but I had to stay in shape.

We returned to Atlanta and barely had time to get the sand out of our hair when we departed for Europe. The pay was $1,000 a week for ten weeks, which may sound great, but that money had to cover Michelle's flight to Europe, most of her meals, and any incidentals. Oh, and don't forget about taxes that were taken out by the U.S. and Germany. Her room was covered since she was sleeping with the Centurions' starting safety.

A breakfast buffet came with the room, so Michelle would join me for a typical German *frühstück*: various breads and rolls, marmalade, honey, cold meats such as ham and salami, various cheeses—many of them smelly—and *muesli*, or cereals. Since the team didn't pay for her lunch or dinner, Michelle would grab an extra roll or two and fill them with ham and salami for a noon-time snack along with a piece of fruit. We would go out to dinner at Vapiano's, an Italian place with good pasta, pizza, and salads. Neither of us went for the typical German fare—Wienerschnitzel and fried pork slathered with heavy gravies and served with boiled potatoes.

The Centurions had a small roster, just thirty-five guys, so I started as safety and played on all the special teams. I was even recruited as the long snapper for field goals and punts. It was like playing both ways in high school. I was exhausted after each game, but every down was worth it. When the season was over, I was named to the All-World team—the NFL Europe version of All-Pro—and gained a lot of pro experience.

Mike

NFL Europe games were played on Saturdays and then televised on Sundays on the NFL Network. I didn't have the NFL Network on my cable system, so I had to go to a sports bar to watch Chris play. From what I saw, he had a phenomenal year.

Chris

What we found is that God had us in Europe for a purpose. Football became a backdrop when we realized that God was going to use us for something far more important. We let everyone know that we would hold a Bible study on Thursday nights at one of the empty meeting rooms at the team hotel. When I told the guys what I was doing, a target was attached to my back that said "Christian guy," but I was used to that because I had been that guy my entire career at Tech. Bible study attendance was sporadic, but we had between five and fifteen guys show up.

Michelle also held a Bible study for several of the wives in Germany. It felt like our calling to do something for others. We ended up developing deep relationships with some awesome people, and God used us for His glory to bring people to Him as we grew in our faith as a newly married couple. I couldn't have asked for a better beginning with my new bride.

The main reason I said yes to playing NFL Europe, besides getting a cleated foot into the door of pro football, was that playing overseas earned me an automatic tryout with the New Orleans Saints. In other words, I was one of the ninety players invited to training camp who could win a spot on the fifty-three man roster.

We came back from Europe in June 2007 and moved into a bedroom above my uncle's garage in the Sandy Springs area. We were in a holding pattern since the Saints' training camp started in July, and who knew what was going to happen. The free rent was nice, and so was not living as a married couple with my older brother and Mom. I spent every day lifting weights and running at Georgia Tech in preparation for training camp. I knew this would be my last shot at playing professional football.

I wouldn't find this out until later, but what the Saints organization was trying to do was pick up guys with character. Sure, they wanted players who had talent—extraordinary athletes who could run like the wind, make open-field tackles, and catch anything tossed their way—but they also wanted players who weren't part of the police blotter the next morning. That was General Manager Mickey Loomis and Head Coach Sean Payton's philosophy, and they were trying to build a solid team around players with character and leadership from the ground up.

Keep in mind that this was 2007, a time when New Orleans nearly lost the Saints after Hurricane Katrina caused widespread devastation and breached numerous levees in late August 2005, precipitating one of the worst natural disasters in U.S. history. Because the Superdome was heavily damaged by Katrina, there was talk that the team would move to San Antonio, Texas. The NFL and then-Commissioner Paul Tagliabue, however, were in favor of keeping the team in New Orleans. Even though the Saints were staying put, the team had to play their 2005 home games in San Antonio and LSU's Tiger Stadium in Baton Rouge,

Louisiana. With a 3-13 record, team morale was at a record low.

Team owner Tom Benson, aiming to turn things around for the franchise, made two bold moves in 2006: he hired Sean Payton, the former assistant head coach for the Dallas Cowboys, as their new head coach; and he acquired former San Diego Chargers quarterback Drew Brees through free agency.

What a turnaround for the Saints, whose emotional return to the Superdome lifted the spirits of New Orleans fans who were still rebuilding their city. The 2006 team played great and reached the NFC Championship game—just one game away from the Super Bowl—before losing to the Chicago Bears.

The attitude in training camp was that this was a team fully capable of reaching and winning the Super Bowl, something that had never happened in Saints history. The attitude of the players toward *me* was light-years different than my experience with the Falcons. Though not forward by any means, guys were more welcoming, and I could tell the culture of the team was something I wanted to be a part of.

Some of the guys were upfront about their faith. I'm sure there were a few "camp Christians" among the group—players who were trying to make the team and attending Bible studies because they were hoping God would bless them for being there and help them make the team. Rub the genie, and all that, but at least they were trying.

I certainly needed God's help to make the team. I was pretty beat up coming into camp since I only had a five- or six-week break from NFL Europe, but I knew this was my final chance. I held nothing back and went all out.

I knew that part of my problem in Atlanta was that I didn't get a chance to get in there and show my stuff. This time around, I wouldn't make the same mistake. I would work proactively to show the coaches what I could do.

Once again, like my freshman year at Georgia Tech, I went full speed all the time on the practice field. When I was playing on the "look" squad, going up against the first team punt or first team receiving squad, the other players didn't like it when I lined up across from them. They knew me as the "try hard" guy.

I had vets get irritated with a young guy like me. *Dude, slow down. This is practice. Stop trying to be an All-Pro on the scout team.*

No way I was taking my foot off the gas. I didn't care if the veteran players thought I was trying to show them up. I wasn't there to make them look good—I was there to make the Saints team and glorify my God by giving everything I had on every play.

For me to win a roster spot, I knew my best chance was to show the Saints that I was an exceptional special teams player. I started that quest by being more physical than my opponent, demonstrating my toughness and relentless effort. To be a dominant player on special teams, you have to have the heart of a lion with a few screws loose in the head to make you dangerous. You can't be scared to throw your body around, and the coaches quickly found out that I wasn't backing down or shying away from any contact or challenge.

There were some great players ahead of me in training camp. I had ten- and twelve-year vets in front of me, guys who had made a strong name for themselves in the NFL. I was probably the sixth safety on the depth chart. There was no reason I was supposed to make that team.

Sometimes it takes one play to make the players and coaches take notice, and I remember one play in training camp that made me stand out. We were doing a run defense drill called the "inside drill"—just linemen, offense and defense, and the quarterback and running back and safeties and linebackers. No wide receivers or cornerbacks. Just the inside box.

Michael Peterson, a third-round pick and a rookie, was the running back. He took the handoff and looked like he was shot out of a cannon as he exploded toward the line of scrimmage on a stretch play to the left. I did the same sprinting downhill, and when the fullback kicked out the defensive end, I spotted a hole opening up. I knew Peterson would run to daylight when the bodies cleared. I came in at full speed, flying in there, and knocked him off his feet behind the line of scrimmage. The Torpedo destroyed the play.

Everybody went crazy. The defensive coach came over, smacked my helmet, and yelled out, "That's what I'm talking about!"

Peterson was a third-round pick, and I was a nobody. He was supposed to run me over, but I blasted him. At the end of preseason, he got cut. It's extremely unusual to see a team cut a third-round pick, but the Saints only wanted the best players regardless of their draft status.

Now I was on the coaches' radar. They started putting me in more and more. And I started making plays, intercepting balls on 7-on-7 drills and doing things on special teams where they were like, *Wow, this guy is not backing down. He's 100 percent every play.*

Halfway through camp, the Saints general manager, Mickey Loomis, approached me one afternoon. "I really like the way you play, Chris," he said. "Don't think that we're not noticing."

I could barely feel my cleats touching the ground. *Maybe I have a chance to make the team. That would be pretty cool.*

NFL teams play four preseason games. Even though I didn't get on the field much for the first three games, I played decently on special teams, so I made the first cut from ninety to seventy-five players. Before the fourth and final preseason game, one of my coaches told me, "You're going to be playing a lot in the second half because we're sitting our starters. You'll be playing with the third team, so be ready."

We were playing the Miami Dolphins in New Orleans on Thursday night, August 30, 2007. I remember the date well because it was my dad's birthday.

Mike

I drove down for the game, which was a great way to celebrate my forty-ninth birthday. I couldn't believe the Superdome was full, but there were more than 68,000 fans there for a preseason game. I could tell that New Orleans loved their Saints.

Chris

I didn't get a chance to play a ton in the first half, but in the second half, I finally got in on defense.

On the first series, the tight end ran a 7 route, which is running ten yards and then breaking toward the sideline but in a diagonal manner. I read the quarterback perfectly, jumped the route, got the pick but didn't score, and Saints fans went crazy. It was my first interception in an NFL game, so I gave the ball to the equipment guy to hold for me as a souvenir.

Five minutes later, I got my *second* pick—making a tough catch on a throw that was tipped up, forcing me to acrobatically dive and cradle the ball in my arms just before the pigskin hit the ground. Yeah, that's right, my second one. I couldn't believe it either. The interception was challenged by the Dolphins but held up under review.

I jogged to the sidelines, carrying my second INT ball. I

remember Charles Grant, the first-string defensive end, boisterously yelling out, "This boy is making the team! This boy is making the team!"

I led the Saints in tackles with six solo tackles—playing just one half. I was all over the field and nearly picked off another pass in the fourth quarter but dropped the ball. When the game was over, I knew I had done the best I could. I retrieved my first interception ball from the equipment manager and jogged over to the stands, where Dad was waving to me.

"Happy birthday, Dad! I love you," I said, handing him the ball.

Mike

I told you he was a great kid. His thoughtful gesture was icing on the birthday cake, as far as I was concerned.

Chris

The next day was an off day. Final roster cuts came the following day. What a hard time that was, sitting in my hotel room all day long, waiting for that dreaded phone call that Coach wanted to see me and bring my playbook.

As the hours passed, my hope of making the roster started to rise until the phone rang at 4 p.m. One of the defensive coaches was on the line. I held my breath.

"Why don't you come over to the facility, Chris. Coach wants to talk to you."

Dang it. Once again, I'm getting cut.

At least I was getting an audience with the head coach before being let go. My mom always told me that if you can look at yourself and say you did the best you could at the end of the day, then you should have no regrets. I had no regrets. To end my

NFL career with a game like that, I knew I would be okay.

I shuffled into Coach Payton's office and sat down in an over-sized leather chair, feeling very nervous. It was just me and him.

"Chris, you had a pretty good game on Thursday night."

"Yes, sir," I said proudly.

"You definitely have some ball skills. You did pretty good."

"Thank you." I didn't know what else to say.

"I have some good news and some bad news. The bad news is that we're going to cut you. The good news is that we're going to pick you up on the practice squad."

My face brightened. "Thank you."

It may not seem like it, but this was good news, as far as I was concerned. I was still part of an NFL team, and my dream of playing in the NFL was still alive. Each NFL team was allowed to keep eight non-roster players on their practice team.

"So this is how it works. After we cut you, you'll get put on waivers. If no one picks you up off the waiver wire, then you'll become part of our practice team."

I cleared waivers. Nobody picked me up. I signed onto the practice squad, which wasn't as glorious as you might think. All you do is practice. You can't play in games, although you can stand on the sidelines. You don't get paid a ton of money, relative to the NFL, but it was a step in the right direction.

The night before the second game of the 2007 season, Michelle and I were praying together before we went to sleep. For some reason God opened up my heart that night. "God, whatever You do, just use me," I prayed. "It doesn't matter what I do—a school janitor or a team grunt or a Pro Bowler. If You want, cut me right now and have me be a garbage man. Just use me for Your glory."

That was a bold prayer for me. A lot of times His will for our lives doesn't match up with what we want in life, but I wanted to surrender my plan so He could use me the way He saw fit. The scary part of this prayer was not knowing where He was going to take me next, but I wasn't worried because I knew He would be with me. I finished my prayer by saying, "Lord, I accept Your will. I'm content with where I am right now. And I thank you."

The next day, Jay Bellamy, the guy in front of me, went down. On Monday morning, Coach Payton called me into his office. "Jay hurt his ankle in yesterday's game. We're going to pull you up to the active roster this week."

Two days later, September 19, was my twenty-fourth birthday, and I was stoked that I would be playing in my first official NFL football game. I did all I could that week in preparation for our Monday Night contest—on national TV—against the Tennessee Titans.

I was in every team meeting, paying attention, taking notes. I was focused. I knew my assignments. I wanted to prove to myself and everyone else that I deserved to be in the NFL and that I could play.

I played what we call the "core four" against the Titans—the four special teams: kickoffs, kickoff returns, punts, and punt returns. I made my first NFL tackle on a punt play, nailing return man Chris Davis for no gain at their 18-yard line.

The coaching staff was pleased with my performance, but let me tell you, the game sure felt a lot faster than preseason. The players were faster and stronger, and everything zipped by. Honestly, it took me a few plays to get into the flow of the game. They don't call it "NFL game speed" for nothing.

I enjoyed participating in the "prayer circle" at midfield following the game, a way of publically professing what we stand for in a subtle way. Players from both teams came together and got down on one knee for a prayer of thanksgiving.

One of Michelle's friends was in the stands that game, and she had brought some people with her. Before the game, Michelle's friend told the people with her about how she knew Michelle and me, and that I played for the Saints. Following the game, they watched as I went to the prayer circle and knelt down with some other players. One of the women with her asked, "What are they doing down there?"

"Chris is praying with the other players," Michelle's friend explained.

That gave her an opening to talk about how I became a Christian and why Christ was important to me.

When Michelle's friend emailed us that story after the game, I was reminded how God can use us in the smallest ways to effect change, and people were watching every move I made even when I didn't realize it. I sure could see where it tied into the "use me, God" prayer.

I ended up playing in every game for the rest of 2007, making about a tackle a game and being a solid contributor on special teams.

I had beaten the odds—an undrafted free agent making the NFL. That's why it had to be a God thing.

Something special was happening, and I couldn't wait to find out what would happen next.

16

Amazing Grace

Mike

Shortly after Chris became engaged to Michelle in the spring of 2006—but before I moved out of my house—I enrolled in a divorce recovery program at North Point Community Church to help me deal with all the turmoil in my life. This program, known as Oasis, ran from April to August in 2006.

There were over one hundred of us who met on Wednesday nights at the church. We'd watch videos on a number of different topics to learn what the Bible had to say about marriage and divorce, forgiveness, the impact of divorce on children, financial management, and dating and sex after divorce. When the videos were over, we'd break up into small groups to discuss what we just viewed.

Most everyone became close friends very quickly because invariably the discussions would swing around to *your* story of how you ended up in a divorce recovery program. Many of our sessions became quite emotional as we took turns describing difficult memories. These were our painful stories of breakups and betrayals. Every story was incredibly personal and tearful. Although I didn't share *one-tenth of* the gory details about my complicated marriage to Donna, even that small amount made me totally transparent to others in the Oasis.

One of the women in our group was named Celia. I couldn't help but notice this very attractive woman with dark hair, big, beautiful brown eyes, and a smile that lit up the room whenever she entered. I wasn't surprised to learn later on that she had been a model for a brief time after college.

Celia arrived late to our first small group session and made a lasting impression on me. After she shared her story, I thought, *That's exactly the type of woman I should be with, but that will never happen because she's so nice, so sweet, has great values, and is a Christian. She would never want to be with someone like me. But someday, that's the type of woman I would like to have a relationship with.*

The short version of her story was that she had been married for twenty-two years and was the mother of two daughters named Lauren and Michelle. Lauren attended Samford University in Birmingham, Alabama, while Michelle was a junior in high school. Celia's husband was a loud, overbearing but ambitious and successful executive. He had a history of having affairs, and he ultimately had a fling with a woman twelve years younger than Celia who worked for him at his company. Celia discovered the tryst when she happened to go through his text messages one night. When she confronted him, he confessed, moved out, and ultimately married the young woman that he was having the affair with just a few months later.

When I shared my story during our first meeting, I talked about how I was trying to sell my house by owner—a FSBO, as they call it the real estate industry. Celia was getting back into the real estate business because she would soon be divorced and needed a way to support herself.

Afterward, she approached me. "You know, it's almost

impossible to sell a house by owner. If you need any help or advice, please let me know."

I appreciated how she had my best interests at heart, although I tease her today about fishing for a listing. Anyway, I enjoyed her company, but like the no-dating rules between FCA staff and students on the Georgia Tech campus, those in the Oasis recovery program were not allowed to date each other.

I had no trouble with that rule, but toward the end of Oasis, my mind began playing with a few *what ifs*—what would it look like if I asked Celia out? I did like her and wanted to get to know her better.

When our meetings ended each week, it wasn't uncommon for a few of us to get together over coffee. Perhaps it was because we needed the mutual support, but I suspected my new friends were just like me. Who wanted to go home to an empty house, or in my case, to a leather couch in a cold basement? So our group—Sandy, Celia, Teresa, Tim, Alan, and me—would descend upon the local Starbucks in Alpharetta and talk about what was going on in our lives and what God was doing to get us through these troubling times.

I was still drinking at the time—nothing had really changed on that front except I didn't drink as many nights as I used to. But I could still tie one on. Toward the end of the program, I happened to go out with Tim on a Saturday night. As we enjoyed our cocktails at The Tavern at Phipps Plaza, I asked, "Tim, are you dating anybody?"

"Well, I had a date for twenty-four hours."

"What do you mean, twenty-four hours?"

"I mean I had a date with Celia when Oasis is over, but she already canceled on me."

Okay, Tim liked Celia. That made two of us. I said to myself,

I'm going to back off. Tim's interested in her, and I don't want to compete with a friend. For once, I was thinking of someone other than myself.

On another occasion, our Oasis group went out for Teresa's birthday. We started with dinner at Garrison's Broiler and Tap and then moved over to a nearby dance club. I had a few drinks, but Celia only ordered a single glass of wine. We got to talking that evening, and she said that while she liked a nice glass of wine to accompany a meal, she was leery of drinking. She also shared that her father was a major alcoholic who had sexually abused her, and the man she married turned out to be a big, big drinker, which caused him to verbally abuse her.

When no one was listening, she leaned over in my direction and said, "I have to ask you something. Are you a player?"

I knew Celia wasn't throwing that question out there to determine whether I was going to make a move on her—or *wanted* me to sweep her off her feet. I think she had an inkling about my past. A woman's intuition.

"What do you mean, *Am I a player*? Of course not. I'm a nice guy. Why are you asking?"

"I don't know. Probably because you've been with a lot of women."

Celia had heard about my two marriages, and I may have mentioned something about having a number of affairs.

"But all that's in the past. I've changed since coming to know Christ," I said.

I don't know if I convinced her, but she didn't probe any deeper.

Understandably, drinking wasn't her scene. Consequently I backed off on my alcohol intake out of respect for her background. I didn't stop drinking completely, but I turned down the volume or tried to hide it from her. On subsequent occasions when we went out in a group situation, I might have one or two vodkas with club soda, but I could control my drinking for the most part. Sometimes I drank nothing when we socialized with Oasis friends.

I asked Celia out on a date toward the end of September 2006, a few weeks after the Oasis program ended. At the time, I thought it would be okay to get back into circulation since Donna and I had been estranged since January and our divorce papers were with the lawyer. I had already moved out of my home to complete the separation. My marriage was over. It was a matter of crossing the t's and dotting the i's.

Celia said yes when I asked if she'd like to go out to dinner with me. I could tell that she had high standards. High values. High morals. Believe me, I treated Celia like we were seventh-graders at a cotillion.

She wore a beautiful black evening dress, and I wore a black suit with an open collar blue shirt. Her daughter Michelle took our picture to commemorate our first date. I escorted her to the Capitol Grill in Buckhead, a very nice upscale restaurant in a mid-rise with an eighth-floor view of downtown Atlanta. Five star all the way.

The entire night, she barely ate any of the lemon-roasted boned-in chicken she ordered. I could tell she was just too nervous to eat. After dinner, we went to Hal's, a high-end steakhouse with a piano bar. When I asked if she would like a glass of wine, she said that would be lovely, and I did the same. We sipped our merlots and danced to several Frank Sinatra songs that I requested.

I looked into those sparkling eyes of hers as we danced to the Sinatra classic *All the Way*, and she looked into mine, and I kissed her. It was very sweet and very innocent.

My divorce was finalized on December 6, and we continued to date in a virtuous manner. Sometimes I'd go to her place and watch some TV with her and Michelle along with her three dogs. When Lauren was home from school, we'd sometimes all go out for dinner and a movie. Celia and I took a Bible study class together at North Point, and on Thursdays it wasn't uncommon for us to go to church to sing worship music.

When Chris and *his* Michelle married in February 2007, I invited Celia as well as a couple of my Oasis mates to the wedding. There were certainly some awkward moments with *two* ex-wives at the wedding and the reception, but I tried to keep everything on the down low between us. The family wedding was a very stressful event to say the least.

There was no alcohol at the reception, which I certainly understood. This was Chris and Michelle's wedding, and adding alcohol to the budget would have greatly increased the cost as well as the chance for inappropriate behavior. When the reception broke up around 7 p.m., though, I was ready for a couple of drinks to relieve my tension from the day. Some habits die hard.

I was with a group that included Celia; my sister Ellen and her husband, Roger; Alan from Oasis and his girlfriend Linda; and Tim and Sandy, also from Oasis. "Say, why don't we all go down to Goldfish?" I suggested. Goldfish had a hopping restaurant/bar scene, and since I was dressed in a tux, I wanted to drink like I was out on the town on a Saturday night.

We hopped over to Goldfish, and I started having drinks. Lots of drinks. I was drinking vodka martinis as fast as they could pour them. My friends were drinking right along with me, but I was drinking them under the table. Celia was sipping one glass of wine.

Meanwhile, I told the cocktail waitress, *Keep 'em coming.*

This was just like the good old days, which meant I couldn't stay in one place too long. I had to keep moving. "Let's go over to Garrison's," I suggested, which was next door to Goldfish. We departed en masse, and I proceeded to have another three or four martinis at Garrison's Broiler and Tap.

This was the first time that Celia had seen me drink more than a couple. I wish I could tell you how big Celia's eyes were getting, but I was a man on a mission. I was drinking to get drunk.

I piled on with a few more vodka martinis. Now Celia was giving me a hard time, no doubt aware of my dwindling ability to cogitate my thoughts. "Mike, you're drinking too much," she said. She repeated herself several more times. I saw the disapproving look, but my addled mind countered with these thoughts: *I'm nearly fifty years old. I'm a grown man. I have a mother. I don't need another. I'll decide when enough is enough. Nobody is going to tell me how much I can drink.*

When we left Garrison's, Celia made a bold move: she took my car keys and insisted on driving. I grudgingly agreed, but I was furious that I was not behind the wheel, taking care of her by driving her home. Having my cars keys taken away had never happened to me before and was quite humiliating.

That's why we got into our first argument on the drive home. Celia was firm in her resolve. "Look, I went through this with my dad and my ex-husband, and I'm not going to go through this with you," she said.

I stiffened in my passenger seat. "I haven't done anything wrong. I just had a few drinks, that's all." I couldn't understand why she was giving me a hard time. It was not like I was doing this all the time with her.

We ended the evening with her angry at me, and me angry with her. But she wasn't going to change me. I still continued to drink a great deal, especially during ConAgra business trips when she wasn't around. But when we were together, she was like Jiminy Cricket, always watching how much I was drinking. I was self-conscious around her and became annoyed when she invariably said, "Do you really need to be drinking that much?"

I was irritated enough to stop asking Celia to go out for six weeks during the early summer of 2007. We had known each other for a year, and I needed to do some soul-searching. After some reflection, I decided that I couldn't lose a godly woman like her. I needed to have her in my life.

We resumed dating, and things progressed smoothly between us. In September, I asked her to return with me to the Capitol Grill in Buckhead for a special evening. I set everything up ahead of time with a reserved table—sprinkled with red rose petals—next to the plate-glass window with a memorable view of Atlanta. After an exquisite meal, I informed Celia that I had ordered a special dessert that should arrive any—

A waiter set a covered silver plate down in the middle of the table and ceremoniously lifted the silver lid to reveal a one-and-a-half carat engagement ring that I had purchased from Solomon Brothers, the same place Chris had procured the wedding and engagement rings for his wife Michelle.

Celia's eyes widened, and she caught her breath. I got down on one knee and asked her to marry me.

When her eyes teared up and she said yes, those seated around us burst out in spontaneous applause.

If there is anything we learned from the Oasis program, it was the importance of going through premarital counseling before remarrying. We met with two different counselors over a six-week period and also sat down with Bob Cargo, the pastor who married us, on several occasions.

There weren't too many things we didn't cover. Yes, I talked about my pre-Christian times, but I didn't go into details. I told her I participated in some "bad behavior" and had swapped partners. "I'm done with that lifestyle now that I have God in my life," I said. Celia demonstrated amazing grace by overlooking my sordid past and accepting me as the man I had become.

We were married six months later on March 15, 2008, at the Primrose Cottage in the historic district of Roswell. Built in 1839, the old plantation home was a beautiful venue. Our wedding party looked picture-perfect as the men wore stylish black tuxedoes with black vests and ties, while the women wore elegant silky rose red dresses with black trim. My oldest son Mike Jr. was my best man, and Celia's oldest daughter, Lauren, was her maid of honor. Chris and Michelle, along with my son Jack and her daughter Michelle, were also in the wedding. Katy was upset about me getting married again, and while she witnessed the ceremony, she didn't want to be part of the wedding party.

I think the biggest adjustment that I had to make was being married to a smart career woman. Celia was a hard-working, conscientious real estate agent who took phone calls and worked on deals in the evenings and during weekends, while I was used to a wife who gave me 110 percent of her time and attention. That was a source of conflict initially for us, but we eventually worked things out.

Chris

Hanging out and laughing with my older brother Mike at Dad and Celia's wedding, I realized how far our relationship had come. It wasn't easy for him to live in his little brother's shadow, but he always supported me every step of the way while I was at Georgia Tech and throughout my NFL career. That's when our relationship was renewed and we started to become friends again.

Our relationship wasn't perfect, but I saw how he had matured and became an upstanding guy who respected the man I had become. And to tell you the truth, I greatly admired the man he had become too.

Meanwhile, as Dad and Celia settled into their new lives together, I prepared for my second season with the Saints.

A melancholy moment hit me when Michelle and I were driving down the road one spring day. I looked at her and said, "Why am I on the Saints? Why does God have us here?"

I felt as though my dream of playing in the NFL had boiled down to nothing more than collecting a paycheck and going home. I became satisfied with that—but found that lifestyle empty and meaningless. I mean, playing professional football was something I certainly wanted to do and was tremendously exciting, but when the dust had settled and I understood better how tiny the odds had been to claw my way onto the Saints roster as an undrafted free agent . . . something bigger had to be in play here. I had accomplished my dream, but why did God have me in New Orleans playing football?

Michelle and I prayed about this conundrum throughout the off-season, and if nothing else, I felt God had put me there to serve others. When you're held up as a "famous" football player and making a lot of money, it's easy to think that you're God's gift to the world, but I didn't want to buy into that lie.

The Lord reminded me of how ignored I felt when I stepped into the Atlanta Falcons locker room that first summer. I decided that I would make a special effort to reach out to any new players—those who came to the team via trades, the draft, or through free agent signings—and welcome them to the Saints fold any way I could.

I haven't forgotten one free agent who was putting his equipment up in his locker near mine. He was wide-eyed from being in a real NFL locker room and appeared nervous. He was also careful not to make eye contact with the other players because they were conducting the "look test": Did he look like an NFL player? Did he have what it took to beat out others—perhaps you—for a job playing football?

I stepped over to him and thrust out my hand. "Hi, I'm Chris Reis, and I just want to say welcome. If there is anything you need, just let me know."

I know . . . that wasn't the most earth-shattering introduction and doesn't seem like much, but I wanted to get across the idea that I valued him as a person and not just another new face in The League trying to take my job. I wanted to serve, even if that meant going against the "dog eat dog" culture of the NFL.

Mike

During the first week of the 2008 NFL season, I received a phone call from my sister Ellen.

"I have some news about Dad," she said. "He has pancreatic cancer. He's terminal. The doctors gave him six months to live, maybe less."

I sighed. I had not talked to my father very much over the last twenty years—and hadn't seen him in person at all. He was living in Dahlonega, an hour north of Atlanta, with his second family.

That night Celia and I went to a gourmet Mexican restaurant named Pure, where I had a lot to drink. That was my normal reaction to stress or bad news. Celia remembers me saying, "Damn, that son of a bitch. Now he's going to make me care about him."

Two days later on a sunny fall day, I traveled to see my father for the first time in two decades. He was glad to see me, but I was conflicted. In a short amount of time, I thought a lot about forgiveness. I thought about God's amazing grace in my life. How undeserving I was of God's love and forgiveness for my sins over the years. How God had sacrificed His own son, Jesus Christ, to pay for and forgive my sins. How God did that so that I could repair my relationship with Him. That's when I decided that I needed to forgive my father and repair our relationship. I wanted to make things right between us.

And that's what I did, but I also felt led to go the extra mile. I had a lot of flexibility with ConAgra Foods, and I could work from anywhere as long as I was logged onto my computer. For the next six months, I traveled to his home in Dahlonega where I spent a part of almost every day with my father up until the day he died.

I took my Bible with me and tried to have conversations with him about Christ and what that meant. I played a teaching series of sermons from Andy Stanley about death and dying and the importance of accepting Christ before you pass away. He seemed to get some comfort from listening to Andy, but he never expressed his need to receive Christ or showed a desire to know Him better. Dad never acknowledged that he was going to die even though he was wasting away before my eyes.

When my father found out about his cancer, he was a strapping guy of 240 pounds, but by the time his seventy-fourth birthday came around on January 16, 2009, he was probably 120 pounds. We knew he didn't have long.

I had bought him a Saints jersey, and we spent a lot of time talking about football and Chris playing in New Orleans. On Christmas Eve, my dad and his family came over to my house for Christmas. He was so sick that day. He could barely walk, but he wasn't going to miss the only time I had ever invited him over for

Christmas. Dad called me the next day to say thanks. He said he was proud of me and loved me. After I hung up, I wept, thinking about a lifetime of missed opportunities to share moments like this as father and son.

It was during this stressful time with my dad that my drinking escalated and almost ended my third marriage. I would frequently hit my favorite bars like Cabernet and Pure while Celia worked odd hours in real estate. Then I'd try to beat her home so she would be none the wiser.

One evening after a challenging week looking after my dad, I decided to go to Miller's Ale House near North Point Mall on a Saturday afternoon to unwind and watch some football. Instead of my usual routine of coming home before Celia, I lost control of my drinking and had one vodka after another. Then I proceeded to hit at least two other bars, all without calling Celia, before going home.

As expected, Celia was furious. We engaged in a fight of epic proportions that was reminiscent of my stormy days with Donna. When the dust settled, I was begging and pleading with Celia to give me another chance, and I promised to stop drinking. That promise lasted four months until March 2009 when I started drinking again. The way I looked at things, though, I had proven I could stop, which meant I had my drinking under control, right?

My dad was hospitalized at Northside Hospital-Forsyth in Cumming at the end of January. I stayed with him day and night to help make him more comfortable near the end of his life. We watched an exciting Super Bowl duel between Kurt Warner of the Arizona Cardinals and Ben Roethlisberger of the Pittsburgh Steelers in his hospital room, even though he slept through most of the game. He died seven days later on February 7, 2009.

As the oldest of his six children from two marriages, I felt I should deliver the eulogy, especially after spending so much time with him during his last months of life. Searching for something positive to say, I said, "Hard work defined my father's life. A legacy he passed down to all of his children, and a trait that I always admired and respected in my dad."

Then I turned a corner. "My dad and I had a rocky relationship over the years, to say the least. But through the grace of God, we reconnected the last few months of his life. Ours is a story of reconciliation and redemption . . . a story of hope and resurrection. It wasn't until I connected with my Heavenly Father through Christ that I had the strength and courage to reunite with my earthly father near the end of his life. To see him and love him as God does. I know that my dad and I felt so blessed to be together again."

I wish I could have talked more about the afterlife with my father when he was alive, but I wasn't mature enough in my faith to say the right things. He never really made any admission of faith, even at the end, and that was sad for me. Indeed, I was surprisingly upset and shed more than a few tears the day he died. But I had forgiven him for all the neglect and abuse, and he knew that.

Larry Roberts, my best friend and spiritual mentor, said I did exactly what God wanted me to do . . . I was there and that was all I could do at that point.

Chris

I knew Dad did everything he was capable of with his father. The fact that he reconciled with his father—whom I don't remember meeting before he was hit with pancreatic cancer—spoke volumes to me and to the man my dad had become.

After two seasons with the New Orleans Saints, I felt more comfortable with my situation because I knew the guys, knew the coaches, and knew the system. I think the coaches saw me as a player they wanted to mold into their key special teams guy and someone who could play some defense, too.

I was excited to be in that realm, but obviously there are no guarantees in the NFL. I knew I had to look at my situation and play like I was on the bubble and could get cut at any time. If I didn't approach my job that way, if I relaxed and got satisfied, then someone else would take my spot. That was the reality of the NFL.

What helped was discovering that a handful of teammates—five to seven guys—were really living out their faith. Jon Stinchcomb, a veteran offensive lineman and former Georgia Bulldog, was a huge FCA supporter. Heath Evans, our starting fullback, had launched a ministry, the Heath Evans Foundation, to help victims of sexual abuse because his wife had been sexually abused as a child for an entire year by a schoolmate.

And everyone knew that our leader and our quarterback, Drew Brees, wore his faith on his black-and-gold sleeve. There was a team chapel every Saturday night in the team hotel before our games, and Drew would be there every time with his notebook, jotting down thoughts from the speaker. I notice those type of things, and you don't take notes if you're a half-hearted Christian. You take notes because you take your faith seriously, and that's who Drew was.

Like many others, I was extremely privileged to have played under a leader like Drew. Here was a guy who had experienced tremendous success as an NFL quarterback, a guy who had all the money he could ever ask for, a stand-up husband with a great marriage to Brittany, but he was also a super humble person who wanted to serve the Lord. I admired that.

Saints fans certainly admired Drew's leadership and pinpoint passing during the 2009 season. We kept winning and winning and winning . . . and winning some more.

We were 13-0 and looking at a perfect season, but we had the angriest winning coaches ever. The more we won, the more ornery our coaches got. We would win a game by 30 points and in the team meeting on Monday morning, the coaches would be all over our butts, picking us apart and screaming like we had lost the game.

I knew what our coaches were doing: they understood that players have a natural tendency to slack off when they're winning. They knew that wouldn't fly in the NFL. You can't turn on and off effort like a water spigot. You have to put in the work before you play, or you won't be prepared when the whistle blows.

The Dallas Cowboys ended our winning streak, but even after losing the following week, we still had the home field advantage locked up before the final game of the 16-game season. When Coach Sean Payton announced that we were resting our starters in a road game against the Carolina Panthers, I got the word that I'd be starting at free safety.

I was enormously excited to hear the news. Turns out this would be my first—and only—NFL start.

Mike

I was thrilled to hear that Chris would be a starter and play some D—defense. Playing both defense and special teams reminded me of his days back at Roswell High School and Georgia Tech.

Chris

Even though we were defeated by Carolina and lost the final

three games of the regular season to finish 13-3, we got our bye in the first round of the NFL playoffs and prepared to play the Arizona Cardinals.

A few days before the game, Coach Mac—special teams coach, Greg McMahon—called me into his office.

"Chris, we got a few guys injured, and we're going to have you sit out this game."

What? I'm not playing?

The team's decision not to let me suit up felt like a slap to the face. I had played in all sixteen games up to this point, had done really well in my special teams role, and felt like I was an important cog in helping the Saints have the best record in the NFC.

What many people don't know about the NFL is that even though the roster allows 53 players, teams can suit up only 45 players plus one quarterback on Game Day. Depending on the dynamics of the team and the players who are injured or hurt, there are a handful of guys who could be "active" or "inactive" from week to week. The special teams players are usually the "flex" guys when it comes to last-minute adjustments regarding who suits up on Sundays.

I remember being in the locker room before the Arizona game and seeing the standard issue sideline gear—a Saints hat and sweats—hanging in my locker. I was feeling pretty mopey when Steve Gleason, who had recently retired after eight seasons with the Saints as a special teams player, tapped me on the shoulder. Steve was a longhaired white guy like me, and a lot of people compared me to him. (After wearing a high and tight military buzz cut throughout childhood and during my playing days at Georgia Tech, I had let my golden locks grow out to shoulder length while playing for the Saints. Several inches of blond hair stuck out from the bottom of my helmet.)

"You're not playing today?" Steve had a shocked look on his face.

"Nope. Some guys got hurt, and they need my spot." I'm sure that Steve noticed that I was feeling down but trying to stay upbeat and positive for the guys.

"Hey, that used to happen to me all the time. Keep your head up and keep working hard. When you get your chance again, I know you're going to make a big play."

"Thanks, Steve."

Little did I know that Steve would prove to be prophetic sooner rather than later.

We destroyed Arizona, 45-14, in the Superdome and prepared for the arrival of the Minnesota Vikings, led by legendary quarterback Brett Favre. I was fired up when I learned that I would be playing in the biggest game in Saints' history.

Mike

And Celia and I were *super* excited to drive down from Atlanta to witness this historic game. If the Saints won, they would be going to the team's first Super Bowl in franchise history. I picked up on a vibe of enormous anticipation—as well as nervousness—from the Saints fans sitting around us inside the Superdome.

The game was extremely close the entire way. At 28-all, Minnesota had a chance to win the NFC championship late in the fourth quarter. On a third-and-fifteen from the Saints' 38-yard line, I watched Favre roll to his right to escape the rush. He had open real estate in front of him and might have run for a first down—or gotten the Vikings a lot closer for a field goal attempt—if he kept churning those forty-year-old legs of his.

Instead, he stopped and threw "backside"—or to his left and back across the field—into coverage. Saints defensive back Tracy Porter saved the day with an interception. Overtime!

Chris

We won the coin toss to start sudden-death overtime, and I was part of the kickoff return team. I helped block and create space that allowed our return man Pierre Thomas to make a 40-yard return to the New Orleans 39-yard line. With a shorter field, Drew went to work and got us down to the Minnesota 22-yard line, setting up a 40-yard field goal attempt by Garrett Hartley.

On the sidelines, several us kneeled down and held hands, just hoping and praying this would be our chance. Holding my breath, I watched as Garrett knocked the ball cleanly through the uprights. Pandemonium broke out. I rushed out onto the field in an explosion of joy that I'd never felt on a football field. *We're going to the Super Bowl!*

I had dreamed about this moment, but I never expected it to come true in my wildest dreams. As confetti landed in my hair, I enjoyed one of the best moments of my life.

Mike

When that field goal won the game, people around me were crying. Real tears. I had never seen so much emotion in one place. Fans boogied in the aisles as confetti circulated in the air. I'm sure the heart-stopping win set off celebrations on Bourbon Street. Locals never could have imagined this happening when their city was underwater after Katrina blasted through.

One of my first thoughts was the same as Chris': *We're going to the Super Bowl!* No way that Celia and I would not be there to see my son play in the biggest game of the season on the biggest stage.

The next few weeks would encompass some of the highest and lowest points of my life. I would get to see my son recover that onside kick to start the second half of the Super Bowl against the Indianapolis Colts, which was a thrill of a lifetime for this football father. Then two weeks after the Super Bowl victory, I was bailing myself out of a holding cell at the Forsyth County Sheriff's Department, where I had been booked for driving under the influence of alcohol.

I had wrestled a number of my addiction demons to the ground before marrying Celia—extramarital sex, codependency, Internet porn, spending money I didn't have, and working too many hours. But there was one more battle I had yet to win—my tug-of-war with alcohol.

It was time to dig my heels into the ground and win this war for my soul.

Once and for all.

17

Sweet Surrender

Mike

I'll never forget the date: February 21, 2010.

I'll never forget that it was a Sunday morning. It's easy to remember these things when you're standing outside the Forsyth County Sheriff's Detention Center in the predawn chill, waiting for a cab to take you home.

The dozen vodkas on the rocks—or whatever the final tally was—had finally worn off. I was sober now—or at least clear-headed enough to experience an overwhelming sense of shame. My arrest was bad news, and it was all my fault. I thought about how much this DUI was going to hurt Celia. *Would I lose her?* That was well within the realm of possibility.

Other disturbing thoughts unnerved me. *What will my family think? What will Chris think?* Four-and-a-half years earlier, I had a conversion experience that rocked my life, but how could I claim to be a Christian now? Was getting drunk, weaving across lanes, and endangering others how a Christian should act?

I felt self-condemnation for letting God down and dishonoring Him with my behavior. I had also let down those people who meant the most to me—my family.

I arrived home around 4 a.m. to an empty house. Celia

wouldn't be home from her Keller Williams business trip in New Orleans until Monday afternoon. I fell into bed and slept for a few hours. The first thing I did when I woke up late Sunday morning was call a friend of mine named Dennis.

"Listen, I got pulled over last night and charged with a DUI," I said. "My car is in the impound yard in Gainesville, and I was wondering if you could drive me up there so I can get my car."

Dennis showed how good a friend he was by not asking me for all the details about how my car ended up being impounded on a Saturday night. "Sure, I'll come over to the house," he said. "Expect me in about an hour."

That gave me enough time to grab a shower and get cleaned up. While hot water cascaded over me, more regret and remorse overwhelmed me. I knew I had to finally surrender every part of my life to God. To stop drinking once and for all. To live a life that my family and I could be proud of.

I stepped out of the shower and toweled off. Up to this point, I hadn't trusted God enough to give Him full control of my life. I had been holding on tight to some areas of my life. But this time, I *had* to let go—and give God complete control.

Once again, it was as if God was speaking to me directly when I heard His voice in my heart. He promised to take care of me, but only if I surrendered my entire life to Him. He said it was time to put all of my faith and trust into His hands. That's when I dropped to my knees and prayed with all my might . . . heart and soul.

"Father God, please forgive me for my behavior. I confess that I have sinned against you, and that I have a drinking problem. Lord, I ask You to remove my desire to drink. Please, Father, give me the strength and wisdom to know what to do next in this area of my life. I ask You to help me become the man that You intend me to be."

I feel compelled to explain to the reader that it wasn't the experience of the DUI that inspired me to quit drinking. Nearly everyone who gets a DUI decides to quit drinking, or at least make a major change in the way they handle alcohol. Many do, at least for a little while. There had been times when I said I would never drink again, but those oaths evaporated like puddles from an August thundershower.

This decision to stop drinking felt much different to me. I thought about Chris' recovery of the onside kick in the Super Bowl. Millions of people around the world watched as the refs pulled players off that pile, but it wasn't the fame and the glory of making that play that impressed me most. No, what impacted me was knowing what it took for Chris to be at the bottom of that pile.

Chris' onside kick recovery was a culmination of his life's work up to that point. The obstacles he overcame as the son of a single parent mom and a father with multiple addictions, the sacrifices he made to better himself on and off the field, and the way he cast aside immediate satisfaction for long-term dreams made him what he had become—a great young man and a successful football player in the NFL. The way Chris had lived his life, and what that play represented, inspired me to make a major change in my life to become sober.

But I also knew that Chris didn't make that play alone. He needed ten other guys on that field to make the onside kick successful, so if I was going to make a "recovery" from my drinking problem, I needed some players on my team, starting with my family.

In the quiet of that Sunday morning, I resolved never to drink again. I had to stop *now*. No halfhearted measures. No "weaning" myself from drinking. No trying to control my intake. I had to stop completely—cold turkey. I resolved within my heart that February 20, 2010, would be the last time I had an alcoholic drink.

When Celia arrived home late Monday afternoon, I nervously asked if she could have a seat on the living room couch. I took her hand into mine. "Something happened while you were gone, and I need to tell you about it," I said earnestly.

I could see the register of shock on Celia's face. I'm sure her first thought was that I had cheated on her, so I quickly laid those concerns to rest. "Around 11:30 Saturday night, I was driving home from the birthday party after making a couple of other stops, and I got pulled over for swerving into the emergency lane just before our exit. I was taken in for drunk driving and charged with a DUI. I was released Sunday morning."

I stopped there and took in a breath, which gave Celia a moment to respond. "I'm actually glad this happened," she said, "because getting caught is the best thing that could have happened to you."

"I know. That's why I've made the decision to stop drinking. I can't go on like this. I now realize that after God, you are more important to me than anything else on Earth, and that includes drinking."

Now it was Celia's turn to catch my undivided attention. "I'm glad to hear that because I don't know if our marriage can survive if you keep on drinking."

So there it was—all the cards were on the table. If I needed any more incentive to stop, I had just heard it.

I was focused on making immediate changes once and for all. I promptly scheduled an appointment with a therapist referred to me by North Point Community Church named John Pruett. Next I decided to attend Alcoholics Anonymous meetings in Cumming several times a week.

These AA meetings helped me prioritize what's important in my life. I realized that if I picked up a drink, I was saying that alcohol was more important to me than my wife, my family, my job, and my friends. But more importantly, I was saying that a drink was more important to me than God, and that was absurd. I didn't believe that drinking was a sin. All I knew was that my drinking couldn't be controlled and invariably led me to sin.

The next thing I started doing was meeting with my wonderful friend Larry Roberts to study the Bible. Every Monday morning at 7 a.m. before our workday began, he and I would get together at a nearby Starbucks to study God's Word and strengthen our walk with the Lord. We started diving into the Word by doing a John MacArthur study on the Gospel of John before moving on to other books of the Bible like Romans and Revelations.

Larry epitomized what it means to be a real Christian man, and I looked up to him as a mentor and friend . . . my best friend. He was a man of God who didn't buy into society's lies and its definition of what it takes to be a real man. Larry lived out his faith by his actions as a husband, father, spiritual leader of his household, and a servant of God.

The next thing I did was disclose my drinking problem to everyone important in my life, starting with my entire family. I never referred to myself as an alcoholic, though. Instead, I said I had a "drinking problem." I don't like using labels, and when most people hear the term "alcoholic," they think of a homeless person huddled under a freeway overpass, clutching a bottle of Ripple in a brown paper bag. They don't think of an alcoholic as a high-functioning member of society, but that was me.

One by one, I met with everyone in my family, starting with my mother. I remember going over to her house and telling her, "Mom, I just want you to know that I've got a drinking problem, and I've decided to stop drinking."

"You don't have a drinking problem," she responded with a bit of irritation. She wouldn't accept the notion that *her* son could do anything wrong or couldn't control his alcohol intake. "I've never seen you act badly or drink too much. I know you like to have a drink every now and then, but I never thought you had a problem."

"Thanks, Mom, but I've apparently done a good job of hiding my drinking from you and everyone else I know. Believe me, I have a problem, and I've decided to do something about it."

I received a similar reaction when I told other family members as well as close friends about my drinking problem. They all said they knew I liked to relax and have fun with a few drinks, but they never thought I had an issue with alcohol. I did my best to set them straight.

I also made the decision to disclose my drinking problem to my colleagues at ConAgra Foods as well as customers that I had known for many years. Again, many found it impossible to believe that I had a serious drinking problem. I think some people, especially my old drinking buddies, just didn't want to admit that they may have a problem, too.

I did not, however, disclose my DUI to upper management at ConAgra Foods for one simple reason . . . I was afraid that I could lose my job. I knew that I wasn't legally bound to do so: I wasn't driving my company car at the time, and I wasn't on company business because the incident occurred on a Saturday night. What happened was a personal and private matter as far as I was concerned.

During the first few weeks after receiving my DUI, Celia was skeptical but supportive. Celia had seen me stop drinking before, but there were always relapses—sometimes within a few days.

I knew I had to back up my words with actions, and that

meant NO DRINKING. A week passed by, then two weeks. I leaned on God and my faith to get me through the tough times of my psychological addiction to alcohol.

Anyone can stop drinking; people do that every day. Abstinence in and of itself doesn't guarantee a better life. Permanent sobriety can be achieved when you create a life so valuable to you that you never want to risk that by taking another drink again. Abstinence just gives you the opportunity to create such a life.

That's why I kept plugging away, day by day, week by week, striving to live intentionally for God and do the right thing each and every day. By the time my DUI case went to court in August 2010, I had a solid six months of sobriety under my belt.

When I appeared before a judge in county court, I felt it was time for me to assume responsibility for the bad choices I had made in my life—to man up and accept whatever was coming my way. I pled guilty with no fanfare.

Even though this was my second DUI, it was considered a "first offense" because my first DUI happened more than ten years before this incident. My first-time offender sentence was still harsh:

- I was fined $1,200 and given twelve months of probation and random drug and alcohol testing.
- I was ordered to take a nineteen-hour alcohol risk-reduction class over a long weekend.
- I was ordered to perform sixty hours of community service work.
- I was sentenced to four days in the county jail. This could be reduced to two days if I met their requirements of reporting to jail on time and good behavior.
- I was ordered to place a Breathalyzer device on my car for six months.

Regarding the last directive, I had the authorities place the

Breathalyzer device on my company car because I didn't want Celia to have to blow into it every time she wanted to start the car—or keep blowing while she was driving.

A little known fact that readers may find interesting is the Breathalyzer device will periodically sound an alarm when you're behind the wheel and moving down the road, which means you must immediately pull over and blow into the device. Failure to do so within six minutes of hearing the alarm will notify authorities and keep the engine from starting again once the car engine has been turned off.

The reasoning behind this is to stop you from having a friend blow into the device to start the car, and then you getting behind the wheel while you're under the influence. I didn't want Celia to have to deal with that humiliating action when driving her vehicle.

I hid the Breathalyzer device from ConAgra for six stress-filled months. When someone in management came in from out of town to work with me or visit a customer, I would meet him or her at the hotel, a Starbucks, or the appointment location. I would never make myself available to pick anyone up at the airport, citing a conflict in my schedule.

If I was concerned that a manager or a colleague would want to travel together by car, I would take my wife's vehicle or rent a car and say mine had broken down and was at the dealership for service. I was *that* concerned one of my bosses would find out, and I would be fired.

For my community service, I worked with a program called SafeRide America. Someone who had been drinking on a Friday or Saturday night could call SafeRide to dispatch someone out to drive him home in his car. I was the "chase driver" who chauffeured a SafeRide employee to the bar or party. He'd get out, find the person who called for help, and then drive his car home while I followed in my car.

These grueling shifts usually lasted from 8 p.m. to 6 a.m., and it was eye-opening to see how people behave when they're drunk, especially when you're not. I had always experienced the other side of that situation.

Staying up all night with SafeRide, though, was a picnic compared to the time I spent in jail. Three weeks after receiving my sentence, I reported to Forsyth Country Jail on a Friday night at 8 pm. It took seven hours to process me.

The experience was so surreal that I felt like I was in a Hollywood movie. Donned in an orange jumpsuit and wearing handcuffs, I was led to a community cell that housed around fifty men. When the prison guards opened the door at 3 a.m., my senses were assaulted by the smell of unwashed, sweaty men sleeping on bunk beds that ringed a communal bathroom in the middle of the large holding cell. Everything was exposed—the toilets, the showers. No privacy.

I felt like there were a million eyes on me as I took the first open bunk—a bed up top. I hauled myself up and didn't sleep a wink. At six a.m., everyone was rousted out of bed for breakfast, which consisted of standing in a long line at the door to the cell and being handed a cafeteria tray with a carton of milk, toast, and some type of oatmeal-looking substance. I imagined that I was in a Dickens' novel being fed gruel.

I had lost my appetite anyway, so I gave my food to my bunkmate, who later informed me that he was a member of the Black Muslims, a term that typically refers to African-American black nationalist organizations that describe themselves as Muslim.

I put my faith out there with the Black Muslim and told him I was a follower of Christ. He smiled and nodded, and then we had a friendly conversation. When I told him that I wished I had a Bible—I wasn't allowed to bring *anything* with me—he said he knew how to get his hands on one. I don't know how God's Word had been smuggled into that holding cell, but my Black Muslim friend did provide me with a Bible, which showed me that God was still working in my life. I had a lot of alone time, thinking and praying. While it was difficult being in that environment, having that time was good for me.

During my stay in jail, I was somewhat concerned for my personal safety and didn't leave my top bunk except to stand in lines for the hideous meals. I didn't eat all weekend, giving my food away to my cellmates. The large holding cell had no windows, was lit with fluorescent lights, and stunk from body odor and toilet smells. Prisoners were not allowed outside to exercise. I found out that some of those incarcerated in that community cell had been there for *months*. I couldn't imagine how they could survive without seeing sunshine or the outdoors.

What really grieved my heart was meeting four or five young men—nineteen to twenty years old—who were in there for taking painkillers like OxyContin and Vicodin and getting pulled over for driving under the influence. They looked like babies. I talked to them about the mistakes they had made and what they could do to turn things around. I also talked to them about God and what it meant to have a relationship with Him.

All I can say is that it was with a huge sigh of relief that I walked out of the county jail after two days, out early because I had met all the requirements. Everything was intact—my faith in God, my marriage to Celia, the support of my family, my sobriety, and my job with ConAgra Foods.

As far as I was concerned, my future was looking good.

Chris

My football future was bright as well. Celebrating in the locker room after the Super Bowl victory, Coach Payton said to me, "Thanks for making me look good."

Coach understood that he made a gutsy call, and if I didn't make that play, then he was a zero instead of a hero. That was the bottom line. Coach took that risk, and it worked out well for the both of us.

Let me tell you, winning the Super Bowl was super fun, and being part of the victory parade through downtown New Orleans was ridiculously awesome. I know what I'm about to say will surprise some readers, but I expected winning a world championship and making an enormous play that changed the momentum of the game to be more than it really was. Instead of filling me up, I felt empty after the confetti had been swept up on Canal Street.

Sure, I wasn't expecting a Super Bowl victory to do this wonderful thing for me or even change my life, but "coming down" after such a big win was an interesting experience. Within days I asked myself, *What do I do next? What's my goal now? Winning another Super Bowl?*

The soul-searching continued through the off-season. When the answers weren't forthcoming, I began asking myself other pertinent questions:

Why did God give me this gift of making a big play in the Super Bowl?

What am I supposed to do with it?

I knew being part of a Super Bowl-winning team was meant for something more. The idea that this could be a jumping-off point to something else stuck in my mind.

Questions also surrounded my father's future because he had just been arrested for driving under the influence. Would he deal with his "drinking problem" once and for all? Could he stay on the wagon?

A DUI is serious stuff, so I was proud of the way he stepped up and decided to never drink alcohol again. But actions are stronger than words, so I knew he had to walk the talk. As weeks of sobriety turned into months, I saw changes for the better in Dad. For a commitment-challenged father, he was finally following through on something he said he was going to do.

I had a great training camp with the Saints as we prepared for the 2010 season. After the final roster cuts, I ended up making the team again, which I was really happy about because there is *no* job security in the NFL.

Coming off a Super Bowl win, the team was still jacked up about the 2010 season. Our first game was at home against the Minnesota Vikings—a rematch of the NFC Championship game nine months earlier.

The day before the game, Coach Payton had told me I was sitting out to make room for another player on the game-day roster. Once again, I was the guy on the bubble as the coaches moved players around like pieces on a chessboard.

I watched from the sidelines as the championship banner was hoisted high above the Superdome rafters while wearing a Saints T-shirt and sweat pants. That stung a bit.

Wow, Coach didn't dress me out. Here you made this enormous play for the team, and one of the reasons they won was because of you, and he didn't let you suit up.

I tried not to take his decision personal, but then I sat out the second game, which *really* discouraged me. I had friends asking me, "Why aren't you out there?"

I also heard that question from fans in the street. Everyone in New Orleans, it seemed like, knew who I was after making that onside kick recovery. That was my fifteen minutes of fame, and now they were wondering why the guy who made one of the biggest plays in Saints history was riding the pine. That was a question I couldn't answer.

Mike

Talk about a bummer. The season opener was a couple of weeks after I served my jail time, and Celia and I came down from Atlanta to celebrate the Super Bowl ceremony with Chris, but he didn't get to play. That just didn't seem right. If it wasn't for Chris' recovery, New Orleans may not have won that game.

Chris

I finally got to suit up for the third game. In Week 4, we were playing the Carolina Panthers in the Superdome with our starting strong safety Roman Harper out with a strained hamstring. When backup Pierson Prioleau injured his chest covering a kick-off in the second quarter, it was my turn to play.

The first five minutes out there, I had three solo tackles. I was playing well and thinking, *Great, this is my chance to show what I can do in a legit game, not an end-of-the-season game where they are resting the starters.*

During the third quarter, I dropped back into coverage and saw Panthers fullback Tony Flammetta flare into the flats, toward the sideline. I moved up to whack him because I could see the eyes of their quarterback, Casey Clausen, looking his way.

I came up, got low, and just as he caught the ball I busted him with a good tackle. At the moment of impact, however, I heard a loud popping sound in my right shoulder, and then an intense pain hit me that was beyond words. I knew something bad had happened, but I had never been one of those guys who stays on the ground. I tried to stumble off the field, holding my arm, but that proved to be impossible. I couldn't move my right arm, and my shoulder had basically slipped down to my armpit. I knew I had dislocated my shoulder.

The Saints trainers rushed out onto the field, and the team doctor confirmed that my shoulder was dislocated. "You're going to have to either lay down, or we have to take you off the field and put it back in," he said. "Your choice."

"Just put it in," I grunted through my mouthpiece.

"Okay, lay down."

I got on the ground and leaned back, and the team doctor stuck his foot in my armpit and yanked as hard as he could on my arm. Never had I felt such excruciating pain in my life, but my shoulder popped back into place. I knew that kind of shoulder injury spelled the end of my season.

The Saints sent me to Pensacola, Florida, where Dr. James Andrews, a renowned sports orthopedic surgeon based in Birmingham, Alabama, had a satellite practice. Well known in the football world as one of the best surgeons out there, Dr. Andrews had successfully repaired the shoulders of NFL quarterbacks Sam Bradford, Colt McCoy, and Drew Brees. After Doc operated on me, he teased me by saying, "I gave you the Drew Brees Special."

Michelle and I moved into a house in Pensacola, and I spent the rest of the 2010 season rehabbing there. However throbbing my shoulder felt during rehab, there was another painful issue that we were dealing with in Florida, and that was infertility.

For two years, Michelle and I had been trying to conceive. Since nothing was happening on that front, we both got checked out. We were fine physically, but I could tell Michelle was struggling, and so was I. At the time, it seemed like all the Saints wives were pregnant—there must have been something in the water—and that put extra stress on us, especially her. Dealing with infertility and a severe shoulder injury made it a tough season of life for us.

We tried intrauterine insemination (IUI), a procedure that involved placing my sperm inside Michelle's womb to facilitate fertilization, but that was unsuccessful. While we were in Pensacola, Michelle—who had been taking hormones to help her produce more eggs—saw a doctor and learned that she had cysts on her ovaries.

Her doctor informed her that she would have to wait until the cysts were gone before starting another round of IUI, and the only way to get rid of them was to take birth control pills for a month. Talk about a deflating, defeating experience. Instead of moving forward, we had just taken a major step backward.

Obviously, we went through this together, and the hurt and disappointment we experienced made us angry at God. We understood that He was in control, but knowing that still didn't make it any easier. My college roommate and best buddy on the Georgia Tech football team, Gavin Tarquinio, came down from Atlanta with his wife, Lindsay, to encourage us. We were sitting around after dinner one evening, talking about our situation, when Michelle blurted out, "I don't think we're ever going to get pregnant. I don't think I'll ever be a mom."

As a man, as a husband, as the spiritual head of the household, hearing Michelle say those words crushed me. Michelle felt called by God to be a mom, but that role didn't appear to be in her future at all.

But we couldn't give up. I remember turning to her and saying sharply, "Don't you ever say that again. Don't you give up on God. We can't give up. We have to trust that He has a plan for our lives."

Sure, we were going through a real struggle, but we had to believe that God was greater and stronger than our infertility problem. He knew exactly what we were dealing with. None of this took Him by surprise.

That night, after Gavin and Lindsay left, we got on our knees. I don't know if we prayed harder, or if we had finally given up control after trying to do it ourselves, but we said, "God, this is on You now. We understand and trust that You have a plan for our lives, even if it's not what we want. No matter what happens, You're still a great God. Your will be done."

It was during the month that Michelle was on birth control that she became pregnant. She took a pregnancy test on Christmas Day in 2010, and we received the best Christmas present ever—a blue line on the stick.

We rejoiced when her pregnancy was confirmed by the doctor. After two years of battling, Michelle and I knew it was a miracle that we got pregnant *while* on the birth control pill. We were overwhelmed with joy and contentment, knowing that we had surrendered to and given Him control of this area in our lives, regardless of the outcome or circumstance, and then seeing His response in the best way.

A few nights later, during the holidays, Dad called. It took everything inside of me not to tell him that he was going to become a grandfather, but I wanted to wait a solid month before sharing the good news—just in case we lost the baby. Dad, meanwhile, had some good news of his own.

"I'm going to get baptized at North Point in a few weeks, and I would love for you to be there," he said. "It'll be on January 23."

"That's awesome, Dad, but I'm not sure if we can make it because I'm rehabbing here in Pensacola. I'll see what I can do."

I could tell he was disappointed, but Dad understood. At the same time, I knew in the back of my mind that I wasn't going to miss his baptism.

Dad had traveled too far for me not to witness this important step in growing his faith.

18

Living for More

Mike

As I rolled into the new year of 2011, I was still on probation and the Breathalyzer device would still be on my company car for another month.

I was feeling like God was calling me to do something more with my life, but at this point, I didn't know what that would be. Meanwhile, Larry Roberts and I started talking about baptism. I made a decision to go public with my love for Jesus, to proclaim my faith, and share my testimony.

Getting baptized at North Point Community Church was an involved and intimidating process that started with an online application and writing out my testimony. Then I met with church videographers to put together a two-minute video of my testimony. My baptism video would be shown to the congregation and thousands of online viewers just moments before I got dunked.

On the day before my baptism, I was out in front of the house raking leaves and cleaning up tree branches from a storm the night before. I knew we were having a lot of people over to the house after my baptism to celebrate, so the place needed to be spruced up. Celia was working hard inside the house to make everything spic and span.

I was raking away when I saw a gray Mustang drive up. *Who the heck was that?*

Next thing I knew, Chris was getting out of the car. I threw my rake down and ran into his arms, crying my eyes out because it meant everything in the world to have him witness my baptism.

"Come on in," I said, and Chris and Michelle followed me into the family room. Michelle was carrying a small gift bag stuffed with pastel paper. They had brought me a little present for my baptism. How thoughtful.

But then Chris said, "This is really for the both of you," which was interesting.

Michelle handed me the gift, which contained a photo frame. It took me a few moments to piece everything together. On the top of the frame was the word "Baby" and on the bottom of the frame was the word "Reis." Inside the frame was a date: September 7, 2011.

It took me a few minutes, but *Oh, I get it!*

Once more, I was overwhelmed, crying and hugging and so happy. Here I was, on the eve of getting baptized and proclaiming that I was reborn into God's family, and then I received the news that there was a new life in our family waiting to enter the world. That was the coolest thing to me.

My baptism was during the 11 o'clock service at North Point, and I had thirty people there supporting me—all of my family and some dear friends. I stood in the baptismal trough dressed in blue gym shorts and a blue T-shirt with a North Point pastor as my video played.

Sitting in a cushioned chair before a black curtain with dramatic lighting, I looked into the camera:

Hi, my name is Mike Reis. Growing up, we attended church twice a year, Easter and Christmas. I went to Sunday school on occasion, and I remember being terrified. I felt unworthy. Condemned. Judged. If this was what church and God were all about, I didn't want any part of it. So I decided to live my life for me and what makes me happy.

I got married in college, had two children, and divorced my wife after seven years because I wasn't happy. My life was a mess. Filled with hurt and pain, I searched to fill the emptiness and loneliness with material things, unhealthy relationships, and alcohol. I married again, had two children, but my pain continued. I was completely lost.

In 2005, my son Chris invited me to an FCA service. I witnessed God's love, and during this service, I felt as if God hugged me and said it was His time now. At the age of forty-seven, I accepted Jesus. I finally had peace and joy through God's love, grace, and His Son, Jesus Christ.

But my life didn't suddenly become perfect. My wife of twenty years decided she wanted a divorce and that led me to North Point Church and Oasis. Today my life is filled with a wonderful Christian marriage, family, and Christian friends, and I live to serve and honor God with my life. I want to thank my son Chris for leading me to Christ and the rest of my children for their love and acceptance.

After the service, a young man visiting our church from Texas approached me. He said it felt like I was speaking to him, and he could relate to my life even though we were decades apart in age. He thanked me for sharing my story and said he had decided to accept Christ that day. Others came up to me and said they learned that it wasn't too late for them to accept Christ and change their lives. (You can watch the video at this link: http://vimeo.com/20580462)

Chris

I probably received five texts from people who said, "Hey, I saw your dad online getting baptized. What a powerful story he shared."

Mike

If this book, *Recovery of a Lifetime*, was a movie, this would be the part where the film fades to black and the credits roll.

And everyone lived happily ever after.

Except things didn't happen that way.

A couple of weeks after my baptism on February 17, 2011, I was leaving the office of my therapist at noon. I got back in my car and started heading from Alpharetta to Cumming when I noticed I had a message on my cell phone. I saw that my boss at ConAgra Foods, who's based in Idaho, had called me. I'm going to call him Terry.

When I returned the call, Terry said, "Mike, you're on the speaker, and you're here with Tom from our HR department." (Tom is not his real name either.)

I wasn't sure why someone from Human Resources was on the call, but I quickly learned why. Tom said, "We routinely pull motor vehicle reports on employees who drive company cars. We found something on your report. Do you know anything about what we found?"

My heart instantly went into overdrive, but I calmly said, "Yes, I do. I got a DUI. "

I confidently proceeded to lay out exactly what happened. That I had gone to a party on a Saturday night, my personal time. That I wasn't driving the company car; I was driving my wife's car. That I was on my way home and got pulled over. That I was booked on suspicion of a DUI. "Because this incident didn't happen on company time and I wasn't driving a company car, I felt it was a private matter and I didn't need to disclose it. Is this a problem? I accept full responsibility for my actions, and I'll understand if I lose my company car."

There was a long silence.

Terry was the next voice I heard. "We need to call you back in a few minutes."

"That'll be fine."

Less than ten minutes later, my cell phone rang while I was heading north up Highway 400.

This time I heard Tom's voice. "This is really serious," the HR person said. "We're going to have to let you go."

Just like that, I was fired from ConAgra Foods. There was no discussion. There was no second chance. I was *totally* shocked at that point because my performance had been outstanding for the last few years. I knew Terry had noticed that I no longer drank at out-of-town meetings or customer functions, and in fact, I had disclosed my drinking problem to him nearly a year earlier. He also knew all the hard work I had done to turn my personal life around.

And yet ConAgra still fired me.

Then there was the matter of the house that Donna and I had owned prior to the divorce. Due to the tremendous drop in real estate values in the greater Atlanta area the last few years, we were under water on the home because of all the borrowing I had done against the house. We were renting out the home since it wouldn't sell.

A few days after I got fired, the hot water tank busted and flooded the basement, resulting in an unexpected $5,000 repair. Then the renters—who had signed a two-year lease—moved out on me when the main breadwinner lost his job.

I was forced to short sale the house for $358,000, but the mortgages I had on it were $444,000. My credit was ruined, and I had to agree to repay $50,000 to the bank before they would approve the short sale.

This was one of the most challenging times of my life. But I chose to react differently. Unlike how I would have handled this type of situation in the past, I didn't let my circumstances control me. I knew that God was in my corner and no matter what happened, I had Jesus Christ and His love for me.

I want the reader to clearly understand that the way I handled these setbacks was much different than the way I had handled adversity in the past. I still retained a sense of peace and joy in my life. But at the same time, I knew the enemy was attacking me after I had been baptized.

Was I upset, even angry at times? Sure, I have human emotions. Was it unfair being fired and losing my old home? Sure, but life is unfair, and I still had to deal with the consequences of my poor decisions and the actions of my past. At the end of the day, though, I knew if I remained faithful to God, He would remain faithful to me.

Faith won out. Within two months of losing my job, I was hired by CTI Foods, a culinary-driven company that provides menu solutions to the foodservice industry, as their director of new business development. Getting a good-paying job at the age of fifty-two within sixty days of losing my position at ConAgra was unheard of, given the poor state of the economy in 2011. I was grateful that in no time at all I was receiving a regular paycheck again.

But I wanted to do more with my life, and as I prayed for direction and purpose, I felt like God was revealing a passion for helping others, especially those struggling with addiction problems. I wanted to make a difference in their lives.

I looked around for opportunities to pursue my passion and decided to enroll in a coach-training program at the World Coach Institute (WCI), where I earned professional coach certifications in addiction recovery and Christian Life. I went on to become a master certified coach and later accepted a position as an instructor for WCI as well. I also decided to become certified to start and lead a SMART recovery group (Self-Management and Recovery Training) in Cumming as another option for people with addictions.

Chris

During the summer of 2011, as Dad was moving into a new part-time role coaching those with addictions, the NFL lockout ended and the players got into training camp. With all the work I had put into rehabbing my shoulder, I felt the effort had been rewarded when the Saints resigned me to a one-year contact. I also had a pretty good training camp.

Midway through our preseason schedule, Piper Mae Reis decided that she didn't want to wait until September 7 to come into the world. She was born three weeks early on August 18, and I got to be in the birthing room at East Jefferson General Hospital near the Saints training facility in Metairie to experience the miracle that is the delivery process. Holding my little girl against my chest, staring into her beautiful brown eyes, I realized that

God just gave me a huge task—being a dad.

At the end of the preseason, though, I didn't know if I would make the final roster. I could tell that I was getting a little older, at least what The League thinks is "old." (I was all of twenty-eight.) I was getting a little expensive for what I do. And I could tell the coaching staff was looking for someone to step up during training camp.

After the last preseason game, Coach Payton called me into his office and asked me to take a seat. The fact that the head coach wanted to see me didn't portend well for my future as a New Orleans Saint. Head coaches cut veterans. Coach Payton got right down to business.

"We're going to let you go," he said. "I appreciate everything you've done for the team and for helping us win a Super Bowl, but we're going in a different direction."

I didn't really have anything to say. The man at the top had delivered the verdict, which was a sign of respect. But I had still been cut from the team, and the news still came as a shock to me.

I thanked Coach for letting me play for him for four years, and he wished me all the best. I went downstairs to clean out my locker and made the rounds, saying goodbye to my assistant coaches.

"What?" said one coach. "I can't believe you got cut. That's crazy." Another assistant told me that when the coaches convened in the team meeting room to discuss who stayed and who got the axe the night before, I was on the final roster.

"I don't know what happened this morning to change Coach Payton's mind," another coach said.

I was just about to leave the Saints training facility in Metairie when I ran into my defensive backs coach, Tony Oden. He was an awesome coach. We had been together since I had gotten there.

We had grown close.

Coach Oden called me into his office, and as I was sitting down, he started to cry. You don't see coaches do that. It's not in their DNA. I started becoming emotional as well. We sat in silence for a few moments, covering our faces and trying to muffle our cries.

Regaining his composure, he took a deep breath. "I want you to understand that I respect you so much as a man," he said. "And I want you to know how you've affected me and my walk with Christ."

His words moved me, but I had never preached to Coach Oden. I had never pulled out a Bible and beat him over the head with it. I was just trying to live out my faith. To have him tell me that how I acted, how I responded to situations, and how I conducted myself day after day in an NFL culture that can eat you up and spit you out and harden your heart, meant a great deal to me. That's the legacy I wanted to leave behind.

I gathered my belongings and left the Saints training facility with my head held high. I was okay with being cut because God had put me in professional football for a purpose. I told myself that this situation was not going to own me. I wasn't angry at anyone. I didn't have any bitterness.

Over the next month, I felt like God was taking me out of the role as a football player and putting me into a far more important role, which was being a father. In a way, being cut was a blessing in disguise because I got to spend a ton of time with Piper during her first few months of life.

During the rest of the 2011 season, I worked out and stayed in shape, but I never got a phone call from another team.

After the season, people were asking me what I was going to do. Some expected me to go into coaching, but I had witnessed firsthand the never-ending amount of hours that coaches have to put in, so the coaching profession didn't appeal to me as a family man.

Besides being a good husband first and a loving father, I didn't know what God was calling me to do.

Then Dad happened to come over for a visit and see how his granddaughter was doing. He said he had been doing some thinking about his legacy and how he wanted to be remembered, and that he had an idea that he wanted to run by me.

"You know Chris, I think we have a great story, both of our lives. What would you think of writing a book together? We could impact a lot of people."

I liked Dad's idea, especially because God had planted that seed two years earlier after we won the Super Bowl. One day while driving home from working out, I felt like God was stirring in me to do something with the famous play He had blessed me with. The soul-searching session continued as an overwhelming wave of silence came over me.

Then it hit me like a ton of bricks. For some unknown reason, I felt like God was calling me to write a book and title it *Recovery of a Lifetime*. But I didn't even know how to write a book—or even what the book was supposed to be about beyond telling my life story.

But when Dad broached the subject with me in early 2012, it was like a light went on. The time was right for us to write *Recovery of a Lifetime*.

Mike

Here's why Chris and I decided to invest a considerable amount of our time, money, and emotional energy to produce *Recovery of a Lifetime*.

The reason I'm sharing my story—and shedding light on my past sins, behaviors, and bad choices—is to glorify the power of God's hand in my life and show you that He can change you from within. I want to inspire you to experience the peace and joy that only comes through God's grace and love.

No matter what you've done in the past, no matter how old you are, you can make a recovery of a lifetime. You don't have to live with the pain, anxiety, and shame of the past. It doesn't matter how old or how young you are, or whether you've done things so bad that you think there's no way God could ever love you, we're here to tell you that it's never too late.

The pattern of generational sin can be broken. Chris is proof of that when he accepted Christ into his heart and began a personal relationship with Him while still in high school. Today, my family's self-serving history of infidelity, domestic violence, alcohol and sex-minded inappropriate behavior is in the past for the both of us, and we're moving through the narrow gate that leads to life instead of the gate that is broad and leads to destruction (Matthew 7:13-14).

I now understand why God led me to read *The Purpose-Driven Life* very soon after I made a decision to follow Christ at Chris' FCA event near the Georgia Tech campus. God was preparing me for my purpose in life, which is to share my story with others to inspire them to make a recovery in their lives.

Chris

Your recovery doesn't have to be as big as my father's or as grand as an onside kick recovery during the Super Bowl. Perhaps it's deciding to put down the iPhone or BlackBerry or turn off the TV when you're spending time with your spouse and children. Perhaps it's going to work a bit earlier so that you can get off in time to see your children's ballgames or share dinner and family conversation together.

When you choose to live for more, it'll be the little things that make a huge difference, and even those little decisions today can and will impact those you love for generations to come.

Mike

I want to leave you with a few verses of Scripture that I hugely identify with. In 1 Timothy 1:12-17 (NIV), the Apostle Paul describes how he, a man who once persecuted Christians but went on to write almost half of the New Testament, was shown grace:

> *I thank Christ Jesus our Lord, who has given me strength, that he considered me trustworthy, appointing me to his service. Even though I was once a blasphemer and a persecutor and a violent man, I was shown mercy because I acted in ignorance and unbelief. The grace of our Lord was poured out on me abundantly, along with the faith and love that are in Christ Jesus.*
>
> *Here is a trustworthy saying that deserves full acceptance: Christ Jesus came into the world to save sinners—of whom I am the worst. But for that very reason I was shown mercy so that in me, the worst of sinners, Christ Jesus might display his immense patience as an example for those who would believe in him and receive eternal life. Now to the King eternal, immortal, invisible, the only God, be honor and glory for ever and ever. Amen.*

Chris

So think about it . . . do you need to make a recovery of a lifetime?

If you do, don't be surprised if you feel like you're at the bottom of a dog pile with a jangle of arms trying to rip that ball out of your hands.

Hold on tight, call out His name, and endure until the whistle blows.

You'll never feel better than when you stand up, lift that ball to the heavens, and give Him the glory.

ACKNOWLEDGEMENTS

Mike Reis

I want to thank God for His amazing grace and love, without which I would not be here today to share my story. Christ freed me from the slavery of sin, and I hope that my life serves as an example to you and demonstrates that it's never too late to become the person God intended you to be.

To my angel on earth and precious wife Celia, thank you for your overwhelming love and support; for having the courage that allows me to publicly shine a light on the sin in my life; for seeing me as the person I am today; and for inspiring me to be a better man. Without you, this book would not have been written. I love you more each day, and I'm so excited to see where God leads us next.

Thank you to my mom, Lois. You were always there for me with open arms and unconditional love. You were the best part of my childhood, and I will be eternally grateful to you for being my oasis in life. Thank you for giving me your strength to battle life's challenges as well as your quick wit and sense of humor. I love you, Mom.

Thanks to all of my children for never giving up on me. You all, as well as my grandchildren, now and in the future, are my reason for writing this book. I'm not proud of my past, but I wouldn't be the man I am today without it. I love you more than life itself. God bless you all.

A special thank you to my cousin, Whitney, for your love, support and inspirational words of encouragement throughout the process of writing this book. I will always cherish the bond we shared as children. I am so proud of you . . . we made it!

To my best friend and brother in Christ, Larry Roberts, thank you for having the most influence on my life of any man on earth. You are my mentor and a true role model of what it means to be a real Christian man. Thank you for living your faith and showing me what it means to be a devoted and loving husband, father and man of God. I love you, my brother.

Thank you to my dear friend of twenty years, Audrey St. Clair, for your love and prayers. You stood by me during the worst times in my life. More than anyone, you've witnessed the miracle of God at work in my life.

Chris Reis

First of all, I'd like to thank God who endlessly pursues me through His son Jesus Christ and is the reason I get out of bed and try to live for more everyday.

To my amazingly strong and beautiful Proverbs 31 wife, Michelle, I love you more than my next breath, and I can't thank you enough for standing by my side and supporting me through this process. I'm so excited to see where God takes us next and so blessed that you're in my life.

To my wonderful little girl Piper, thank you for your smile and life that constantly reminds me of God's indescribable love. My love for you will never end. Your life is meant for great things so hold fast to God, no matter what you go through.

Thank you to my mom, Stephanie. You've always demonstrated amazing love, and there aren't enough words to thank you for all the sacrifices you've made. I'm the man I am today because of you, and for that, I am forever grateful.

And thank you to one of my best friends and older brother, Mike. We've been through some rough times together and it hasn't always been perfect between us, but I want you to know how much I respect and love you. Thank you for being such a selfless brother and supporting me through everything.

Mike and Chris Reis

To our collaborator Mike Yorkey, thank you for all your love, support, hard work, and for having the God-given talent to make our stories come to life. Grateful thanks also go to his wife, Nicole, who kept us well fed with her amazing culinary skills during our long interview sessions, which were emotionally difficult. Thanks to both of you for our budding friendship and the bond we share as brothers and sisters in Christ. We've only just begun our journey together.

Finally, we'd like to give a special thank you to our entire family and to all our friends who have touched our lives and played a part in shaping our story. Your prayers, love, and support will not be forgotten.

INVITE MIKE AND CHRIS REIS TO SPEAK AT YOUR EVENT

Mike and Chris Reis are a dynamic father-and-son speaking team whose mission is to encourage others to live life with thoughtful and selfless intention.

If you would like to invite Mike and Chris Reis to speak at your next event, please contact:

Yolanda Harris

The Keynote Group

P.O. Box 2444

Mt. Pleasant, SC 29465

Yolanda@thekeynotegroup.com

843.654.9344

www.thekeynotegroup.com

For more information about Mike and Chris Reis or this book, visit: www.recoveryofalifetime.com

About the Authors

Mike Reis

Mike Reis is an author, speaker, and master-certified addiction recovery coach who firmly believes that it's never too late to become the person God intended.

After becoming a Christian in 2005, Mike was eventually able to battle the cycle of his own alcoholism and other addictive behaviors, and today he lives a life dedicated to God, family, and serving others. He feels most called to help men live a purposeful life and to carry his message that being a good father, husband, and spiritual head of household is about much more than living for yourself, your income, or your possessions. He travels to churches, retreats, men's groups, business organizations, and rehabilitation centers to share his own story of enlightenment and redemption.

Prior to coaching, Mike enjoyed a hugely successful career in executive sales with companies like Hallmark Cards, PepsiCo, and ConAgra Foods.

Mike graduated with honors from Georgia State University with a B.A. in liberal arts and business. He is a Certified Master and Professional Coach, and he is also certified in Recovery and Christian Life coaching, all from the World Coach Institute (WCI), where he is also an instructor. Mike is a member of the International Coach Federation (ICF), Georgia Coach Association (GCA), and Recovery Coaches International (RCI). He also holds a certificate of ordination from the National Association of Christian Ministers.

Mike is the proud father of six adult children and two grandchildren. His son is NFL Super Bowl XLIV champion and former

New Orleans Saints safety Chris Reis, who became a part of football history when he recovered the onside kick at the beginning of the second half of the game, which is credited for altering the mood—and the course—of the entire game itself.

Mike and his wife, Celia, live in Cumming, Georgia, with their two golden retrievers, Buster and Bennie.

Chris Reis

Chris Reis is a loyal follower of Christ, devoted husband and father, author, inspirational speaker, and former NFL football player who played four seasons with the New Orleans Saints.

He is best known for his historic, game-changing play made during Super Bowl XLIV, and ultimately helping to lead the Saints to victory. As the first onside kick recovered before the fourth quarter of a Super Bowl game, NFL.com named Chris' play one of the "Top 10 Greatest Super Bowl Plays of the Decade," and the actual ball he recovered now resides in the NFL Hall of Fame.

Chris is a graduate of Georgia Tech, where he was the president of the Fellowship of Christian Athletes (FCA) throughout his entire college experience. It was through the FCA that Chris met his wife, Michelle. It was also within these walls of fellowship that Chris' father, Mike, felt his own calling to surrender his life to Christ.

Chris is passionate about helping others to improve their lives. He serves on the board of lüō, a nonprofit organization that works on empowering children in impoverished global communities by providing them with sustainable solutions including nutrition, biblical curriculum, education, and medical care. (For more information, please visit www.luo-setfree.org.)

Today Chris travels the country speaking to men's groups,

youth groups, churches and religious organizations, Rotary Clubs and other service organizations, touchdown clubs, and corporations, inspiring others by sharing his story of living a faith-based lifestyle in an ego-centric culture. His "Live for More" motto inspires many who may find trusting God in today's culture to be more and more daunting.

Chris lives in Cumming, Georgia, with his wife, Michelle, their daughter, Piper, and their dogs Kolsch and Tyger.

Mike Yorkey

Mike Yorkey is the author or co-author of more than seventy books, including these collaborative efforts:

- *Believe: The Eric LeGrand Story*, the story of Rutgers football player Eric LeGrand, who was paralyzed from the neck down on a kickoff play in 2010
- *My Big Fat Greek Diet* by Nick Yphantides, M.D., who lost 270 pounds
- *Play Ball* by former San Francisco Giant pitcher Dave Dravecky
- *Holding Serve* by tennis star Michael Chang
- *Every Man's Battle* by Steve Arterburn and Fred Stoeker (there are nine books in this series that have sold 2 million copies)
- *Up, Up and Away: The Story of Marilyn McCoo and Billy Davis Jr.* (they were part of the Sixties music group, The Fifth Dimension)

Mike grew up in La Jolla, California, and graduated from the University of Oregon with a B.S. degree from the School of Journalism. After a stint as a newspaper editor, he was editor of *Focus on the Family* magazine from 1986-1997 and also held other titles at Focus on the Family, including editorial director and editor-in-chief.

Mike has been married thirty-three years to Nicole, a native of Switzerland. He is the co-author of two World War II novels, *The Swiss Courier* and *Chasing Mona Lisa*, which are set in Switzerland, France, and Nazi Germany.

Mike and Nicole are the parents of two adult children, Andrea and Patrick, and make their home in Encinitas, California.

His website is www.mikeyorkey.com.